What they ar

"Samantha Rose's mastery of words is a gift—*Giving Up the Ghost* is an intimate, unfiltered, heart wrenching and, at times, hilarious account of a family story forever changed by suicide. In these confusing and increasingly lonely times for us all, Rose's memoir is a must read for anyone coping with grief and surviving loss."

—Eve Rodsky, author of the *New York Times* bestseller and Reese's Book Club pick, *Fair Play*

"A beautifully written and piercing reflection on grief, the bonds between mothers and daughters and the importance of finding your own voice. Rose's journey of resilience inspires us to dig deep for the answers that will set us free and that have the power to ripple outward and offer hope and healing to us all."

—Cathy Heller, podcast host *and* author of *Abundant Ever After*

"Heartbreaking, raw, honest, and inspiring . . . Samantha Rose may have just put herself out of business as a ghostwriter because she is anything *but* in this deeply personal and moving account of her firsthand experience with suicide. In her refreshing voice, she takes us on a compelling journey as she bravely navigates her way through grief's darkness, moving from the depths of shadow and transcending into higher light. This book serves as a powerful reminder that love never dies and we are never truly alone."

—Rebecca Rosen, author of the national and international bestseller, *Spirited: Connect to the Guides Around You*

Giving Up the Ghost

A Daughter's Memoir

SAMANTHA ROSE

Published in the United States by Sibylline Digital First,
an imprint of All Things Book LLC, California.

Sibylline Press is dedicated to publishing the
brilliant work of women authors ages 50 and older.
www.sibyllinepress.com

eBook ISBN: 9781960573414
Print ISBN: 9781960573681
LCCN: 2024951851

Cover Design: Alicia Feltman
Book Production: Sang Kim

For Mom and for Derby, who share the top spot for favorite.

PRELUDE

Have you heard the one about the ghostwriter who walks into the afterlife?

ME: "People aren't going to like it. They'll say I'm making it up."

MOM: "Just tell them you're a ghostwriter who's written books for all types of people."

ME: "Right, for people who are still living."

MOM: "Who's to say I'm not still alive?"

ME: "Your obit, for starters."

MOM: "A minor detail, and plus, the best books challenge readers to suspend disbelief, to see things in a way they haven't before."

ME: "And if they still accuse me of making it up?"

MOM: "Blame it on me."

ME: "Well, that'll be easy. I blame it all on you."

MOM: "Ha, I'm sure you do, but this isn't a story about blame, is it, darling? It's about secrets and shame."

ME: "It's about the stories we tell."

PART ONE

Unravel

That Day

I was getting my toes painted the color of spring lilacs at the moment you jumped fully clothed into the sea. I had always imagined, or maybe I'd read it somewhere, that when someone close to you dies, you know it. You feel it, like a little tremor that quakes within, nudging you awake, whispering in your ear: Something significant has happened to someone you love.

When it happened to me, I missed it. I felt nothing shake or seismically slide. I detected nothing out of the ordinary as I reclined in a salon chair, attempting to capture twenty minutes of restorative downtime. I missed it because I was lost in my own head or because feeling an atmospheric change when someone leaves this Earth is a myth. As scented bubbles circled my soaking feet, I was unaware that you were drifting out with the tide, already gone from me. I had no idea that after the Coast Guard recovered your body, they'd immediately started looking for me. I felt no instinctive warning when an officer pulled up to my former home in Texas at the moment my toes began to dry in California, and when this officer was greeted by someone at the door who wasn't me, he turned and left without being able to relay, "We're sorry to inform you, ma'am, but your mother is dead."

I'm grateful to have missed that unwelcome knock on the door, although outdated records only spared me a few hours. When I left the salon and walked to my parked car in disposable flip-flops, I was still on the side of unknowing. It was just a Tuesday. I was leaving for a work trip the next morning, my carry-on bag was packed, and I felt confident my week would unfold according to plan.

When you didn't answer my series of texts later that afternoon: *Hey, just wanted to check in one last time before I leave tomorrow* . . . followed by, *Where are you?* and again, *Mom, can you call me?* I started to become not suspicious, but questioning. And when you didn't call me back and I texted again, *Will you please call me?* and you didn't, I became cautiously concerned and called my sisters. You weren't responding to them either, they confirmed on our three-way line, and that's when I offered: "I talked to her this morning, and she said she was going out to the beach."

"Oh, shit," said my older sister, Jenni. "I'm hanging up and calling CHP."

I thought this reaction was bigger than the concern. Our mother had gone to the beach and had probably lost track of time, and she probably didn't have cell service and was likely driving back right now. I was sure she was somewhere along the Pacific coastline, and calling the CHP to look for her would create a false alarm. After all, I'd spoken to her for nearly an hour this morning. We'd talked about the neighborhood I'd recently moved into, and she asked me about my upcoming work trip to Los Angeles.

"I'll be back by Friday," I said, "so let's get together over the weekend for wine in the garden."

"Sure, that should work."

"Let's plan on it."

"Okay," she agreed.

* * *

As I waited for Jenni to call me back, I allowed some anxiousness. "C'mon, Mom," I said out loud. "Where are you?" To say I didn't suspect my mother of getting lost wasn't entirely true. After all, she was grieving the recent death of her husband, and there was a part of her that had become unreachable, and not only by phone. When we spoke earlier that morning, she admitted to feeling "blue" and that she might feel this way "for a long time."

"I think we're all going to be grieving for a while," I said, attempting to soothe her. "And we'll get through it together, like we always do."

"Yes, I guess you're right," she said quietly. "I think I'll go out to the beach and take a walk."

This was not uncharacteristic of her. She loved the beach, wherever she could find one, and had just returned from visiting her sister in Massachusetts, where she'd walked along the North Shore in frigid single-digit temperatures, an activity most people would rather avoid and trade for the warmth of hot cocoa and a wood-burning stove, but that she described as "exhilarating." Indeed, she'd had a restorative glow when I'd seen her four days ago, fresh off the plane.

I texted again. *Mom, can you call me and let me know where you are?*

Still holding the phone in my hand, I nearly jumped when Jenni called back.

"Hello?"

Silence.

"Hello?"

"They found her." Jenni's voice cracked.

"What do you mean? Where is she?"

"They found her body."

Body?

"What do you mean?" I asked again.

"She's gone," Jenni whispered.

My chest tightened and I pushed back. "No, that can't be right. I just talked to her. I talked to her this morning."

"They found her at the beach."

"What are you talking about? I *just* talked to her," I asserted, as if underscoring the recentness of our conversation would void Jenni's claim.

Jenni began sobbing and stringing words together that I didn't understand nor wanted to hear. Something about a fall, a 911 call. I tuned her out, shoved her words to the background so I could focus on what I knew to be true. I quickly rewound the details of the day. I spoke to Mom at nine, went to the salon at ten. Had Jenni just mumbled something about an officer looking for me in Austin? At noon? It was now almost five o'clock on the West Coast, and none of this made sense. My head began to spin. I silenced Jenni's voice and refocused. I spoke to Mom at nine, I went to the salon at ten. I first texted her at eleven, or was it noon? The timing of the day was accelerating; it was adding up too quickly and it wasn't right, like when you're in the grocery checkout line and the numbers increase faster than you can add them in your head. *Why is the total climbing so high? I can't keep up!*

"Sam," Jenni broke through. "I'm with Gretta. We're coming to you right now."

She hung up and I didn't move. I tried not to breathe. If I stood perfectly still, maybe I could stop time from ticking forward, maybe I could stop the Earth from spinning, maybe I could stop whatever this was from happening.

What was happening?

I needed everything to stop so I could think. I needed the world to please pause so I could think.

I couldn't think.

It didn't make sense.

It didn't add up.

Did Jenni say Mom was *dead*?

No, no, no.

Impossible.

My mother cannot be dead.

This couldn't be true.

I'd just talked to her.

She was here, this morning. I heard her voice. I can still hear her voice. Why isn't she answering my texts?

I took a shallow breath. I didn't move. Could I stop this thing in its tracks if I didn't move? Or, maybe, if I ran out the front door right now, I could get to her. Where was she? It wasn't too late.

Was it?

Was it *too late*?

I shook my head. No, no, no. I refused to believe this.

How can someone be in this world at nine thirty a.m., sipping coffee and talking to their daughter on the phone, and no longer be in their body by noon? I stood barefoot and unmoving on my hardwood floor for another ten seconds, twenty, thirty, barely breathing, until I felt it—a tremor shifting the ground beneath me, upturning my world. I could hear it too: the sound of deep roots pulled violently from the Earth.

"NOOOOOOOOOO!" I screamed, and that's when the floor gave out.

I realized I was on the ground, leaning against a wall, when there was a knock on the door. I was untethered in darkness, floating in space, scared and alone. Had someone come to rescue me? Another knock.

I stood as Gretta and Jenni opened the door. Their regretful faces confirmed what I didn't want to believe, and what I now felt undeniably in my bones: Our mother had done something out of our control. We silently arranged ourselves in a loose circle in the living room. Jenni was the first to speak—"She wrote a note"—and offered me a typewritten sheet of paper with Mom's distinctive swoop signature at the bottom.

I stared at it. She'd written a *note*? I wanted to grab it, this physical piece of her, this written explanation of the horror unfolding here, but I was also repulsed by it. Reading it would legitimize it—whatever *it* was that she'd done—and I wasn't ready for tangible evidence.

"Not yet." I shook my head and looked away.

Jenni placed it on the coffee table between us.

We sat in silence.

"I talked to her this morning," I said finally. I looked at them both as tears rimmed my eyes. "We made plans for the weekend."

"I didn't talk to her, but she texted me," Jenni said quietly. "After I'd left for work, she stopped by to walk Maisy." Jenni pulled up the message on her phone: *Fed and walked your pup, now going out to the beach.*

Gretta sat forward. "She texted me too. Thanked me for helping her with the bills this past Sunday."

"She did?" I asked Gretta. "What time was that?"

"About ten thirty."

Again, I shook my head in confusion. I didn't understand when this seemingly ordinary morning had taken such a hideous turn. I glared at the typewritten note on the table. When I'd called her this morning, she said she'd been, "drinking coffee, doing a little writing." Was this *that* writing? I'd assumed she was writing in her journal, as she often did, or taking notes on a new fiction piece.

"I found it on top of her laptop," Jenni said.

I still made no move to pick it up, although I could see she'd dated it at the top.

This was deliberate. This was no accident.

When I'd suggested we make plans for the upcoming weekend, she was noncommittal, and now I understood why—she'd already made plans of her own.

She'd planned this. *She'd planned this?* Before we hung up, we'd exchanged our standard, "Love you, bye." I played it back now. Was she saying goodbye? Goodbye forever?

I felt gutted, sick to my stomach.

No, this couldn't be right. I commanded my mind to take over. Maybe there was something here I didn't understand. Something I could still prevent or undo?

"Tell me what the sheriff said. Can you repeat it, please?"

As Jenni recounted their conversation, I mentally assembled and dissembled the timeline, the minutes and hours, the what-happened-when—turning over what I knew and what I thought I knew, searching for a loophole, an alternative ending, one that contradicted the details provided by the sheriff, who received an emergency call at approximately twelve thirty from a hysterical woman reporting an "incident." Someone had jumped from Bodega Head, the favorite tourist destination along the rugged Northern California coastline, most known for its dramatic cliffs rising above a crashing sea. Before jumping, the person had identified herself to a group of women at the famous lookout as Susan Swartz from Sebastopol. "Call 911," she'd instructed them before stepping off the edge.

"That sounds like her," I interjected. "Responsible, even then."

"She didn't want us looking for her," Jenni speculated. "And they would have found you sooner—her next of kin—if they'd had your forwarding address."

I shook my head in confusion. "I've been back in California for seven years."

Jenni shrugged.

"Why didn't they call me when they couldn't find me? My number hasn't changed."

"Don't know."

We played this guessing game well into the evening, searching for some discrepancy in the timeline to make it not true. Round and round we went until it finally hit me: This was what people did when they felt powerless; they feigned control. We were acting as if we had a say in the matter, in what was already done. By nine o'clock, we hadn't undone anything, and I fell back against the couch, weary. "I still don't understand. How can this have happened?" Jenni and Gretta returned no answer, so I asserted, "Really. How can *this* have happened? This is not our family story."

Not ours.

As soon as I said it, I regretted the presumption, my sense of false privilege. It was true that a darkness like this had never touched our family directly, and as far as I knew, it wasn't a thread woven anywhere in our family's history. Because we hadn't ever confronted it up close, had I come to believe our family was somehow exempt from suicide claiming a family member? I'd read the statistics. Upward of 50,000 people die by suicide in this country each year, and in Sonoma County, where we lived, the rates were higher than the California state average.

Still, suicide doesn't happen to *us*. We're immune. Why did I believe this?

I turned it over.

Suicide doesn't happen to *her*. That's what I'd meant. Suicide doesn't happen to my mother, the local celebrity columnist and outspoken feminist. As if there were some governing body determining those of us most likely to succeed, Mom—I believed—was an unlikely candidate for suicide because she thrived at living. Excelled, even. In her early fifties, she'd written a series of books about what it meant to live a full, "juicy" life, and for as long as I could remember, she walked her talk. On the West County trails that she frequented on foot, my mother could become easily arrested by the drifting scent of an overripe fig tree and rendered speechless by an ancient redwood around the next bend. In San Francisco, where she periodically indulged in arts and culture, she might delay entering Davies Symphony Hall to provide an audience of one for the homeless man plucking his four-string violin on the street corner. My mother was enthralled with life, in love with its color and complexity, and it made no sense, no sense at all that she would abandon it.

Someone offered me a glass of wine—Miriam, I think, one of Mom's best friends and her next-door neighbor, who'd joined us in my living room, although I don't remember when she walked in.

"Here you go, Sam," she offered gently, setting the glass down in front of me.

I appreciated that the wine was an effort to help me soothe, to blur the edges of this grotesque picture. Drinking to disappear, to hide and un-feel was an act I did well, but if what we were confronting was true—that my beautiful and vibrant mother died today, that suicide dared to claim her, and that she was, perhaps, at this very moment, transitioning somewhere between this world and whatever comes next—I didn't want to be soothed. I quietly pushed the wine aside. As much as I didn't want to acknowledge this surprise twist in my life story, something told me to pay attention, to not let this moment pass by in a haze of alcohol. My mother's death, the most sobering moment of my life, deserved my vigilance, my presence.

I noted the time. It was 10:13 p.m. on Tuesday, February twenty-fifth. This morning, my mom had been alive. We'd talked on the phone. I listened to her familiar voice. I told her I would see her on Friday. She said she'd been doing some early-morning writing. She said she might drive out to the beach. Because neither of these activities were irregular to her, I didn't give them a second thought. We hung up and I had my toes painted the color of spring lilacs, unaware of the darker shade of violet spreading out before me.

⋆ ⋆ ⋆

At a quarter to midnight, Gretta squeezed in next to me in my queen bed. She had the sensitivity to know I could not, or probably should not, spend this night alone. We stretched out, back-to-back and side by side, two heavy hearts motionless in the dark, done talking for the day. I closed my eyes and willed myself to sleep, and then stopped my body from allowing it. *I can't sleep. I won't do it.* The restorative act felt inappropriate, indulgent on a night like this, when I was still breathing and Mom was not. I stared into the void and silently let my mind race, returning back to my stubborn insistence that suicide doesn't happen to us.

Not us.

An abrupt ending like this doesn't happen to us, Mom—not to me and you, the mother-daughter duo with the same bright smile and upturned nose. It doesn't happen to us because we were something more. We'd grown into adult friends and colleagues who swapped writing tips and fashion advice. What is it you used to say? "We're so good together." And you were right. We were lucky. We were envied. And not only because we looked alike and both worked in the world of words. Our intimacy ran deep and wide. We talked every day and about everything—poetry, politics, parenting, perimenopause, and, inevitably, collagen loss and what to do about our aging men. We shared it all, the big and the small. We trusted each other, too, didn't we? Why didn't you trust me with the biggest thing, that you were on the edge of falling?

How could you keep this from *me*?

I shuddered under the sheets, imagining the final scene that had been described to me. Mom on the edge of a cliff. Jumping into the sea.

Why did you do it? How could you do it?

I rewound back to our phone conversation, searching for what I might have missed. A word out of place, an extended pause that might have given her away. She said she was going out to the beach and was returning in the afternoon for a book group event, wasn't it? Her story seemed solid. Nothing to question. Nothing to doubt.

But you weren't telling me all of it, I understood now. Only a part of it, not all that you'd planned—because if I'd known your intentions, I would have followed you there, chased after you, caught up with you before you took that final step. I would have grabbed your hand and held it tight. If I would have known, I wouldn't have let you go. Because I am yours and you are mine.

I stared into the shadows, a forty-nine-year-old woman searching for answers, searching for her, feeling as disoriented as I'd been at five years old when I'd lost her in a crowded airport. *Mommy, where are you? You were just here. Where did you go?* Suspended in the dark, I curled into the fetal position, a scared little girl who'd lost her navigation, her compass rose. Throughout my life, my mother grounded me in time and space. She was my constant, my past, present and future. My home. Where I belonged. Without her, I was displaced, and I couldn't imagine what happened next. I'd never taken a single breath without her moving somewhere among the living, walking within the crowd, and I wasn't sure how to be in the world if she was not. I didn't know who to be. Careful not to wake Gretta, I cried blinding tears into my pillow and summoned her forward. *Mommy,* I pleaded, *please don't leave me. Please don't go. Please, please, please, don't do this.* I pleaded with God, with the unknown, with anyone who would listen to please undo this horror, until I finally exhausted myself to sleep.

★ ★ ★

At four o' clock in the morning, I was startled awake by the distinctive sound of seagulls outside my bedroom window, which is not unheard of in many parts of Sonoma County but is uncommon in my inland neighborhood. My sleepy mind drew a fragmented line between their overhead cries and Mom's last sighting at the beach. For a groggy instant, I wondered if a flock of coastal birds had rescued and returned my mother to me. I cried out a disoriented, "Mom?"

Gretta opened a wary eye and looked over at me in the early-morning shadows, and without a word, we acknowledged the awful truth: Birds had not carried her home. She wasn't returned, nor was she coming back. I closed my eyes and hoped sleep would take me. My earlier bravado to feel my pain had passed. I now desperately wanted something to blur the edges, to mask this terror, to carry me away to the land of forgetting.

The Day After

I pulled myself out of bed the next morning.

Hazy.

Surreal.

I stumbled into the bathroom and regarded myself in the mirror. Devastation had been hard at work. A crease ran down the length of my cheek that, I was quite certain, wasn't there before. My eyes had retreated behind my brow bones, as if to hide from the new reality I'd been forced to wake up to, and my neck and jaw felt tight, likely from suppressing screams throughout the night.

There ought to be an anti-shock serum for days like this.

I had no context for the bombshell that had landed in my living room. There was the unbelievability of her death, and also, I couldn't reconcile how to operate without a mother. A part of me was missing. I felt hollowed, like a cantaloupe that's been scraped down to the rind, and I stared at myself in the mirror, uncertain how to exist on the most basic level.

"What do I do?" I wondered aloud. In the absence of normalcy, of a dependable routine, nothing felt important, worth doing. *I could get dressed*, I finally considered. I could likely do that.

I plodded into my closet and mindlessly sifted through clothes, deciding finally on pink cargo pants, a polka-dot knitted sweater, electric-orange running shoes, and a turquoise ball cap. It was a questionable combination that begged for an answer: Is this some kind of joke?

Was it?

My mother jumped off a cliff.

It sounded like the start of a bad joke; except she really did jump. Did that mean the joke was on me?

I tucked my hair into my cap, a look that was part resignation, part defiance—a colorful "F-you" to the universe, and when I met Gretta in the kitchen where she was already pouring coffee, I preemptively explained, "I've decided to dress like a traumatized party clown today." She smiled weakly and handed me a cup.

"Thanks," I said, dropping my act. Who was I kidding? There was no lightness here. I sipped the strong coffee. "So, what do we do *now*?"

Gretta looked thoughtfully out the kitchen window. "I don't know." She returned her gaze to me. "But whatever it is, we'll do it together."

That was enough for me.

Gretta's dad married my mom when I was nine. I'd been an only child, and then Gretta came along, freckled and kind, an instant playmate and a new sister who didn't leave my side. This morning, I would depend on her to help me navigate this unexpected derailment of our blended family line. I searched her face and recognized our shared sadness. While our biology was different, she'd also lost a mother.

⋆ ⋆ ⋆

We'd decided the night before to meet Jenni at a local bakery because sugar and caffeine seemed like necessary ingredients for surviving this impossible day. We spotted her in the back, her slender athletic body swallowed by an oversized café chair. With her Nike ball cap pulled low, she didn't see us until we were standing in front of her.

"Hi," we said quietly.

She looked up and tried to smile but abandoned the effort.

We sat down next to her, the three of us together again in the stark morning light. Only fifteen hours had passed since everything changed and now it was the next day and we had decisions to make. I was about to ask if anyone wanted coffee when I noticed Jenni silently surveying my outfit. She cocked her head to the side, as she were about to comment on the clashing color scheme, when I raised both hands in defense. "I don't know why. It just came together this way."

On any other day, she wouldn't hesitate before delivering a sarcastic jab, but given the circumstances, she gave me a pass.

"Okay, let's get started." She sat up, took a slug of her coffee, and opened her laptop. "I started a Google doc of all the things I could think of for us to tackle. Obviously, we're not going to get to it all today."

Gretta and I pulled our chairs in closer and read down the list.

"I divided it into professional calls, personal calls, and services to suspend. I think we should start by sending out work emails."

"I already called for a sub last night," Gretta said.

"And I sent mine already too." After I'd been woken up by seagulls, I crept out of bed and wrote a shaky email to my client with the subject line: Death in the family.

"All right," Jenni said. "Moving on."

This was our training: My sisters and I knew how to *do*. Jenni was a lawyer turned executive director, Gretta was a thirty-year veteran of the public-school system, and I was a television producer-turned-ghostwriter, a profession I'd seen described in a *New York Times* feature as a "shadow scribe who writes books in someone else's voice without leaving fingerprints."

"Next," Jenni said, "I think we should all plan to take the full week off, maybe longer."

Gretta and I nodded in agreement, although excusing myself from work responsibilities was uncharacteristic of me. The day after my son was delivered by an emergency C-section, I took a client call in my hospital bed, and less than a week later, I returned to work by balancing my laptop on his nursing pillow to write between feedings. Setting professional boundaries wasn't a strong leaning of mine, but in this rarified case, I felt justified. My mother was dead. If there were ever a time to cancel a flight the morning of travel, this was it.

We returned to Jenni's list.

"What's next?" Gretta asked.

"We should order the death certificate," Jenni said. "Remember that it takes five to six weeks to get it, and we're going to need it to do practically everything."

Where our level of productivity the morning after our mother's suicide may have appeared premature or even distasteful to some people, we were only following protocol. You see, we'd been through this before. Only three short months ago when we'd lost Klose, my stepdad, Jenni and Gretta's father, and Mom's second husband of nearly forty years.

★ ★ ★

Bob Klose was a local icon of print journalism—one of the old guard—and his newsroom buddies had called him by his last name since he started in the business as a fresh-faced, twenty-year-old copy editor for the *Oakland Tribune*, and when Mom introduced him to me as one of her "work friends" in the late '70s, "Klose" was what I called him too. When he evolved into more than a friend and became my stepdad, he was still Klose, and for the forty years I knew him, he called me Sam.

He'd always been an active and healthy guy, traveling to Russia, Vietnam, Israel, Somalia, and Bosnia as an investigative reporter, and as he got older, he stayed in shape at his local gym, maintaining his stamina for cross-country motorcycle rides with his college buddy from Kansas. When, a year ago, he was diagnosed with metastatic cancer originating in his lungs, Klose said something succinct like, "Well, shit . . ." and quickly dug in as he was professionally trained to do. He educated himself on his disease and the available treatment plans, he followed his doctor's recommendations, he took the prescribed medicine and showed up for every blood draw. He treated his condition like a serious assignment, one for which he gathered all the facts, trusted his sources and science, while also believing in faith over fear. When his cancer metastasized, spreading throughout his body, he leveled with us: "I think this thing is going to outrun me . . . unless"—he winked—"I outrun it first."

The joke in our family since the movie came out in 1981 was that Klose was the real-life embodiment of Norman, Henry Fonda's cantankerous and relentlessly difficult character in *On Golden Pond,* but as it turned out, when faced with crippling cancer, Klose was dependably calm and the most level-headed of all of us. One week before he was admitted into the ICU with internal bleeding that would start a domino effect of irreversible organ failure, my sisters and I ordered takeout pizza and gathered around their kitchen table. Klose was in great spirits and equally outspoken about his preference for dinner talk. "Let's change the subject for once, shall we? Haven't we all had enough of cancer?"

"I'm going through menopause," Jenni cheered.

"Me, too." Gretta jumped in.

"I'm on the fence." I shrugged. "Not sure it's for me."

As Jenni recounted an exaggerated night sweat that nearly flooded her bedroom, he grinned across the table at the three of us who'd become sisters well before pimples and periods.

"So do you mean to tell me"—he leaned forward like his favorite evening news anchor, Dan Rather—"that when I wasn't paying attention, you three grew up into adult women?" He dropped his voice with mock seriousness. "Now, tell the truth, girls—When did this happen?"

He'd put up an honorable fight, and even with a hopeful elixir of experimental drugs and a mastermind oncologist, Klose lost the battle. He'd always been a realistic man, and still he'd been determined to hang on until his first grandchild's high-school graduation. We'd all believed he had more time, but cancer makes its own schedule. On the morning his body gave in to the relentless disease, we gathered around his hospital bed, drinking coffee and listening to NPR, as was his habit, and for the past three months, my sisters and I had been grieving his absence while also helping Mom, a lonesome new widow, attend to the Business of Dying.

And now she was gone too.

⋆ ⋆ ⋆

"What do we need the death certificate for?" I scratched my head, trying to remember.

"To close bank accounts, and probably to pay their mortgage. Also to access life insurance . . ." As Jenni listed each item, she typed them into the Google doc.

"And we should call the crematorium," Gretta added.

"Jesus," I exhaled. "We were *just* there."

"I know. Poor Joe at Pleasant Hills is going to do a double take when he sees us again."

"We should get a punch card for repeat business," I muttered.

"Or, at least, a two-for-one urn," Jenni added without looking up from her laptop.

I appreciated that this wasn't everyone's way to handle crisis, but it was ours. Last night, we sat in paralyzed shock, and today we had things to do and frankly, we needed a lift; we needed to laugh. If we allowed ourselves to insert a joke here and there, and if we could busy ourselves with organization and details, we might be able to fend off the horror and the heartbreak. Or, at least, postpone it until after we made a few important calls.

"I'll call the county clerk's office," Jenni offered.

"I'll call Joe," Gretta jumped in.

"I'll call . . . ?" I asked.

"How about you get us more coffee, and take the next call?" Gretta suggested and handed me her empty mug.

After another round of coffee and successfully crossing crematorium, county clerk, and credit union off the list, Jenni said gently, "We should probably make some personal calls before the obit comes out."

Oh, God, the obit.

I vaguely remembered Jenni calling the regional newspaper last night and speaking to the executive editor, a longtime friend of our family. "You're going to get a report," I heard Jenni say in hushed tones from my son's bedroom, "about a woman who jumped from Bodega Head." The editor had already seen it; she'd received a police report a few hours before Jenni's call, identifying the woman as local columnist Susan Swartz, who'd written for the *Press Democrat* for forty-five years. I heard Jenni pleading into the phone, "Can you please hold the story for at least a day, until we can tell our families?"

Gretta sunk back in her café chair. "I don't know what to

say to people. I mean, what *do* we say? People knew Daddy was sick, but this . . .". She shook her head "This will be shocking news and I don't know how to deliver it, and honestly, all I can think about is what we're going to tell the kids."

"I have to call Nancy." I looked at them both. "If there's one person I have to call *right now*, it's her."

* * *

I pulled down my turquoise cap and walked outside, slogging up and down the sidewalk and mumbling to myself, "I don't want to do this, I really don't want to do this," until I summoned enough courage to dial the 978-area code. As the phone rang, I hoped my aunt wouldn't answer the call. I took a measured breath and slowly exhaled. My nerves began to settle on the third ring, but when she finally answered a chirpy, "Hello?" my throat constricted.

"Hi, Nancy, it's Sam."

"Hi, honey . . . what is it?"

Mom's older sister, Nancy, was a hardy New Englander and a retired ER nurse. Throughout my life, I'd observed my aunt weathering life's volatility like every nor'easter, with equal parts sensibility and fortitude. She'd lost a mother to Alzheimer's, a son to jail time, and a husband too early. "My sis-tah is the strongest woman I know," Mom liked to brag in an exaggerated Boston accent. Nancy, now well into her eighties, had proven herself to be tough and resilient, but losing her baby sister, the one who'd just returned from a two-week stay at her North Shore beach house?

I whispered, "Something has happened to Mom."

Steadily, she commanded, "Tell me."

We talked for nearly thirty minutes and because she asked me to, I recounted every detail I could remember from the past twenty-four hours.

"I talked to her on the phone yesterday morning," I said, "and she told me she was going out to the beach . . ." My voice broke. "I didn't question it because, *you* know . . . she loves the beach."

"I talked to her too. At about seven thirty."

This was a detail I hadn't factored in, that Mom had spoken to someone else besides me. "That was before our call," I said, reconfiguring the timeline.

"We often checked in about that time. Not every morning, but most mornings. Especially after Klose died. She didn't like waking up alone without him, and it gave her something to do first thing."

"What did she say?"

"Not much, really. She was up early, drinking coffee. She said she was doing some writing . . ."

The note.

"We only talked for about ten minutes, and she seemed . . . fine."

"She'd seemed fine to me too, or, at least, fine enough."

I rewound our conversation in the context of this new information, attempting again to locate anything that might bring the picture into sharper focus.

"I just don't get it," I said, stunned all over again. "If I'd known . . ."

Nancy stopped me. "Honey, it's not your fault. You couldn't have known, and if I had any indication she was considering something like this, if I thought she was feeling that bad, I wouldn't have let her leave Massachusetts. I wouldn't have let her get on a plane. And trust me, if I thought she was in that kind of state yesterday morning, I would have called you right away and told you not to let her out of your sight."

Mom had fooled us both, and I wondered how Nancy was processing her sister's deceit, her disruption of the natural order.

For the past half hour, my aunt had held my hand and monitored my heart rate as she'd professionally been trained to do, to treat the patient first and foremost and not become emotionally involved, but this was her sister and I knew, because I'd watched them openly adore each other my entire life, they were woven tightly, and that bond had just been broken.

"Nancy, how are *you* doing?"

"Go be with your sisters," she deflected. "That's what's important right now."

⋆ ⋆ ⋆

I joined Gretta and Jenni back inside, collapsing into a chair.

"How'd that go?" Gretta asked.

"Oh, that was wonderful."

Gretta put a hand on my arm and sighed.

"What?" I asked. "What *now*?"

"In one hour, the school bell will ring."

I recoiled, regretting the next thing on the list. I stood up and forced a gritty smile. "It really is amazing how much bad news you can deliver in one day."

School Bell

The activity of the day, the busyness of doing and tackling lists, had served to keep my mind occupied, and the near-constant company of my sisters had further insulated me. I sat in the car, unmoving, staring out the windshield at the stenciled letters of Village Bakery. *I don't want to do this.* Hadn't Nancy's call been enough for one day? I dug deep within me to find the courage for what came next when I tapped an emotional water line, sending a rush of shock back to the surface. *She's dead?* I leaned back against the head rest, replaying every line of dialogue we'd exchanged the day before as if she were sitting in the seat right next to me, chasing the question that continued to have no logical conclusion: If I can still hear you, if your voice is still ringing in my ears, how can you be gone? Yesterday, you picked up the phone. We talked for an hour. And today, you will not answer? Nor tomorrow, nor the next day? How can it be that I will not hear your voice ever again?

"I need to talk to *you*!" I screamed. "I need to talk to you about *this*! I need you, my mother, to help me understand. Explain this to me. What happened?"

* * *

When things happened in my adult life, Mom was the first person I called, and she'd promptly answer—"Hi, sweetie, what's up?" She was a natural journalist—a great listener, compassionate and curious, and I depended on her to talk me through it, whatever it was. And now, the one person I needed most was the one who'd gone missing. The unfairness of this revolted me. I made certain the windows were up when I screamed louder this time. "You cannot leave me! You cannot do this! Mothers don't leave their children!" A couple glanced my way as they entered the bakery, and I glared back through stinging tears. Whatever, I thought. I don't care who sees me, the hysterical woman in a clown outfit. I slumped in my seat, limp and defeated. I cried for ten minutes, or maybe it was an hour. I'd lost my sense of time, but when I saw the same couple exit the bakery, I resolved that my time was up and I ought to get it together. I blotted my eyes and put the car in reverse, lasting long enough to merge onto the freeway when I erupted again, this time accusing. "How dare you? How dare you die! You didn't ask my permission!" followed by a searing, "And I don't remember you asking anyone's permission to kill yourself!" I accelerated and crossed into the fast lane. My shock had upshifted to anger, and everyone had better get out of my way before I exercised my American right to road rage.

"It's one thing to leave me," I continued screaming, "but how do I explain to your grandson what you've done?"

Until this moment, I'd been experiencing Mom's death as her daughter, but as soon as I exited the freeway, I'd have to assume another role, as mother to my own child. My eight-year-old son, Derby, was still on the safe side of unknowing. Last night, somewhere between my initial near collapse on the floor and settling into a haze of disbelief, I felt some relief that my son was with his father. While my sisters and I debated whether or not to read Mom's suicide note, Derby was protected by a shared custody agreement that, because it was Tuesday, spared him this scene. He'd been afforded one more day of innocence, one more day than the rest of us to believe that things were as they were, that his grandmother was still alive. And that was about to change. In less than thirty minutes, I would have to tell him that his "Mutti," his pal of the past seven years, was gone.

⋆ ⋆ ⋆

Soon after Derby's first birthday, my then-husband and I intentionally relocated to Petaluma, California, from Austin, Texas, so our son could grow up alongside his West Coast grandparents. Eager to be involved in his life, Mutti and Granddaddy, as they liked to be called, soon instituted "Derby Fridays" where I'd drop him off at their house in the morning and find a nearby café to write for the day. While I worked, there were gardening projects with Mutti, trips to the hardware story with Granddaddy, and afternoon strolls with them both to the local library. Once Derby started kindergarten, they kept Friday afternoons intact, and where they picked him up from school in Granddaddy's truck and took him to a nearby park or to get frozen yogurt until my workday was done. Derby Fridays were a reliable and recurring date in my young son's calendar and they'd continued, nearly uninterrupted, for seven years, and this past Friday was no exception. Mom had been there, waiting for her grandson outside his classroom in Audrey Hepburn sunglasses and skinny jeans. How was I going to explain to him that this standing tradition was now over? That he'd never see his grandmother again?

My second-grader was not immune to bad news; he'd lost his grandfather just three months ago, and I'd had to deliver that news at the end of a school day too, and while the loss was painful for him, he had at least understood that Granddaddy was sick, that sometimes his neck hurt and he had to use a walker, that on other days he might be extra tired and not able to pick him up from school. That he had a disease called cancer that was making him feel bad and that he was doing his best to feel better. Mutti, on the other hand, hadn't presented as sick. At seventy-six, her energy remained boundless, her curiosity endless, and her ability to entertain appeared effortless. The only indicator of suffering was interpreted as sorrow. In the three months since Klose died, there'd been scattered times when I'd notice her focus drift as she was reading a book to Derby or making him a snack. She'd be mid-sentence when suddenly she'd go quiet, as if she'd become lost in a memory, and Derby would notice it too. "Mutti," he'd ask tenderly, "are you okay?"

I explained to him: "Sometimes Mutti gets distracted because she misses Granddaddy so much."

"I miss Granddaddy, too."

"We all miss him, and it really hurts to miss somebody, but feeling sad is how we're supposed to feel right now. It means we love him."

Explaining grief in these terms seemed to make sense to Derby. What I was called to explain to him today would be much harder.

Suicide.

My eight-year-old who only recently revealed he knew what the F-word was—"It's *fart*"—had not yet heard of the word that slithers with an *Sssssss*. Suicide was not in his second-grade vocabulary, and today I would not only introduce it to him—the word that I didn't want to say, or hear, or feel—but also, I would attempt to define it.

As I took the exit off the freeway, I tried to recall what Gretta and I gleaned from the child psychologist we spoke to in a hurry last night. In the midst of the swirling confusion, Jenni had the smart idea to call her friend, Dr. Karina, to help us with some quick dos and don'ts when introducing kids to this topic:

Don't avoid it because it's difficult.

Keep it simple.

Speak clearly.

Be truthful, but don't offer too many details.

Express strength while acknowledging that it is sad.

This seemed like a tall order, and as I rehearsed a few clumsy lines in my head, I worried I wouldn't get it right, and that whatever came out would have a life-altering and lasting impact on my child, and definitely an immediate one. This assignment enraged me. That I had to introduce my son to something inherently dark and scary that hadn't existed for him before today made me furious at Mom: You have forced suicide on my son. You have made this part of his life story. You decided this for him. And your choice will change him forever.

I pulled up at the house, fairly certain I'd throw up before I made it to the front door. I'd asked a family friend to pick Derby up from school because I hadn't wanted to show up on campus, where I'd likely run into parents I knew and where I wouldn't be able to act as if it were just another Wednesday. I worried that the first person to flash me a friendly smile or show me any kindness would unintentionally trigger a breakdown episode, and I was in no mood to star in that *Afterschool Special*. I slowly got out of the car and willed myself toward the front door, my body resisting every step. Five cobblestones later, I took a deep breath and instructed myself to: *be the grown-up.*

"Hi, Mommy!" Derby smiled brightly as soon as I opened the door. He ran over to greet me and I wished I could freeze him in time, happy and innocent. *Oh, baby, you have no idea what's coming.* I wrapped my arms around him as my heart sank with apology; if I didn't tell him right away, he'd soon be the one holding me. I gently pulled back and looked into his sweet face. "Let's go sit outside."

He followed me without question onto the patio, and when he plopped down beside me on the little couch in the sun, I took his hands in mine. "Honey, I want to talk to you about something important. It's about Mutti."

His little brow crinkled. "What?"

I hesitated. Once I said it, I couldn't unsay it. Once I said it, everything would change, he would change, we would change. He'd be introduced to a horror he couldn't unknow, and I didn't want to hurt him, I didn't want to tear away the safe and protective layer of his childhood—but it had to be done and I was the one to do it. I looked at him and tears filled my eyes.

"What is it, Mommy?"

"Mutti has died," I said as gently as I could.

His eyes flashed confusion.

"I am so sorry, baby."

He stared at me speechless, unblinking, and when he registered my seriousness, a single tear fell down his face and he dropped his head to hide it.

We sat together on the couch in silence. I rubbed his back and asked nothing of him. Minutes passed until he lifted his red-rimmed eyes and asked—

"How?"

A logical question. How could she die if she'd just picked him up from school? Six days ago, they'd eaten ice cream together on this same patio and talked about his upcoming talent show. After I'd finished work, I'd joined them. We opened a bottle of white wine, and when it was time for her to go, we casually said goodbye like we'd see her again soon. At the latest, by next Friday.

I remembered my coaching—don't provide too many details,

but be honest—so I said, "You know how Mutti has been sad since Granddaddy died?"

Derby nodded his head.

"Well, I think her sadness became so big that it made her sick. Not sick on the outside like Granddaddy's bad back, but sick inside, where we couldn't see it."

I paused and searched for the right words. I wanted to give Derby an answer that was truthful, but I didn't know the truth. I was only guessing, an amateur faking it as an expert. I said, "Mutti's mind got mixed up, honey. She wasn't thinking clearly, and so she made the choice to end her life."

End her life?

Derby looked at me with appropriate confusion. Really, how is a child expected to understand this concept? To most any eight-year-old, this is unthinkable, an inconceivable act. I was sure Derby hadn't ever considered this was a possibility, that there were things one could do to stop being alive, that the people you love could choose to be gone one day from the next. They can choose to leave, to "end" it. They can choose to be gone forever.

"Why would she do that?" He stared at me, incredulous.

I'd been asking myself the same question. "I think her sadness became too big and scary, and she wanted it to stop."

He looked up at me with furrowed brow. "How did she make it stop?"

Oh, Jesus. I hadn't anticipated a follow-up.

"The details aren't important," I wavered and hoped he'd drop it.

"I want to know *how*." His eyes filled with tears.

"Honey . . ." I shook my head. "I want to answer all your questions, but let's save this one for another time."

"No!" He stood up, his hands forming into little fists. "I want to know how, or I'll imagine the worst thing. Mommy," he pleaded, tears streaming down his face. "Tell me. Tell me how Mutti died or I'll never be able to sleep."

I was conflicted. My maternal instinct was to ease my child's pain by giving him what he said he needed. I well understood that our imaginations could take us to dark and scary places, especially for children, but knowing the "how" of her death had disrupted my sleep last night and would likely do the same for many nights to come. I was haunted by the image of my mother on the edge of a cliff. Jumping to her death. Floating out to sea. I did not want to share this horror with him, and I knew she would not want him to imagine her that way. But Derby was insistent.

"Mommy, tell me!"

If I didn't tell him the truth, I feared he'd lose trust in me, and I had the foresight to know that in the days and weeks ahead, he would have more questions that needed answers, that deserved answers, and I wanted him to know he could come to me and ask me anything, and I wouldn't lie to him.

So, I told him. Mostly.

I told him she drove out to one of her favorite beaches, and she walked into the ocean, and when the waves came, she let the ocean take her away. Even without the cliff, it was a terrifying picture and I regretted painting it for him, but as soon as I did, Derby settled. He unclenched his fists and sat down quietly, as though he were thinking it through. "So, she drowned?"

Drowning was a word in his second-grade vocabulary. Since he'd started splashing around in a pool, this cautionary term had been introduced and repeated every time he pulled on his swim trunks. The potential danger of water had been drilled into his head, and he understood people could die by drowning.

"Yes." I nodded. "She drowned." Except I didn't know this for sure. Did the sheriff tell us she drowned? There were so many unanswered questions. I slid over to Derby and put my arm around him. "The most important thing for you to know is that Mutti loved you very much and she'd never want to hurt you. She'd never want to hurt us. Remember that, okay?"

"Then why would she do that? Why would she leave us?"

"I don't know, buddy. I don't know."

★ ★ ★

Later that evening, after dinner, dishes, and bath, Derby appeared in my bedroom doorway. "Can I sleep with you tonight? I don't want to be alone."

"Yes, of course, get in." I scooted over, making room for him in the bed, as if I were accommodating him when I needed him close as much as he needed me. As he slipped under the covers, he asked, "Mommy, are you sad about Mutti?"

"Yes, honey, I am very sad." I pulled him closer.

"And are you still sad about Granddaddy?"

"Yes, I am sad about Granddaddy too."

"So, will you do what she did? Because you're sad like she was sad?"

I looked into his curious eyes, understanding the dots his young mind was trying to connect: If Mutti was sad and Mommy is sad, will Mommy do what Mutti did?

"No, I said firmly and touched my forehead to his. "I will not do what she did. I am sad, but it's a different kind of sad." His Mutti had been grieving and was likely depressed, if not something more, but I wasn't about to introduce any more words to his vocabulary; at least, not tonight. "I will never leave you." I held him tightly until he fell asleep.

★ ★ ★

I woke up in the middle of the night. The image, again—Mom on the edge. I got out of bed and paced the room, wishing I could shove suicide to the back of my dresser drawer like I had her goodbye note. If I could cast it into the shadows, would it stay there?

I wished suicide would leave us alone, but it was too late for that now. It had shown up unwelcome and still, it was here. There was no un-saying it. There was no undoing it. It wasn't leaving. It was in our lives now. And what happens to us, I wondered, now that it's here? How do we stand guard against it?

I got back in bed and stared at the ceiling. If I relegated suicide to the dark, would it stay there? Would it stop hurting us? Or, if ignored, would it only grow into a bigger monster?

Life Interrupted

The next morning, Derby woke up and went through the motions like it were any other day: a bowl of cereal, socks and shoes, backpack and coat, and out the front door. I drove him to school, relieved to dip back into the normalcy of a routine, even though there could be no pretending this was a normal day. I tried to convince myself that keeping Derby to his regular school schedule would help him feel like a normal kid living a normal life. I walked him to his classroom and forced a reassuring smile before leaving him with his buddies. I looked back once, heartened to see him goofing around. Maybe, I hoped, he could escape into the insulated walls of second grade and forget about what had happened on the outside. Although, even if he could temporarily forget, I had a duty to share our news. Again, I reluctantly pushed my body forward, this time in the direction of the school office, and positioned myself outside the principal's door until I heard her hang up the phone. I nudged open the door and peeked my head around it. "I'm so sorry to interrupt, but I have to talk to you."

Her expression of mild annoyance softened when my eyes welled up with tears. She waved me forward. "Come in. Is everything all right?"

I sat down across from her, hoping that if I spoke quickly, I could get ahead of my emotion, but as soon as I said, "My mother took her life two days ago . . ." the words caught in my throat. I buried my face in my hands, unable to say more. I heard Principal Schultz get up out of her chair and come around her desk and kneel next to me. "I'm so sorry."

I gulped for air, embarrassed to be unloading on this woman before eight in the morning. I felt her hand on my shoulder, and once I caught my breath, I lowered my hands and dared to look at her. "I told Derby yesterday. He's very sad and confused, so please tell his teacher to be extra gentle with him today. He might not show it, but he's going through a lot."

"Of course." Ms. Schultz met my eyes.

"Thank you," I whispered and stood up abruptly, desperate to exit her office before I erupted again. As I hurried through the quad toward the parking lot, I spotted a group of moms waving me over. For them, this was a normal Thursday drop-off and I envied them and their innocuous morning conversation, their easy smiles and steaming coffee cups. On any other day, I'd have joined the group, but I no longer fit in. I was on the outside of normal now. I pointed toward the parking lot and mouthed, *Sorry, I have to go.* I hid behind my dark sunglasses and disappeared.

Secure in the car, I collapsed into the seat. I can't keep doing this, I thought, reliving this horror with every single person I see, or avoiding people so I won't have to tell them. I reversed out of the parking lot and reassured myself I had a reprieve, for the next six hours, anyway. I'd be solely in the company of my sisters, and with them, I didn't feel the need to divulge my feelings nor hide them either. I could just *be*, in whatever shape I took, and I was quickly learning my emotional state could shape-shift from moment to moment.

* * *

We'd agreed to meet at the house. No one had been inside since Tuesday, when the deputy sheriff called Jenni and confirmed they'd found a woman they identified as our mother at Bodega Head, and Jenni had rushed over to the house to discover Mom gone and the note she'd left behind. When I pulled up in front of the familiar address, my sisters were standing together, huddled on the sidewalk in puffy vests with take-out cups of coffee. I appreciated that they'd waited for me to climb the front steps together, the ones Mom had painted blue to add cheer and make their shingled cottage look "more French." The Parisian charm was notably absent this morning, and as we solemnly took the steps together, I dreaded what we might find inside.

Jenni was the first to reach the porch, and before she unlocked the door, she turned to us. "Ready?"

I felt uneasy, reluctant, not how I typically entered this house. My routine was to fearlessly climb the steps to the tiny porch with the two mismatched chairs and the potted geraniums. Just inside the glass-paned door, Klose would almost-always be sitting cross-legged in his favorite armchair, where he might be watching a Giants game or MSNBC. Positioned next to him: a red thermos full of coffee, a half-empty cup, a yellow legal notepad, and a scattering of felt-tip pens. With a push of the door, their cockapoo, Olivia, would sound the alarm, barking—*an intruder is here!*—and Klose would look over without hurry or alarm. "Hey, kid, what's up?" This was my standing invitation to enter, and no sooner than I stepped inside, Mom's bright voice would sing out from the kitchen or from one of the back rooms. "Who's that?"

"It's me," I'd sing back, and seconds later she'd glide into the room, flashing her signature smile. "Is that my daughter?" she'd ask with a playful tilt of the head.

"Hi, Mom."

"Hi, baby." She'd embrace me, typically with a kiss on the cheek. "Nice to see you."

This routine was so predictable and safely reliable—how could it be any other way? As we huddled together in the entryway, the first thing I noticed was the absence of noise. No barking dog. No hum of the TV. No one to greet us. Silence surrounded us, along with stale, flat air and dim light, but beyond the stillness, as we moved through the room turning on lights, things appeared as they typically would. Mom's slippers, kicked off, next to the couch. Her laptop on the red table by the window. A bookmarked novel on the couch. A coffee-stained cup on the side table. I followed my sisters through the living room, hesitant to touch or pick anything up, as if it were a crime scene—which I supposed it was, and we were the investigation unit. I scanned the room, wondering what clues Mom might have left behind. Would we find some thread that we could follow that might help us understand her mind?

The living room was in order—if I didn't know different, I'd assume she was at her morning yoga class, soon to return and start another pot of coffee—and in the bathroom, everything appeared ordinary, with her plastic ivory comb and a squeezed tube of toothpaste on the counter, towels hanging on the hook by the shower, a half-roll of toilet paper at the ready. I ran my hand along the sink counter when I spotted them—Mom's silver hoops. *That's strange.* Her earrings, though not expensive nor family jewelry, were sacrosanct to her. They were an integral piece to her look, completing nearly every outfit she wore, whether it was jeans and a Gap T-shirt or a Johnny Was tunic blouse. She wore the earrings daily, and here they were. Why had she left them on the counter, almost as if on display? I stared at them, perplexed.

Had she left them for us? Had she intentionally not worn them? Had she thought ahead of time that silver hoops weren't appropriate for the occasion of her death, that what she planned to do shouldn't be accessorized? This was a crass thought, but I could imagine Mom thinking like this, and even if I were wrong, I still felt certain that leaving them here was a deliberate act, one that meant something. But *what?* I took a picture of them, determined to sleuth it out later, and wandered into the kitchen and opened the fridge. There were fresh groceries: a few apples, a head of romaine lettuce, and a bowl of tuna salad covered with Saran Wrap. This struck me too. I pulled it out and smelled it. The tuna salad, with sliced pickles and chopped red onion, was freshly made. I stood frozen in place, seized by the gross contradiction, the finality of her death and how recent her life. I reasoned there must have been a part of her who'd made the tuna salad because she planned to stick around and eat it. I slowly closed the refrigerator door, sickened by the alternate truth: There was another part of her who'd made other plans.

"Have you seen this?" Jenni called out.

In the guest room, neat piles were stacked on the bed. Tax documents, Mom's life insurance policy, credit-card statements, and a typed list of computer passwords. Here it was, evidence of her intention, her forethought. We'd stumbled on the scene of a life interrupted, I thought, and then edited myself: No, this was the scene of a life abandoned.

"It's kind of giving me the creeps," Jenni said.

"Me too," agreed Gretta. "Let's go sit out on the deck."

⋆ ⋆ ⋆

For the next several days, this became our new routine—meeting at the house, typically on the side deck at the weathered wooden table with the bright red umbrella. We'd show up with coffee, sometimes sandwiches, and, if it were later in the afternoon, we'd open wine.

"I transferred everything to a whiteboard I took from my office," Jenni said one afternoon as Gretta and I walked through the side gate. I sat down and scanned the organized list written in black marker:

Cancel health insurance
Call DMV: transfer title / sell / store vehicles
Cancel cable
Pay utilities and water
Turn off phones
Pay outstanding bills
Cancel credit cards
Close bank account
Taxes? Prep a joint return or extend?
Meet with financial guy: IRA accounts
Life insurance policy?
Check homeowners' insurance / pay mortgage

"Holy shit," I exhaled. "That's a lot. I'm exhausted just reading it."

"I hate it," Gretta concurred.

"These are the big items," Jenni said with neutrality. "And then there's the smaller stuff."

"Don't tell me there's another whiteboard." Gretta braced.

"No, just another column." Jenni pointed to a shorter list titled *House Stuff* on the right-hand side of the board:

Bring in the mail / forward mail
Water the garden, check drip system
Take out trash / recycling bins
Clean out fridge / freezer

Rotate the lights
Stop newspaper delivery

"I hardly have enough time to do this stuff at my own house," Gretta said.

"What's 'rotate the lights'?" I asked.

"Turning on and off lights in different rooms so it looks like someone is home," Jenni explained. "Because, you know, robberies after a death is a thing."

"Really, it's a *thing*?"

"Rotating lights," Gretta corrected, "isn't a thing. It's a full-time job."

I voiced the obvious. "And we already have full-time jobs."

"It is a lot to do," Jenni agreed and looked at us both. "And at some point, we're going to have to decide what to do with the house."

"What do you mean?" My voice went up a notch.

"Meaning," Jenni answered . . . "do we keep it, or do we sell it?"

I looked across the deck to the double French doors, the ones that Mom and Klose preferred to keep open on sunny days, a welcome invitation for visitors to stroll into their kitchen with the long oak table that Klose built in 1968. As the story goes, after Jenni was conceived, he said to his buddy, "The best thing you can do after knocking up your college girlfriend is to build a family table," and that was what he'd done. Then, after marrying his girlfriend, having a second baby and surviving a divorce and an eventual move across country, the table had become a fixture in our blended family, one we gathered around for birthdays, Thanksgiving, and Christmas dinners because it could accommodate up to fifteen people, maybe more if you squeezed in tightly and were willing to sit on a stool or share someone's chair. Even after decades of use, with the nicks and water stains to show for it, Klose's table maintained its sturdy charm, and when it wasn't being used to host a gathering, he and Mom could easily fill the space with a thermos full of coffee and a stack of newspapers between them.

I zoomed back out of the house and let my eyes wander around the garden, landing on the blue hydrangeas at the base of the towering redwood tree, the smaller Meyer lemon and persimmon varietals across the front gate, the old grapevines growing in wild, tangled threads along the fence line and the still-blooming orange nasturtiums weaving underfoot. Even though it was now hard to be here, I didn't want to not be here, to lose our accessibility to this sacred land and the rooms that housed so many of our best family memories.

I appealed, "Can we agree to keep it for now, to keep paying the mortgage for at least a few months until we're able to get through some of this other stuff? Putting the house on the market, on top of what we're already doing, sounds extra overwhelming, if not impossible right now."

"I agree," Gretta said. "This feels like more on top of more."

I sat back in my chair. "Remember when Miriam told us it takes at least one year to finalize a death and we were like, 'no way, we're wrapping this up in a month, tops?'"

"And we were so smug about it." Jenni laughed. "'*Miriam, there's no way it'll take that long. We get shit done.*'"

"Where did she hear that anyway?" Gretta asked.

"Probably some article in the *AARP*." I shrugged. "To be fair, I did hear something similar from a friend of mine who also lost her mom. Said the hardest thing was closing her QVC account. She told me, 'I'll probably be paying for my mom's discount jewelry for the rest of my life.'"

"Susan wouldn't be caught dead shopping on QVC," Jenni deadpanned.

"So true." I nodded toward the whiteboard. "You'll notice that QVC is not on our list."

"Well, I do think we've underestimated the process," Gretta inserted. "Even with three of us, this is going to take *a while*."

"You know," Jenni said with the brightness of a new idea, "there may be an opportunity here. The market is full of end-of-life and estate-planning businesses—you know, support for families *before* someone dies. But I haven't heard of many 'what to do *after* someone dies' businesses. Basically, an outfit that creates an action list of all the things you have to do after a family member dies, then helps you execute them. Most people don't know where to start. Think about it, sissies, by the time we check everything off our list, we're going to be experts."

"Kind of like the Marie Kondos of dying?" Gretta said with interest.

"Not *of* dying, of *post* dying," Jenni clarified. "The Marie Kondos of the After Life. Get it?"

"Pretty sure we'd be sued for calling ourselves that," I interjected.

"Okay, hold on . . ." Jenni looked skyward, searching for a better idea. "How about 'Three Orphans Aftercare' because, you know, we're orphans now."

Gretta stifled a laugh. "Jenni, that is an awful name."

"Really," I joined in, "who wants to open their door to three grieving, middle-aged women with a whiteboard?"

"Three Orphans After-Party?"

Gretta raised an eyebrow. "Because this is such a party?"

"Come on, you have to at least agree that Three Orphans has a ring to it, you know, like Three Twins ice cream?"

"They went out of business," I said.

Gretta smirked. "Yeah, and do you see any ice cream at this after-party?"

"Not a bad idea," Jenni said. "I'll add it to the list."

Solo Trip

The following week, I returned to the house alone. Until now, I'd been in the company of my sisters, and this had been an intentional choice. I hadn't shared it with them, but I was afraid. As I ascended the front steps, I feared that without my sisters and the three-way chatter between us, I might be engulfed by a sadness too sad for me to hold alone. I unlocked the door anyway, driven by a compulsion to step inside on my own, to both feel the presence and absence of our parents without distraction. I called out into the empty space, "Hi, Mommy. Hi, Klose." I stepped lightly into the foyer and quietly closed the door behind me. "It's me." I stood still for a moment, unsure what to do, then proceeded slowly, walking through the living room like a lost little girl. "Mommy, I'm here."

I entered the bathroom, running a finger over her silver hoops, unmoved since I first discovered them. I opened the refrigerator, now empty, and closed it. I walked through the house finding nothing new, just the same frozen scene. I lingered over the photographs that had hung on the walls for years, the stacks of books in every corner. I walked slowly through every room like a quiet shadow until I halted at the back bedroom, the one room I hadn't gone into yet. I'd been consciously avoiding it because it was so intimate, so unmistakably Mom. I cracked open the door.

"Mom?" I entered the room delicately, afraid of what I'd find. Afraid of what was missing.

My mother did not appear with outstretched arms like I'd hoped she would, yet she was everywhere. In the yellow-and-white striped duvet cover, in the slender volumes of Billy Elliot poetry on her nightstand, in the crystals and coins, in the beads and stones that she'd arranged in small decorative dishes on the windowsill. She was in the oval mirror on the antique bureau where she'd tucked a faded black-and-white photograph of her own mother into the wooden framing, along with another of her and Nancy laughing as little girls. She was in the view of the open sky out the picture-frame window, the one she greeted every morning like an old friend. "Hello, sky," she'd croon, still nestled in bed with Klose, Olivia the dog, and a steaming cup of coffee.

I took in every detail of the room with a heavy heart, my eyes finally resting on her open closet with the sliding door. Mom's clothes hung dutifully—a turquoise cotton blouse, a plaid button-up, a cashmere V-neck—all waiting patiently for her to return and slip them on. What would become of her clothes, I wondered, without her slender frame to give them life? That someone else might wear them seemed absurd to me, wrong somehow, yet I supposed they couldn't hang here forever. I sat down on the bed and faced the closet, studying every piece of clothing hanging there, the basket of scarves, the clumsy stack of well-worn T-shirts, her red leather boots on the floor. I remained unmoving, afraid to go any closer, afraid to touch them, confused by the sight of them. How can you be gone, vanished into thin air, when your clothes are still here? I could not reconcile her physical absence. I stood finally, and walked over to the closet, pushing my face into the cluster of hangers, pulling the fabric around me, breathing in slowly.

It's *you.*

A mix of lavender laundry soap, mint tea, and something I couldn't identify but that I recognized in my cells, a smell so familiar, so intimate. The smell of my mother. I sat back on the bed, dizzy from the presence of her, still here and yet—gone. How can someone just disappear? I felt sick all over again. Oh, the agony. The yearning.

I flashed back to when Derby was a new baby. During the day, I left him in the care of a nanny to bottle-feed him and put him down for naps while I struggled behind the door of my home office to meet a looming book deadline. When I needed to take a bathroom break, I'd sneak down the hallway with silent footsteps and still, there was no disguising it—my breast milk gave me away. My baby could instantly and unmistakably smell me, and he'd shriek from his crib with the deafening cries of a newborn—*I want my mother!*

This was how I felt now. I could smell my mother, but she was not here. I craved the physicality of her touch. My body mourned her. It ached for her, was in withdrawal from her, and I could not stand that I could not touch her, that she could not touch me.

In an attempt to bottle her before she drifted away from the wardrobe and my memory altogether, I grabbed her Cabochard perfume off her bureau—the French fragrance she reserved for special occasions like Christmas Eve cocktails, anniversary dinners, or public-speaking events, for times when she wanted to feel elegant and beyond expense. I popped the top and inhaled. The spicy, sweet, and earthy notes rose upward as if they might magically summon my mother from the bottle, only to quickly fade.

"I want you back," I cried. "I want you here!"

Frustrated by what I couldn't have, I stomped around the room, wounded and despairing, reasoning that if I couldn't have her, I'd steal her perfume. I stashed it in my bag. *You're mine! You belong to me!*

Right then, I heard Gretta call out, "Sam, are you here?"

I'd been caught in the act, the greedy daughter. I slowly walked into the living room, where she welcomed me with a smile.

"Jenni can't meet us today and I only have an hour. Wanna try to tackle one thing on the list and then have a glass of wine in the garden?"

"I took Mom's Cabochard," I blurted.

"Huh?"

I pulled it out of my bag. "Mom's perfume."

"Oh," she said as she recognized the bottle.

"I can put it back . . . I'm sorry." I turned back toward the bedroom.

"It's okay, Sam. You should have it."

I shamefully met her eyes.

"It's okay," she said again.

Was this understanding? Forgiveness? A simple act of kindness? Whichever it was, Gretta was allowing me this indulgence without question.

"Thank you," I whispered.

She tilted her head in the direction of the garden. "Maybe today we skip the list and go straight to the wine?"

"I'll grab two glasses."

⋆ ⋆ ⋆

I relaxed back into the weathered director's chair, the one Klose preferred. "Shouldn't we try to tackle something today?"

"What do you have in mind?" Gretta tipped her glass, catching the sunlight on the rim.

"The phone?"

"Oh, no, not the *fucking* phone."

"We can do it," I said, my cheer returned. "It's going to go better this time."

Twice already, we'd attempted to pay Mom's outstanding

phone bill and discontinue the service. We specifically picked this task from the whiteboard because we assumed it would be simple, but after sitting on hold both times for, no exaggeration, forty-five minutes while being fed an audio loop of synthesized jazz, Gretta had hung up, and not happily.

She took a measured breath and another sip of wine. "I'm not sure I can do that again. Can't we give that job to someone else? Like Jenni?"

"Let's try it one more time and if we don't get anywhere, we pawn it off. Deal?"

"Okay," she moaned and dialed the customer-support number.

"Put it on speaker," I said.

The number only rang once before someone answered. Gretta looked at me in disbelief and I flashed her an encouraging thumbs-up.

"How can I help you today?" the phone rep chirped.

Gretta explained we were calling on behalf of our mother who recently passed away, and that we'd like to please pay the balance due, turn off the phone, and close the account.

"I'm so sorry for your loss, ma'am," said the rep. "I can help you with that. I'll need to first ask you a few identifying questions. What is your mother's password for the account?"

Gretta shrugged and I shrugged back.

"We don't have the password for the account," Gretta returned in a clear, unapologetic tone, "but I have the account number and the most recent bill right here. Also, we're calling from her phone. Is that enough?"

"I'm sorry, but I need her password to access her account."

Gretta whispered to me, "They do realize we're trying to pay them money, right?"

"I can give you the hint to the password," the rep offered, and I nodded encouragingly.

"Okay," Gretta said thinly. "What is the hint?"

"The hint is: 'Who is your favorite actress?'"

"Oh, I got this." I spoke directly into the phone. "Is it Jane Fonda?"

"It is not Jane Fonda," said the rep.

Gretta and I looked at each other in surprise.

"Is it Susan Sarandon?"

"It is not."

Gretta covered the microphone. "Who's the woman with the cool, short silver hair?"

"Is it Judy Dench?" I said to the phone rep.

"It is not Judy Dench."

"Okay, let me think . . . oh, I know who it is! I know who it is! Of course, it's Katharine Hepburn." I smiled triumphantly; certain I'd finally guessed correctly.

"I'm sorry, it is not Katharine Hepburn."

"It's not Katharine Hepburn?" I returned incredulously, and mouthed to Gretta, "Who the *hell* is it?"

I scanned my mental catalog of strong female leads and remembered the first so-called "grown-up" movie I watched with Mom as a kid, the 1977 Oscar-winning drama called *Julia,* which I remembered nothing about except that Mom loved it and it starred Jane Fonda and—

"Vanessa Redgrave!" I exclaimed.

"It is not Vanessa Redgrave."

I threw my hands in the air. "I give up! We've named all her favorites. There's no one else. I mean, are you sure it's not Katharine Hepburn?"

"Do you want the second password hint?"

Gretta leaned in like a contestant on *Jeopardy*: "I would like the second password hint."

"'Who is your favorite *actor*?'"

Gretta straightened with confidence. “I know this! It’s Robert Redford.”

“No, ma’am, I’m sorry,” sighed the rep, equally exhausted by our efforts. “Do you want to think about it and call back?”

“Oh, we will not be calling back.” Gretta hung up with her middle finger.

We finished the bottle of Sauvignon Blanc as the sun set behind the redwood tree. While we were no longer strangers to death, we had a long way to go before we’d become experts at this, if we ever would. Unless you’re a mortician or a gravedigger, death is lost on amateurs, I thought, which was most people like us who still felt like kids and who now identified as orphans, and who weren’t prepared for what this new job entailed.

Open the Door

As Gretta predicted, this new job—the one we hadn't applied for nor expected to get—became a nearly full-time job as we put our paid work on hold. I could do this because as a writer who worked for myself and from my own home, I set my own hours. On the day Mom died, I was packed for a one-day writing retreat in Los Angeles. The following week, I was scheduled to meet my client again in New York City to fine-tune her messaging before she took center stage to discuss gender equity with a handful of prominent female leaders, including fashion icon Diane von Furstenberg. When I was first invited on the trip months ago, I'd called Mom right away.

"Guess who I get to meet in New York City?"

"Who?" she returned with matched enthusiasm.

"The one and only DVF."

"Diane?"

"That's the one."

"Well, tell her I said hi," Mom replied, trying to sound cool. "You know, she and I go way back."

Since the early '70s, Mom had confidently worn the design that Diane became most famously known for: the wrap dress. As a nod to them both, I'd packed one for the trip—not one of Diane's, but a contemporary knockoff from H&M. I wasn't often invited by clients to step away from the computer screen and interact with them in the real world, so I'd been excited for my East Coast trip, where I might rub elbows with a celebrity and also give my writer's wrist a break.

But then I'd had to cancel when Mom changed my plans.

"Don't worry about it," assured my client. "There'll be more trips. You need to be with your family right now."

As my sisters and I continued to meet at the house and diligently work the whiteboard, including field trips to close bank accounts and wrestle with the DMV, people came forward to help us with the Business of Dying. "What can I do?" was the general ask, and we assigned jobs to a select few who were happy to come over to the house to water the garden and bring in the mail. The news had spread by now, through social channels and the old-fashioned way—people talking—and when the obit ran, the calls, texts, and emails flooded in.

The dreaded obit.

When Klose's ran on the front of *The North Coast* section of the local paper, with a picture of him on a trip to Puerto Vallarta, wearing his summer straw hat and a blue button-up with a pen in the right pocket, I thought, how did *you* become the subject of an obit? While most people skip this section unless they expect to know someone in it, Klose had a habit of reading the obits every Sunday with great attention. He believed that giving people their proper tribute was the honorable thing to do, and he'd read aloud, to whomever was in the room, the ones that stood out to him, that touched him in some way or revealed something about a person that he believed ought to be noted and remembered.

"Jim, here, took a leave from GE and spent five years as an

officer aboard the USS Rowan," he might say. "And ninety-year-old Beatrice sailed from Hawaii to Alaska when she was a young woman. Loved a crabcake. Big advocate of water conservation. Sounds like a pretty cool dame."

On the day he appeared in the paper, staring back at me in his straw hat, I struggled to make sense of the reverse image—him layered within the text instead of on the other side of the page where he ought to be, reading glasses falling down his nose, drinking a cup of black coffee.

And now Mom had her own corner of the page, and I refused to read it, to settle my eyes on the picture of her sitting in a field of Northern California wildflowers with the sun brightening her face, an image from another time when she was invincible, my mother who would live forever. I didn't want to acknowledge her death in this way. It was so public, and as far as I was concerned, her death was between me and her, between a mother and a daughter. It was private. A family matter. Yes, Mom was a well-known figure, but my loss was mine; she belonged to me. Maybe my reaction was selfish. She'd been important to so many people, and still, I didn't want to share her with a wide circulation of readers.

I folded up the paper and opened my dresser drawer, the one that was beginning to collect a variety of things I was hiding in the shadows: the note, her perfume, and now this. I slammed the drawer shut, and harder than I meant to, pinching my finger and cracking a nail. The tears came fast and furious as I slunk to the floor. "Goddammit, Mom! You're not supposed to be an obituary!"

Throughout my life, my mother's name, Susan Swartz, had appeared regularly as a byline, attached to words that were vibrant and alive—a syndicated column she'd written, a keynote speech she was giving, her name highlighted in a program or underneath the sweeping letters of a book title. And now, here, in black and white—*Susan Swartz, longtime reporter, columnist, dies at 76.*

"You're more than a headline," I cried.

To be fair, her obit was more than a headline. The full article was a generous half-page, six columns wide. This was more print space than most anyone receives, and Mom would have been honored by the amount of attention, and I could imagine the playful banter between her and Klose.

"Now what just a minute," he'd tease. "You got the front page of the section, plus a jump to the top of A5?"

"Hey, you got a color photo," she'd poke back. "Mine's in black-and-white. I'm all washed out."

A colleague of theirs had written it, a man named Chris who'd worked at the newspaper as long as they had, and who'd been a friend of our family for decades. Always brought a pie to Friendsgiving and gave me a generous check when I graduated from high school.

He'd called me the day after, still in the early hours of shock.

"I'm so sorry, Sam." His voice cracked and I knew he was crushed by the news, like we all were, wrestling with the loss of his friend and colleague while still trying to do his job. "I'm writing the obit, and I know this is hard, but can I ask you a few questions?"

"Chris, I don't know how to do this."

"Just tell me what she meant to you. Can you do that?"

I'd paced the room, searching for words. "I don't know what to say," I whispered. There was no quote that could capture my sense of loss, of what it meant to be Susan's daughter. I'd eventually said something in an effort to say something, an incomplete sentiment that I preferred to leave forgotten in the back of my dresser drawer, but plenty had read my stumbling quote and reached out after the obit ran to offer their own.

Oh, my God . . . Just oh, my God, messaged a friend.

I just saw the paper. I am stunned. Just numb, wrote another.

My oldest childhood friend texted in all caps: *THIS IS SO FUCKED.*

I appreciated their uncensored honesty. It was far easier to digest than platitudes like "at least she's in a better place now" or "at least she's no longer in pain." I appreciated that the words were hard to find. And I didn't fault people for their discomfort around the topic, for their awkwardness or resistance to approach it. Whatever they said was welcome, it was okay, because there was no right way to talk about it. Hell, I still didn't know what to say. I was learning that some terms were outdated; there was new language to use and saying the correct thing was tricky—no doubt the reason why Target didn't stock "Sorry for your suicide" sympathy cards. Not a sentiment that rolls off the tongue, nor one that's easily stuffed into a pink envelope. I almost preferred finding gifts left on my doorstep without the sender, like the pot of red tulips I discovered after returning from a walk, the sweet little packages of tissues tucked into the screen door, and the bag of groceries that happened to magically appear along with the daily mail. The simple notes attached, *I'm so sorry* or *Love you!*, were enough. They didn't require lengthy conversation, yet they communicated the most important message: You are not alone. I needed this reminder because most of the time, my grief felt like my responsibility, mine alone to hold, and I staggered around my house, unsure when my heavy heart might drop out of my body and knock me backward onto the floor.

In the days after Mom's obit ran and people kindly stepped forward in their own ways, I began to understand I wasn't suffering singularly; I was surrounded by a community of people who were sharing our family's loss, some of whom had personal experience in this dark arena and the resilience to steady me into a chair. This helped. I thought, this is how I will get through this. This is the only way I will get through this. I will surround myself with friends and family and I will let them help me. I will invite them into my house to sit with me, to be with me, to talk or not say anything at all.

I'd always been equal parts independent and introverted, the Go It Alone type, so this private declaration was notable for me. To mark the shift in my personal evolution, I wrote a message to myself on an oversized index card—*Open the Door!*—and stuck it on the fridge. On the night that Miriam arrived at my house with a Zabar's Bagels and Spreads Kit that her nephew had overnighted from New York, we feasted on smoked whitefish and salmon pâté, scallion cream cheese, and sparkling wine. There were eight of us, passing bagels and exchanging containers in a hungry frenzy around my round table designed for four, and when I looked around at the group of us squeezed together, sharing laughter and a lighthearted moment, I thought, this is not awful; we are together in this.

I baited Miriam, the only Jewish person in the room. "Well, if this is what it means to 'sit shiva,' I'm in."

"Sam . . ." Miriam rolled her eyes. "This is not sitting shiva. It's just bagels."

"Either way, could your nephew send us a box every month?"

The following morning, when I fetched the cream cheese for a leftover bagel, I smiled at the command—*Open the Door!*—thinking that if Mom were here, that's what she'd advise me to do because that's what they did. Before Klose got sick and she became a widow, their door was always open, either literally or symbolically. On any given day, they welcomed people into their home, and when they weren't hosting, they were frequently out with friends or engaging with their community in some way. They lived by the mantra *Open the Door!*, which is why

I regretted that Mom had died alone, isolating herself on that steep cliff, removed from her fabric of friends and family.

"I will do this differently," I asserted out loud between bites of bagel. I will open up. I will let people in.

And then, within a week, my plan for building community was upended when the governor of California issued a state-mandated shelter-in-place order to safeguard against the spread of a deadly virus. I was forced to shut the door.

Lockdown

Two weeks before Mom died, I'd moved across town into a new home, my first separated from my husband and as a single mom. Before I signed the lease, Mom toured the single-level house on the sunny corner and approved with a smile. "I can see you happy here." She compared the downtown neighborhood with the wide, tree-lined streets to Albany, where Klose grew up. "He'd approve too, and you bet I'll be over all the time."

That had been our plan, and while she was back East visiting her sister, I moved in and began to unpack. When she returned from Massachusetts, I thought, now we can start our new life together, one that included not only Derby and me, but also, Mom. I'd even joked with her. "Now that you're a widow, and I'm nearly divorced, we can double date."

It had been only a month since I'd moved in, and my original plans had dramatically changed. I was surrounded by packing boxes of my own and additionally, I was sifting through what remained of my mother's life. I'd started a pile of her forwarded mail on the kitchen table, and many smaller stacks of her tax documents and credit-card statements occupied a corner of my home office. The newness of the house held the finality of her death, and I wondered if her prediction could come true under the new circumstances. Could I be happy here? I was doubtful, but I guessed that time would tell and, in the meantime, or at least until the state mandate was lifted, I had nowhere else to go.

Due to the COVID outbreak, I was able to create my own version of sitting shiva on my living-room couch. Elastic pants and a lime-green pullover became my daily wear, a look that suited both grieving and living primarily indoors. On the day Mom's obit ran in the local newspaper, the front-page headline read: *Pence to Lead Virus Response*. I'd mostly overlooked it because I was consumed by the bigger story impacting my family, but there could be no ignoring it now. News of a deadly virus was impossible to miss, and as the country had been advised, I dutifully retreated indoors and began stockpiling canned goods, hand sanitizer, and toilet paper. Until the threat cooled off—probably in a couple of weeks, at most, we figured—Jenni, Gretta, and I agreed not to see each other, to conduct family business over Zoom, and in the meantime, to put a memorial on hold.

"I'm kind of relieved," Gretta said into the camera phone. "We just had Daddy's memorial a month ago and . . ." She paused.

"And it was a *huge* production," I finished her sentence, remembering the reception hall packed with more than three hundred people drinking Zinfandel and eating handfuls of nuts. We'd landed on an abbreviated menu of Costco cashews, chocolate-chip cookies, and California wine because "that's exactly what he'd want," Mom asserted at our memorial planning meeting at the Unitarian Church, underlining all three items—nuts, cookies, wine—in her pocket notebook. We didn't argue and even agreed that Klose's directive would have been more concise: For God's sake, don't make a big deal of it.

"I'm with Gretta that we need to take a break before planning another event," Jenni agreed from her little square on the screen, "especially given the circumstances. No one can safely attend a memorial right now, although that leaves us with five cases of unopened wine. We overestimated how much people drink at these things."

"Red or white?" Gretta and I jumped in at the same time.

"Red, you freeloaders."

"Oh, you can have it," I relinquished. "Red gives me headaches, plus . . ." I leaned into the frame. "I just learned that my favorite local winemaker will deliver Sauv Blanc to my doorstep. At least, that's one pandemic perk."

I missed being in the physical presence of my sisters, and even though I'd just committed to "open the door," I closed it without much resistance. I knew how to retreat, how to be alone. Solitary hours had always been okay with me: safe, quiet, controlled. While many of my friends were already voicing panic at the idea of shrinking their social circles and locking their doors to the outside world, I easily adjusted to the isolation. In a way, it was a welcome reprieve. There was nowhere to go, to put on a false smile, to act like I was keeping it all together. Since Mom died three short weeks ago, my energy had been consumed and directed toward *doing*—making phone calls, filling out paperwork, helping to manage the details of their estate—and now, in the stillness of my own home, I was left alone to do that thing therapists love to prescribe: sit in your loss, face the darkness, become intimate with it. The surprise uncertainty of the virus slowed everything down, and within the forced pause, I found room to grieve.

In those first days of paralyzed inactivity, Mom's absence stepped forward in a new way, making its own kind of noise that reverberated in the silence. It could sound like a slowly dripping faucet, one melancholy note in the distance, the bow of a violin slowly crossing a single string. In other moments, it sounded like howling wind, glass shattering on the floor. Furious screams. Most days, Mom's absence stood alongside me in the shower, a hallowed outline in the corner that didn't move as I wept against the wall. I soon got used to the soundtrack of my grief, an unpredictable but constant ache, a pain that wouldn't quiet, that wouldn't subside. And since it was always there, I adopted a new routine and a new pace, one to accommodate my loss, to absorb the shock of her death. On the days Derby was with his father, I'd wake up early and make coffee. I'd walk around the block in the early light. I'd come back inside to write. I'd stare into the void and wonder how all of this had happened, shuffling from room to room, shaking my head in confusion. How can you be *dead?* How can *you* be dead? I struggled to make sense of it, to put her death in context. It was as if the Earth had swallowed my mother whole. *Where did you go?* When no answer arrived, I'd rub my tired eyes and write some more. I quickly lost track of the hours.

I understood that many people were losing their jobs due to forced lockdown and sickness, so I was careful not to complain that I had full-time paid work, but I wasn't sure how I would get through it. Writing required long hours of uninterrupted focus and I was distracted a lot of the time, somewhere else, in the shadows of grief. I willed my mind to go quiet and cold, to push myself aside and give voice to someone else. This is the work of a ghostwriter, after all, to compartmentalize your own thoughts, and eventually, for at least four to five hours a day, I could zero in on the page and leave my loss temporarily in my periphery.

Most days passed like this, with mechanical repetition. Early morning coffee. Walk. Write. I'd break mid-afternoon to bring in the mail, much of it forwarded to Mom. Her J. Jill and L.L. Bean catalogs now came to me, along with her

AARP publication, her subscription to *Yankee* magazine, and pleas for support from the Sierra Club, Planned Parenthood, Doctors Without Borders, the Alzheimer's Association, and the American Red Cross. By a landslide, it was more mail than I received on any given day, and I dutifully carried it in and wiped it down with disinfecting sanitizer, a new FCC recommendation that added to my heightened state of unease. At lunchtime, I'd prepare simple food—cheese and crackers, maybe an apple—only to quickly lose interest in eating. Not yet ready to return to work and unsure what else to do, I'd wander into the bathroom and stare at my reflection. I remembered once reading that grief ages a person, expediates the process, and I saw the truth of this now. I looked worn, like I'd been chain-smoking and sitting in the direct sun without sunblock. At least, I reconciled, no one can see me like this, hidden inside, growing older behind the door.

Throughout my solitary evenings, I watched *The Great British Bake Off*, one of the only things I found palatable. Everything else on TV was either too intense, too flip, too confrontational, or too irrelevant. Some nights, I watched *The Crown*, because in a lot of ways, Princess Di seemed to have it worse than me. This was a consolation.

I retreated from social media: no scrolling, no posting. I didn't want to share my grief with a wide community, and it was too painful to watch others live without it. I fell behind in my responses to people's texts, emails, and letters. I was glad to receive them, they were comforting, but I had limited energy to respond in kind.

I also stopped reading novels, a favorite pastime of mine, but escaping into fiction felt more indulgent than watching baking shows. *I need to stay out here*, I thought, *in my own bad story*. Several well-intentioned friends sent me books on suicide and grief that might explain what I was going through, and these also piled up on my nightstand. I couldn't open them. The titles alone caused me to recoil. Maybe I'll read them later, I told myself. Until then, I couldn't make space for anyone else's horror. Mine was enough, mine was too much. I refused to look beyond my own experience, and I felt apologetic about this.

I knew I wasn't the only person grieving my mother, and I understood that the world was experiencing a collective sense of loss caused by a pandemic and political polarization, but my grief occupied its own space. It was uniquely mine, always with me, always near, and I wore it like an old sweater I dragged behind me on the floor.

Because of my shared-custody agreement and because my profession prefers the solitude of a home office, I had the privilege to grieve in a way my sisters could not. They both had public-facing jobs and other people to attend to in their homes.

"Between teaching a classroom of kids on Zoom and managing my own kids who are at home twenty-four hours a day, I don't have a second of quiet time to myself," Gretta lamented.

"There is no time," Jenni agreed, who was winding down a law practice and starting to head up a new organization.

It soon became evident to me how little time our culture allows for grief. Most employers only permit two-point-five days of bereavement leave to grieve the person who gave us life, or for the child we gave life to, or for the partner or friend with whom we've shared our lives.

Two-point-five days? Sometimes less. And not often paid.

That's the equivalent of rolling your car through a stop sign and slowing down just enough to look both ways before putting your foot back on the gas and accelerating into the fast lane. Jenni, Gretta, and I all took one full week off from our jobs after Mom died—much longer than what is typically permitted—and then we each had to jump back into our separate work to relieve substitute teachers, meet looming deadlines, and fulfill client needs. The three of us agreed we needed that first week, at least, to start processing the practical repercussions of Mom's suicide in the wake of Klose's death, and when that week was over, we understood that navigating the emotional wreckage caused by losing two parents within three months would take much longer. Unfortunately, we couldn't afford to take much more extended time off. The cultural expectation was to keep going, to push through. Grieve during your free time. Or bypass it until later.

But grief doesn't like waiting. It's impatient, really, and until you are hit with it, you don't know how much time grief demands and how imperative it will be to give it what it needs: breath and space. Grief insists we slow down, sit quietly, and hibernate for a while before getting *back to life.*

I gave in to my grief because I could, and because what life was I in such a hurry to get back to, anyway? The life I had before Mom's suicide was no longer available to me. There was no returning to before, and I was in no rush to start my life without her. While forced isolation created unexpected complications and hardships, it did allow me time to reckon with death, to absorb the shock of it while wandering aimlessly around the house, to stare out the back window into the dormant garden without anyone from HR to tap me on the shoulder and nudge me back to my cubicle.

In an unexpected way, the pandemic presented me with the gift of time, and given the cultural attitude that grief deserves no more than a long weekend, I regarded it an act of rebellion to allow myself open-ended hours to miss Mom. I also considered it a necessity, fearing what might happen if I didn't give myself permission to feel her absence. If I didn't let myself go there, if I buried the hurt and the horror, I worried what it would do to me. Pain like mine didn't want to be ignored. Oh, no, if ignored, it would wait me out, and I couldn't know when, but at some point and absolutely, I was sure it would return and hurt me all over again. Even though it would have been so much easier to numb—I knew how to eat, drink, and binge-watch my way through discomfort—the pain of avoiding and not feeling presented its own kind of suffering, so I deliberately roamed my quiet house and willed the tears to come forward until they burnt rivers down my face.

⋆ ⋆ ⋆

What was grief, anyway? I wondered as I endlessly wandered. I had been heartbroken. I had been sad. I had been lonely before. But I'd never known grief. Was it an emotion? A condition? A state of being? I'd always regarded it as a nebulous and shapeless thing, and now, grief felt like its own presence, so physically heavy, so tangibly near. I felt my grief on me, coursing through me, filling the room. It was both internal and external; it plugged my ears and pressed on my chest. Wherever I went, it was always there, touching everything.

In the space that Mom vacated, grief slipped in. It wasn't a replacement for her but because it was so insistently present, so intensely painful, it kept her close, within reach, still alive in some way. And this aliveness extended to me. I'd never felt so awake. Alert. In my body. And not in the way people in probiotic commercials jump in the air and proclaim, "I feel alive!" No, I didn't feel alive in the good way, but rather in the way that there was no hiding, no forgetting the aching hole in my chest, the raw sensitivity of my skin, the understanding that I'd been cut so badly, I might never fully heal. My version of grief kept me in a heightened state of physical pain. It forced an acute awareness that wouldn't let me close my eyes, it wouldn't let me un-see, it wouldn't let me un-feel. If ever I started to nod off, it would nudge me awake. Hey, you, I'm here. Look around. Look at me. I'm everywhere. Inside you. Around you. Everywhere.

Mirror, Mirror

It was becoming easy to lose track of the isolated days, wandering the twenty-five feet between my home office and the kitchen to reheat my coffee for the third or fourth time, and to check the front porch for mail. Today, as I passed the hallway mirror between the two rooms, I caught a glimpse of myself and abruptly stopped. There she was—Mom, staring back at me.

Where I'd always delighted in our resemblance, in the look-alike comments when we went places together—"Mother and daughter?"—now, my reflection haunted me. It hurt to look at my own face because it served as a painful reminder of what was missing, of who was missing, and I'd observed this effect on other people too. Just a couple of days before the shelter-in-place order, Sara, a longtime friend of the family, showed up at the house and when I greeted her at the door, I saw a flash of the same startled recognition in her eyes.

"I'm sorry," I said and covered my face with my hands. "I look too much like her, don't I?"

"It's okay." She stepped forward and hugged me. "It's a good thing. I recognize her smile from happier days."

When Mom was alive, she'd say to me, "I see my younger self in you," and I'd proudly return, "And I see my older self in you." Mom's face, creased by years of laughter and active curiosity, provided me with a glimpse of my own bright future. At some point, I would have her knitted brow, the upturned lines fanning her eyes, and I welcomed this face.

Her face.

I knew a lot of women who outwardly groaned at the suggestion they looked like their mothers. "Oh, please," my friend Katy said when I noted the obvious resemblance between her and her mother, Joan. "I don't want to look anything like her, *especially* the older version." I understood Katy's opposition because I was privy to their complicated history. But I felt the opposite about my face. It had always been my honor to look like Mom. She was radiant until the end. Even at Klose's memorial, three months before her own death, she entered the room with her dazzling smile and her head held high, expecting to be warmly welcomed by a crowd that did not disappoint; three hundred faces smiled back at her. At every age of my life, I'd wanted my own face to reflect my mother's confidence, her optimism, her relentless anticipation of what came next. But now that she was gone, my future felt uncertain.

Oh, mirror, mirror on the wall, who am I without you? Where is my bright future if you are not in it? I stared at my solitary image in the mirror. Who would I become without my mother looking back at me, without my twin reflection reminding me who I was, from where I came, from whom I belonged?

Playing Detective

This felt like an existential identity crisis, this questioning of who I was without my mother. I began to wrestle with an uncomfortable suspicion. It went beyond: *Who am I?* I started to wonder about Mom's true character. *Who was she?* Her suicide continued to perplex most everyone who knew her. Her childhood friends, her early colleagues and most recent contemporaries—truly, everyone I talked to didn't understand it, and many didn't trust it. Her own therapist, even, who'd had a session with Mom just days before she jumped, stammered with shock when we called her with the news. "Are you sure? Are you sure it was *her*? Are you sure it was Susan?" No one could believe that my mother, famously full of life, had ended her life.

In the two weeks that became four weeks that became an entire spring of lockdown, I opened my own amateur investigation into Mom's death. In the stillness of the evenings, either alone in the house or after Derby was tucked into bed, I hunkered down on the couch with a notebook and pen, chronicling her last days, hour by hour. Who was she with on Saturday and Sunday? What was she doing on Monday? Had she dropped any hints that indicated what was to come the night before? I reached back into my memory as far as it would go to identify anything—a throughline in my own life or hers—that might explain this hideous ending.

On many nights, exhausted by my own efforts to connect the disparate dots, I'd call someone who knew her even before I did, people who predated my arrival: her sister, her college roommate, her longtime bestie from San Diego who remembers the day I was born.

Help me see what I'm missing, I appealed. Is there something I don't know, something in her past that might explain her unraveling?

I was chasing after an explanation to help me make sense of the nonsensical, to help me find my footing again, to help me regain some control in this new reality that was upside down and underwater. If I could understand the "how did this happen?" then maybe I could accept that it had happened at all. And if I could understand its origin, then maybe I could stop punishing myself for what I hadn't stopped and couldn't undo. My questions wouldn't release me, and my pleas for answers went unmet—

"I'm in as much shock as you."
"I would have never expected this from her."
"It just doesn't sound like the Suzi I knew."

Mom's suicide evaded us all.

I knew from reading about the deaths of comedian Robin Williams and celebrity chef Anthony Bourdin that suicide doesn't claim a type—the lonely and alone, the fringe misfits, the addicts, the outwardly troubled and disenfranchised. Suicide doesn't discriminate; it isn't reserved for certain categories of people, and for me to think so was an unfair assumption. One can be successful, brilliant, vivacious, and adored the world over and still suffer silently, in ways that aren't easily detectable or diagnosed.

I knew this. Intellectually, I knew it, yet when it came to my own mother, suicide didn't fit. It felt like the wrong ending, an inconsistency in the story I'd been told my whole life, a gross error on the last page that needed to be retracted. I sat back on the couch after hanging up with her college roommate, Karen, who reinforced popular opinion: "She was always up for anything, so happy, so much fun." Karen was right that Mom was upbeat much of the time. She didn't have a history of depression, anxiety, or even bad moods. At her lowest, she might report that she was feeling "crummy" or "blue" and quickly reverse: "But not to worry, all is well."

What happened to my happy mother? When did her story change?

I thought about her favorite mantra, all is well. She said it so often, and now I wondered what definition of the term she'd most identified. Adequate, satisfactory, competent? Fortunate, healthy? I might not yet be able to accept Mom's suicide, but there was no denying she hadn't been "well" for a while, and I thought I understood why—caretaking Klose for over a year as he traveled a maze of cancer ups and downs had exhausted her. Managing his medications, his oncology appointments, his walker and mobile oxygen tank, his special dietary needs and restrictions, his fluctuating pain levels, their escalating medical bills, and shared fatigue had started to wear on her.

"I'm overtired," she admitted one night when Jenni, Gretta, and I stopped by to visit them both. "And I'm also really sick of cooking," she said with an exaggerated sigh as she poured herself a glass of wine. "I've never been the overly domestic type, as you all know." She'd meant it as a joke, but there was truth there. In addition to her extended caretaking role, Mom had assumed full responsibility of the household—washing dishes, doing laundry, grocery shopping, and preparing countless meals—a domestic workload that had historically been shared between them, and that she'd never fully embraced. Even after she'd retired from the newspaper a few years prior, she'd remained professionally active. She started a blog, aptly called, *My "So-Called" Retirement*, and she was close to finishing her first novel. Mom continued to be asked to speak at local literary events about writing, feminism, women's health and aging, and how they intersected. She never said it, for it was implied she would forever remain the "writer" over the "wife," and I wondered if her new caretaking role rubbed up against her sense of visibility and relevance.

"Can I order a pizza?" Gretta had offered and shot me a helpless look. "Or can I make you dinner?"

"Klose ate earlier and I'm not hungry." Mom waved her off, but not dismissively. "I just need to sleep." She took a seat at the kitchen table, out of earshot of Klose watching news in the other room.

"Is there *anything* we can do?" Gretta asked again.

Mom sighed. "I think if I could sleep, I could do this, but when it's time for bed, I can't. I just lie there, listening to Klose breathing, staring into the dark. Sometimes I'm still awake when the sun starts to come up. When I hear the birds begin to chirp, at least then I have hope that it's a new day and that Klose will get good news and that we will get through this."

She didn't say it outright, but not only was she overtired, she was scared, we all were. Even though Klose had battled his cancer into temporary submission and his oncologist was enthusiastic about a new cancer drug with a high success rate, an unwelcome turn remained a possibility. "There are no guarantees," his doctor cautioned us. "A good outlook today could change tomorrow." Mom was trying to stay positive and upbeat, but her smile had started to thin.

Her primary doctor prescribed her sleeping pills for insomnia. Mom had never taken a sleeping aid and was averse to pills in general, summarizing her resistance with simple distaste: "Yuck to pills." At first, she opted not to fill the prescription, until one afternoon when I stopped by, at her request, to help her edit the final draft of her novel. We were in the middle of a sentence fix when she looked across the table with worry. "I hate taking pills, but I don't know what else to do. I just can't *think*," she emphasized, "if I can't sleep."

"If you're still not sleeping, maybe try the pill, and see?"

She didn't refuse, which told me she was suffering more than she was letting on, and within a few days, she reported gladly over the phone, "I slept through the night!" The buoyancy was back in her voice. But a week later, a different doctor told her the particular sleeping pill she was taking was linked to early-onset dementia in people over age seventy. "I have to stop taking them," she asserted. "I won't let them turn my brain into mush."

I recognized this comment had less to do with her than it had to do with her own mother, whose beautiful mind had drifted into the engulfing fog caused by Alzheimer's disease. I was about fifteen when Mom explained that "Grandma Helen is going to live in a nursing home where people can help her with her memory. She often forgets things, like when she last ate or where she put her purse or sometimes where she is, or . . . who she is."

Nearly every summer, Mom returned to New England to visit her sister and also to see Helen in a nursing home in Newburyport, a few towns over from Ipswich, where Nancy lived, and although she didn't say much upon her return, I imagined that the act of observing her mother's mental decline and being incapable to stop it was deeply painful. Once, when I pressed her for details, she said, resentment in her voice, "This disease is cruel. It has robbed my mother of herself. That woman in there isn't her."

Throughout my teenage years and well beyond, I watched Mom channel what I perceived to be helplessness over her mother's illness into her own health. She adopted the mantra: You're only as good as your brain. Determined to beat the genetic odds of Alzheimer's passing down to her, she followed the latest studies and research, read every article on brain health, and adopted fitness and food regiments that proposed to prevent mental decline. When Mom learned that turmeric was considered a "brain booster" with cognitive advantages, she started sprinkling it on everything. When she read that blueberries were a superfood linked to slowing down the symptoms of Alzheimer's, they showed up every morning on her Cheerios.

★ ★ ★

After Mom died, there were people who asked my sisters and I separately if we knew she was compromised. They were careful with how they posed this question. No one asked explicitly: Did you know your mother was suicidal? Did you know she was going to jump off a cliff? Instead, they carefully suggested, "Did you have any idea?" They hinted, "Were there any indications?" They wondered aloud, "Did you know she was thinking about this?"

I understood well their confusion and I appreciated that they, too, were searching for answers, for something they overlooked, but no, I did not know my mother planned to do what she did and if I had, I would have moved heaven and Earth to stop her.

Yes, we knew she was overtired. We knew she felt trapped and stir-crazy in her own home. We knew she worried about following her own mother into a mental fog. Were these indications of what was to come? Were these warning signs of suicide? I asked myself this now. Should I have known better? Has anyone who's lost someone in this way *known better*? Has anyone who's lost someone in this way prevented it? At the time,

I thought her fatigue, her stress, and her worry were appropriate reactions to the situation. Her husband was battling cancer and she had stepped into the demanding and exhausting role of full-time caregiver. I thought she deserved some grace to go a little off the rails, to not keep it together all the time, to be able to say, this is a fraught time.

Did I think she was *unwell*? Yes. Did I think she wanted to die? No. Did I think she was capable of doing what she did? Never. Plenty of people get tired and stressed and worried, and they don't write a suicide note, and carry it out.

She did.

My mother was compromised.

And the question I continued to ask myself throughout the seemingly endless nights of lockdown was: how did this happen? When did her mind take this fatal turn? After his autopsy report, Robin Williams's wife learned that he had Lewy bodies, abnormal clumps of protein in his brain cells that can cause anxiety and paranoia, memory loss, insomnia, and dementia, and lead to an incurable brain disorder that has an associated risk of suicide. For Williams, Lewy bodies was an explanation, not a definitive answer, but a solid start to unraveling the yarn. What was my mother's explanation? Age, diet, DNA, friendships, sleep, geography. Doctors say these factors play a significant role in our mental health, yet they don't provide a reliable or definitive forecast, because when someone like my mother, who had a long history of health and happiness, steps off the edge—how do you explain that? When someone appears to be doing everything right, how do you explain when things go so terribly wrong?

Looking back, there was a point when the effects of not sleeping while trying to outguess, outsmart, and outrun Klose's cancer seemed to become something else. Heightened agitation. Impatience. Quick to frustration and new lows that weren't characteristic of her. My sisters and I privately acknowledged that she'd reached an unfamiliar stress point, but more often than not, our attempts to help alleviate her workload were declined. "I can do this," she'd insist, and sometimes resentfully.

The morning Klose called me and appealed, "Hey, Sam, can you come up here? Your mom needs some help," I was relieved. His request was casual, and still I heard his seriousness, an unspoken acknowledgement that he saw it, too. When I arrived thirty minutes later, her defenses were down and she welcomed me warmly. "Do you want some tea? I just put the kettle on." She smiled and still I could see it, the cloaked sadness in her eyes.

"Sounds good." I sat down at the table and watched her prepare our cups: a bag of chamomile and hot water to the top.

She took a seat across from me and slid a spoon across the table. "Thanks for coming," she apologized. "I know you probably have a busy day of work."

"It's fine. I'll catch up with work later. Tell me what's going on."

She took a deep breath, as if preparing to say something she didn't want to vocalize. "I'm not sure I can do this," she admitted weakly. "I don't think I'm very good at this, taking care of Klose, taking care of me." She looked down and stirred honey into her tea.

"Mom." I leaned forward, reaching my hand out to touch hers. "You've taken on *a lot*." I glanced around the table, covered with a scattering of handwritten lists, an oversized paper calendar scribbled with upcoming appointments, unopened mail, pill bottles, and empty glasses. "These lists alone would make anyone crazy. Let me help you. Please."

She lifted her eyes. "Okay," she relented. "Thank you."

By the time I left later that afternoon, she'd accepted my offer to pick up groceries and take Klose to his bloodwork appointment the following day. We'd also created a master list that included the Post-it notes she'd stuck here and there—on the fridge, the bathroom mirror, the bedroom doorframe—that called attention to things that needed immediate attention: *buy toilet paper, take out garbage, reorder prescription.* I drove home feeling happy to have provided her some relief and hopeful that we'd get through this together, as a family.

A week later, the narrative changed.

I called early one morning to check in. "Hi Mom, how's it going?" And she snapped with impatience. "Sammy, I don't want to do this. I just can't do this anymore."

"What do you mean," I repeated her words slowly, "that you don't want to 'do' this?"

"I mean," she said, her agitation returning and her voice growing louder, "I don't want to *do* this anymore." She underscored every word.

In our family, words were carefully chosen and delivered intentionally. The difference between "I'm not sure I can do this" and "I don't want to do this" was worth noting, and I noted it instantly. The first sentiment spoke to ability and the second referred to willingness. In the days since I'd sat across from her at the kitchen table drinking tea, something had changed. She'd flipped the script, and this revision of her original statement alarmed me. As soon as we hung up, I contacted her primary doctor, who didn't share my alarm but nonetheless referred her to a psychiatrist.

★ ★ ★

"Oh gawd, no," Mom protested when I showed up two days later to drive her to the intake appointment. She stood in the middle of the living room with her hands planted firmly on her hips. "Sammy, we already have enough doctors between the two of us and I don't need a *psychiatrist*," she said with distaste. "I just need to get organized. And plus, I can't leave Klose alone."

"Sweetie, I'm fine." Klose looked up from reading the front

page of the *Times*. "Plus, I have a date with Rachel [Maddow] this afternoon. Listen to your daughter and go."

It was a short visit in an unremarkable room. Mom reluctantly answered questions and I filled in with the details she chose to leave out. The doctor listened, took a few notes on a pad of paper, then suggested Mom might be suffering from anxiety, perhaps circumstantial depression due to Klose's cancer, both treatable with more pills. Mom groaned under her breath as she took the white slip from the doctor's outstretched hand. As she and I walked out, I gestured down the hallway. "Should we go to the pharmacy now and have your prescription filled?"

Mom leveled her eyes at me. "I am not depressed, and I don't want to take any more pills."

I'd crossed a line, I knew it instantly, stepping in to parent my own mother. It hadn't been a conscious overstep, a deliberate usurping of her power; I'd just done what I thought was right, what I believed was needed in the moment, and she made it clear as she turned on her heels and walked out of the hospital with me trailing behind—she wasn't ready to step back, or even step aside. She was still the matriarch, she told me on the drive home, if anyone needed reminding.

* * *

This cascade of scenes is what continued to nag me during the long quiet hours of lockdown—

Why wouldn't you step back? Why wouldn't you take the damn pills? Why wouldn't you let us help you?

"Your mom was kind of a feminist icon, a leader of the community, always so independent, so strong, so cool. It was probably really hard for her to admit she was struggling," surmised Stacy, an old friend who'd spent many overnights at my house growing up and whom I'd called after receiving her condolence card.

"That's bullshit," I rejected. "If she was the fearless leader she proposed to be, she should have set a better example by accepting help."

"Wait, are you *mad* at her?" Stacy's tone shifted. "You know, suicide is the result of mental illness. You can't be mad at someone for being sick, Sam. She deserves your compassion, not your judgment. You really should think about talking to someone about your anger."

Meeting B

I paced the floors of my house for the next several days, pissed at Stacy and angry at Mom. I raised my voice, charging into the empty house. Yes, I am mad at you. I'm mad at you for leading us to believe you were okay, or, at least, okay enough. After you finally relented to taking antidepressants, you still insisted there was nothing for us to worry about, and every time we sat in the psychiatrist's office waiting room filling out the requisite forms that asked—*Are you sleeping enough? Eating enough? How is your mood?*—you insisted: "Fine, fine, fine." I sat right next to you, looking over your shoulder as your witness, and every time you came to the section about harming yourself—*Do you ever have suicidal thoughts?*—you'd roll your eyes, and check the "no" column with exaggerated annoyance, like: how dare anyone ask me such ridiculous questions? And when you didn't check the boxes to indicate alarm and initiate a distress signal, your doctors didn't check them for you, either. They took you on your word. We all did. At most, they'd adjust your medication, suggest meditation and other "stress-reducing" practices, and send you home. This was their error. Was it negligence, or was it medical protocol? If a patient insists they're healthy, and if they present as clinically healthy and do not check the boxes to indicate otherwise, then is it safe to conclude they're not a risk, a threat to themself? I don't know the answer, but as your daughter, I wanted to believe you were healthy enough, I see that now. I recognized that long-term caregiving had drained you, and when Klose began to lose his battle with cancer, I knew you were scared, and when he died, I could see you were in shock, as we all were, and grieving deeply, as we all were too. But this other thing you kept hidden from us, this darkness that had silently slid into your mind without invitation, this undercurrent that had begun to wrap its tentacles around you, this was your secret. And, maybe, that was my error—my oversight—because I trusted that if something menacing was lurking, feeding your mind with thoughts of doing harm to yourself, you would, of course, tell *me*, your daughter who was sitting right next to you in the waiting room and who would have helped you without question had you checked the other column: *Yes, sometimes I have thoughts of harming myself.* I'm mad at you for keeping this from me—for burying the lede, as you journalists say—and I'm mad at me for not reading further into the story, for not knowing how very close to the edge you were teetering.

This regret forms into a hot stone that I carry around in my pocket until it begins to sear my skin, and I consider that Stacy may be right about one thing—maybe I ought to talk to someone about my anger.

⋆ ⋆ ⋆

"You should call my brother," my friend and colleague Rebecca suggested.

"Your brother, the rabbi?"

"He's not practicing anymore. He's a grief counselor now."

I immediately pictured an older guy with a beard, wearing an itchy cable-knit sweater and polyester slacks, an Elliot Gould look-alike in a stuffy office surrounded by books. It was a snap stereotype and I was embarrassed I'd done it, but my mind had gone there without asking. While Rebecca continued talking, I Googled him, hoping an accurate photo would correct my wrong assumption. And there he was—aha!—early forties was my guess, fitted black tee, shaved head, wide smile, and hold on—were those tattoos? Standing at the base of the Colorado mountains, this rabbi looked very cool, very unstuffy. Still, I felt compelled to clarify: "You know I'm not Jewish," and considered sharing I'd been "sitting shiva" in Target sweatpants. I resisted.

"That doesn't matter," said Rebecca. "It's not religious counseling. He takes a spiritual approach to grief. It's nondenominational, totally unconventional, and he's worked with a lot of survivors of suicide."

Survivors of suicide.

It took me a moment before I realized she was referring to me. I'm the survivor? I hadn't thought of myself as a survivor; I'd been focused on how Mom hadn't survived and how I'd been left behind. I hadn't considered another title for myself beyond orphan, and especially not one that identified as more empowered than victimized. I sat up a little taller in my chair as I rolled it over—I have survived Mom. I am surviving her suicide. An interesting reframe, and perhaps one worth exploring. A day later, I called the rabbi.

* * *

Rabbi Baruch HaLevi answered on the first ring. "My sister said you might call, I'm so glad you did." His familiar greeting disarmed me right away. I'd been nervous as I dialed, unsure how grief counseling worked and already, he'd pushed clinical weirdness out of the way. "You can call me 'B' or Rabbi B or whatever you want, really. It's nice to finally meet you, officially," he said with a smile in his voice. "My sister's talked about your writing collaboration over the years, so I feel, in a way, like I know you, but"—he paused—"I know that talking about books is not the subject of this call."

"No." I hesitated, not sure what else to say, and hoped he'd continue to fill the air.

"I understand your mother has just passed away," he continued, more somberly. "I'm sorry for your loss."

It was the perfunctory line, the standard platitude—I'm sorry for your loss—but the way Rabbi B said it, I believed he meant it; they weren't empty words, he wasn't performing or reading from a script. As a ghostwriter, I've trained my ear to listen for what's really there or not there, to discern what's underneath or between someone's words. In pitch and tone, in a pregnant pause or an exaggerated run-on sentence, I hear what's implied, what's withheld, and what I heard from B was no subtext; he was on the level. Finally, I thought, someone who will tell me the truth, and allow me to speak mine.

"So, do you want to tell me what happened?"

I wavered. "Do you mean, tell you *how* she died?"

"If you can, if you want to."

I did, I felt this strongly. I did want to talk about how Mom died without having to skirt around the *ssssss* word, or whisper it, worrying about how it would sound, how it might create discomfort, invite judgment, and deciding—ultimately—to change the subject because most people would rather not talk about it.

"She died by . . . suicide," I said, stumbling myself. It hadn't been a word in Derby's vocabulary, and I was equally surprised when it had found its way into mine. I still hesitated to put "suicide" and "my mother" in a sentence together, as if they shouldn't touch or occupy the same line.

Rabbi B didn't react, he didn't flinch or recoil. He didn't change the subject. In fact, he nudged the door open a little more. "Do you want to talk about what she did to end her life?"

I conjured the scene: Mom on the edge of a cliff, the dramatic Pacific coastline below, and the final moment I wasn't there to witness and still couldn't shake, the one that consistently woke me up at three in the morning and felt too horrific, too damning, to speak out loud. Certainly, this man on the other end of the line didn't want to know specifics? I waited, expecting Rabbi B to retract his question once he realized what he'd asked.

He didn't take it back. He sat quietly, allowing the empty space to swell.

"Well, what she did was pretty awful," I said, eventually.

"Okay."

The subtext: I'm not afraid. I can see it. I can hold it. It's *okay*. With one word, I understood that Rabbi B was grounded in something I wanted for myself, a daring to open the dresser drawer and hold what was dark and painful up to the light.

"Okay," I returned and for the next fifty minutes, I told him all of it, at least as much as I'd had the courage to tell myself up to this point. He listened with a quiet seriousness, not interrupting, permitting my words to wander around in circles until I finally shared what I knew about the final moments of Mom's life. I spoke it all out loud: my guilt, my anguish, my hurt.

I let it all bleed into the phone line, and when I was finished, he asked, "How old was your mother?"

"She was seventy-six, but a young seventy-six," I defended. "She was vibrant, physically healthy, sharp."

"Still, seventy-six is not a shocking age to die. It is a shocking *way* to die. As you've likely learned from knowing my sister, I lost both my grandmother and my father to suicide, and what you're feeling is real, and it's complicated. Suicide is a shattering; it creates chaos and a disruptive void unlike other deaths. It can be very difficult to process, to orient to a new reality, when someone is here one moment and then, suddenly and surprisingly, they are gone. As someone who's been through it, what I can tell you is that suicide is dark and painful, it can be hideous, and for those of us who survive it, it leaves deep cuts and scars. Your challenge is not to cover them up, but to wear them. Your challenge is not to look past or bypass your complicated feelings in an effort to feel better, but to go toward them and feel your deep pain, to be in it. That's where you will find clarity and meaning and a way forward that redeems your mom's choices. Not right away, but eventually. There can be openings and new beginnings in endings—even in suicide—and finding them is the work."

His words were sobering. And also consoling, although where he was encouraging me to go or how I was meant to get there was foggy at best. I did understand one thing—I wasn't alone. Rabbi B was offering me a hand in the dark. I made another appointment for the following week.

* * *

Suicide is like a sneaker wave. Sudden. Taking. Selfish.

This insidious force can appear out of nowhere, run up a beach in seconds, and grab driftwood, sweep away beach chairs, snatch a child and the father who chases after him.

As a kid who grew up along the Northern California coast, I'd been warned of sneaker waves since I could stumble down to the ocean's edge. *Don't get too close*, Mom would say. *It's not as safe as it looks. Why don't you play in the high dunes instead?* I listened and I'd been cautious. I didn't wade in beyond my knees. More often, I didn't go in at all. I kept my distance. I played safe. And when I became a mother, I issued the same warning to Derby, and when he dared to dip a toe and chase the edge, I stood near, ready to pull him back with a firm word or a strong hand.

What makes sneaker waves deceptive is that they don't even look like waves; they appear to be steady water until suddenly they're upon you, pulling you down with a strength greater than your own and with a swiftness that catches you defenseless, helpless. Mom's suicide crashed to the shore on a day that appeared clear and calm. When we spoke on the phone that morning, I didn't detect imminent danger. On the surface, her words were consistent, her mood predictable, and I didn't see what was churning below, the dark current that was taking form, gaining momentum and force, and that would reach out a cold hand and grab her before I could pull her back. I'd been watching her; I had. I'd been cautious and careful not to look away for too long, standing by on the ready, in case she needed me. And still, I didn't see it coming until it was too late.

Suicide is a sneaker wave. It took my mother. And now its unforgiving tentacles had a hold on me.

⋆ ⋆ ⋆ ⋆

In the days leading up to our next call, I replayed B's words. Could something redemptive, even meaningful, come from this—what did he call it—a shattering? I liked to believe redemption was possible, but it sounded like such a high-minded goal. What did it mean, anyway, to redeem someone's death? I did a quick flip through my mental thesaurus. Was it the same as repairing? Repenting? Rectifying? Was redemption something I was supposed to do, or was it on Mom, wherever she was now? I'd have to clarify this point with B. For now, the only thing my shattering had revealed was what I'd lost. She was gone and I couldn't see beyond the sharp edges of my grief. Was there something hopeful up ahead, something less cutting? If there was, it hadn't yet appeared.

In a flash, I was reminded of something Mom said to me a few days after losing Klose. She was sitting on my couch, in almost the same spot I found myself now, and wondering aloud:

"I cannot imagine my life now. I just can't see it." She looked over at me with searching eyes, as if I might have an answer, a future vision that would calm her present worry, but I had none to offer. Her eyes wandered around the room. "I just can't *see* it, Sammy."

I understood her limited view much better now, along with the assurance she sought that her life would go on without him, that her best days were not behind her, that she would feel whole again. I could have told her what she wanted to hear—*it's all going to be okay*—but I couldn't assure it, and I realized I could not provide that assurance for myself either. Mom was gone and there'd be no returning to the happy scenes in the framed photos on the wall, those that captured a shared laugh or a knowing look between us that said: We belong to each other. Those moments were in the past; they existed as memories only and what lay ahead was uncertain, blurry. I puttered into the kitchen to refill my coffee, wondering when the camera would refocus, and that was when I spotted them—the packet of wildflower seeds behind the coffee maker. I remembered unpacking them from one of the boxes marked "kitchen" and tossing them on the counter where they'd gotten pushed out of sight. I pulled them out of hiding and felt my heart fall as I read the handwritten note on the colorful package: *For your new garden. Love, Mom.*

Oh, Mommy, in the midst of your own grief and a darkness descending, you'd still paused to buy me California wildflower seeds to plant at my new house. A hopeful gesture, and so *you* to prioritize beauty even when your world was growing bleak. I slipped on a jacket and carried the packet outside to the raised bed in the corner of the side yard, the one that looked like it had been abandoned for a while. I sank to my knees in the wet leaves and dug my hands into the old, crumbly soil. As I worked my fingers through the dirt, I reflected back to a brighter time—Mom in her garden, cutting spindly sweet peas to put into a vase, watering a showy wall of pink-and-white cosmos, delighting at the first yellow pop of daffodils in the spring and the fragrant surprise of narcissus in the winter. I worked the soil slowly as a form of moving meditation until my little garden plot looked restored; enough, anyway, for me to scatter the seeds and rake them in. So maybe, there's no assurance of what comes after loss but there can be hope in the form of a seed, a small but sturdy commitment to persevere in the March cold.

On the Plus Side

In little more than a week, my wildflower garden showed the stirrings of life when the first perky green tip broke through the surface, interrupting the monotony of my grief and reminding me that beauty endures even in horror. I'd become so accustomed to my daily habit of mourning that I was surprised by how much I enjoyed a new routine of padding out to the garden at sunrise to check on the garden's daily progress—so much so that I determined to create more spaces for color, for lightness and life. And Derby was my best partner in this endeavor.

Like much of the world on house arrest, Derby and I were in each other's company for long stretches of time, for days at a time, and without much interruption. I was thankful he was still at an age when he liked me and outwardly showed it. I'd been forewarned by friends with older children that this time was fleeting, if not imminent, and that I ought to maximize the moment. So, in the afternoons, once he was finished with Zoom school, I encouraged us to migrate to the outside patio where we played Uno and Old Maid, made up silly songs about our tabby cats, adorned ourselves in costume jewelry, and drank mocktails from antique stemware. For both of us who gravitated toward warmer weather, the premature temperatures that felt more like summer than spring enhanced our moods. "Chase me with the hose," Derby said one afternoon, emerging out of the shadows of the house, already in his swim trunks.

"You'd better start running!" I turned the spray gun on him, abandoning the pink petunia in the hanging planter and watering him instead. The following afternoon, thanks to overnight shipping, I surprised him with a Slip 'N Slide that he tirelessly played on until his belly was chafed, and the lawn was so oversaturated, it ran off into the street.

When Derby was with his dad, I allowed myself my erratic grief, but when he was with me, I willed myself to show up for him. We spent afternoons in the yard, and in the evenings, we snuggled together on the couch, watching episodes of *The Great British Bake Off* and re-runs of *Modern Family*, a new favorite for him. If the warm weather extended past sunset, we'd slip outside in jammies and light jackets and walk around the block holding hands, stopping to pet the neighborhood cats and to gaze up at the moon. While I wanted many things to end—my grief, the pandemic, the loose ends of my divorce—I didn't want moments like this to stop. In a sea of sad, what my son and I had was good, and I recognized its importance as not only a respite, but also a reminder that our relationship deserved as much, if not more, of my attention than my relationship with Mom. Derby needed a mother who was present, available, safe. I no longer had one, but I could be that mother for him.

"What better way for him to feel comforted during this time?" said Aunt Nancy. "You're both home together so he doesn't have to think about it; his mom is always there." I called her at least once a week to check in, and her reassuring voice gave me comfort. "Enjoy your time together, as much as you can, okay, honey?" My aunt had lost her only sister. She was eighty-five years old, isolating in New England where in April, the streets were covered in snow. If she could get through this chilly time, so could I.

Rage

Derby's presence in the house helped to keep me grounded and not swallowed whole by grief, but as my moods were prone to do, they'd slip and slide into each other, typically without warning, like when I carried a load of laundry through the living room and stubbed my toe and because it hurt so bad, I kicked the offending furniture. In this case, I sent an oversized barrel chair across the room while screaming, "You suck!" The harshness of my voice cut through the room, causing Derby to go wide-eyed with Legos in hand, regarding me like he no longer recognized me, the clumsy monster that wandered into his living room. Watching him watching *me*, I quickly attempted to course correct. "I'm sorry, babe." I assumed the position of apology: slumped shoulders, a conflicted smile. "I didn't mean to scare you. That was a really dumb thing to do." He continued to look at me without blinking until his stunned expression broke into laughter. "Oh, my God, Mom. You just kicked *a chair.* You are seriously losing it." He added, "Maybe you should talk to someone."

Two people now, who had made this suggestion.

I plopped down in the barrel chair I'd just kicked across the room. *Was I losing it?* Was my outburst misdirected? Or was my reactivity appropriate? I understood the contemporary reframe that grief isn't a ladder where one levels up from denial to acceptance, and that it's more truly like a spinning top that can land any which way—depression on Monday, back to bargaining on Tuesday, and sometimes both on Wednesday. I resonated with the spinning top analogy, but I actually preferred to think of my grief in terms of food, specifically as a serving of spaghetti in which a variety of emotions shared the same plate, often overlapping each other with no clear beginning or end, and where the meatball in the middle was my anger. Whether I was sucking on the noodle of sadness or winding my fork around confusion, I always came back to the meatball. Usually on Monday, Tuesday, *and* Wednesday.

⋆ ⋆ ⋆

"Tell me about your anger," B said on our second call.

"Anger?" I played dumb.

"You talked last week about how you're mad at your mom and that you wonder if you shouldn't be. That some of your friends, even, have suggested that your anger is inappropriate."

"Is it inappropriate? To be mad at someone who died, to be mad at someone who was clearly suffering?" As soon as I asked it, I knew what B was going to say—of course it was inappropriate to be mad at Mom. And then he surprised me.

"It depends on who you ask, but as far as I'm concerned, you shouldn't feel wrong for the feeling because you feel it. Your anger is there; you're not making it up. Her suffering was real too, but it doesn't negate your feelings. Your anger is honest and if people don't like it because it makes them uncomfortable, that's their business and it's not your job to change their mind about you."

I would have to pass this note on to Stacy, and anyone else offended by my rising temper.

"Personally, I think your anger is appropriate. Justified," B continued. "But you tell me: What are you mad at? If your anger could speak, what would it say?" Here again, B wasn't soft shoeing with idle chitchat. He was inviting me to step right into it, to go deep. "If you could give words to it," he encouraged, "what would your anger say to your mother?"

What would it say to *her*? B's invitation was tempting. As far back as I could remember, no one had ever encouraged me to get mad, and while my anger wanted to be released—oh, boy, it really did—I held back. It was one thing to raise my voice alone in my empty house, save for the cats, and quite another to speak it out loud to someone whom I respected, whose opinion of me mattered. This was only my second call with Rabbi B, a man I hardly knew but who seemed to see and accept me in a way others didn't, even those who'd known me for much of my life. I needed him. I was already depending on him to stick with me through my complicated grief, and I had a flash of worry that my unedited angry side might turn him away. I had a reputation for being agreeable, likeable, and mostly kind, and what if that's what he expected from me, too?

He interrupted my inhibition. "My personal mantra is that if you're not pissing people off, you're not being honest enough. It's a spin on the popular Bette Davis quote: If everyone likes you, you're not doing it right."

I took a deep breath. "This call isn't being recorded, is it?"

"Nope. It's just you and me."

I threw cautious likeability to the wind and let my anger speak out loud. It said to Mom—

"I am furious that you left me.
That you lied to me, that you betrayed me.
That you fooled me into thinking you were okay.
That instead of telling me the truth, you wrote a note.
A suicide note!
I'm angry that you made a plan.

That you intended to do this.

That you drove out to the beach and jumped alone.

I am mad that you gave up.

I am mad that you gave up on me, on Derby, on all of us.

I am mad that you died alone.

I'm angry that strangers, people you didn't know, saw you do it.

That you told them your name and to call 911, and then you stepped off the cliff before they could stop you.

I'm angry that you were being pulled out of the water by the Coast Guard while I was only miles away. Getting my toes painted—my toes painted!—when you were departing this Earth.

I'm mad that I had no idea. Until many hours later, when there was nothing I could do.

I am furious that I had no power, no say.

You made this choice without me.

I'm mad that you didn't give me a chance to say goodbye, that you left this world without saying goodbye to me, your other beating heart, your daughter.

I'm mad that you denied me your final moments. I missed your death, and that's left me with an impossible sadness to hold, a heartbreak I had to share with my son, your grandson, who carries this pain now, as his own.

I am angry that you hurt us, that you burdened us with suicide, that you introduced this 'option' in the narrative of life.

I'm mad that you changed the ending of our story. And I can't change it back.

I'm mad that I'm not supposed to be mad at you. I'm mad because I miss you. And you're not here when I need you the most."

I paused and took a shaky breath. "And for all of this," I said to B, "I am outraged."

"Yes," he returned softly. "You should be outraged. It's a testament to how much you loved her. Outrageous love deserves outrageous rage."

His words dropped like a pin on my heart, quelling my anger and releasing a river of tears.

"I loved her the most," I said, hardly above a whisper. "And I miss her so much. Next to Derby, she was my favorite person of all, and she was with me first, so that makes her number one."

"She was number one. She was your mother. And there's another piece to this—the act of her death was dramatic. Disruptive. Violent. Public. It demands a big response, especially from you. Her death deserves outrage and anything less from *you* wouldn't be enough. As horrible as it was, you honor her by honoring her death. By looking at it, not past it."

He was right. Jumping off a cliff was not a subtle move. It deserved a reaction, and I imagined Mom would have expected one. I sat with this as he continued. "I counsel a lot of people who've lost parents, and while losing a parent is always significant and can be one of the hardest transitions of our lives, not everyone mourns the loss as intensely as you're mourning your mom. For any number of reasons: Some people aren't as close to their parents, maybe they'd become estranged as adults, or they had a difficult relationship from the beginning. Everyone has a different dynamic and not everyone is as shattered as you. Consider yourself lucky that you loved your mom so deeply."

"Lucky?" I bristled.

"Well, lucky and angry."

"So, what do I do now? Just go around pissed off all the time?"

"That's what I did for a long time, and I don't recommend it. After my dad died, I was so furious at him, and I took it out on everyone around me. Eventually, I knew if I didn't release my rage in a more constructive way, it would consume me, so I started writing nasty letters to him, really nasty letters, listing all his errors and the ways he disappointed me. I wrote letters until I'd exhausted my anger, or at least a good amount of it, and then I burnt them."

"What did you say in the letters?" My writer's curiosity had to ask.

"That's between me and him. The point is—I encourage your anger. It's real. It's honest. Allow it, feel it, channel it. Anger is like fire. It's a powerful energy that wants to breathe, to speak, and when you suppress it, or if you try to rename it as something false like 'I'm not angry, I'm fine . . .'"

"It burns out?" I interrupted, certain I knew how the sentence would end.

"No, it burns the house down."

* * *

I was eight years old when my parents told me they were getting divorced. I felt blindsided by this news that they delivered on what I'd thought would be a typical afternoon—and then suddenly, Dad was packing a single suitcase, throwing it into the hatchback of our Honda Civic and driving away from our house. *Where will he go? Where will he sleep tonight? When will I see him again?* To help soften the blow to my young sense of safety, Mom suggested a run to Jack in the Box, where over bacon cheeseburgers she told me everything was going to be okay and, "Oh, there's one more thing . . ." She'd fallen in love with another man. "You know him. Klose, from the newspaper. We'll be moving in with him and his two daughters really soon." She gave me a reassuring smile and I sensed she wanted me to swallow this down in one big gulp in the parking lot of our favorite fast-food restaurant and because I loved her, when she squeezed my hand and said it again—"We're going to be okay, *okay*?"—I smiled back at her and nodded my consent.

As I thought back on this pivotal scene a day or so after my call with B, I saw clearly that my eight-year-old self didn't think she had a choice. I sensed the unspoken expectation of me in the moment—be easygoing Sammy, amenable, the sweet child who accepts the sudden collapse of her family with an agreeable nod of the head—and if that doesn't work, to stuff it down with French fries. And now, forty-one years later, I began to imagine how this scene might have played out differently, how my life might have played out differently, had I been invited to get mad. To protest. To scream, *hell, no!* To ask questions: Why is this happening? How will it affect *me?* Would this scene have changed into something else had I been emboldened to take a moment and feel what I was actually feeling—*I'm sad, I'm scared, I'm confused*—and to say what I was actually thinking—*I don't like this, I don't want this*—even if it conflicted with what Mom wanted me to feel? In fairness, I wasn't told not to express myself honestly, but I wasn't encouraged either. Was this *the* moment I'd learned that the best way to get along was to smile and go along, even if it meant keeping silent? That the best way to preserve the peace was to make others happy by doing what they wanted of me even if I wanted something different? Was this the moment I'd made an unconscious agreement to suppress my own voice, to play small, in order to give Mom what she desired, a new marriage, her version of happiness—and by making that agreement, I'd guarantee my safety, my mother's enduring love and protection? If this was that moment, I was unaware. As eight-year-old me sat in the dark car, eating a bacon cheeseburger while trying to reconcile the surprise plot twist in my young life, I really only knew one thing for sure: Mom was my everything, my center, my sun. If she said it was going to be okay, I trusted her. She was in the driver's seat, after all, and so I buckled up and let her lead the way.

★ ★ ★ ★ ★ ★

Over breakfast the next morning, I looked across the table at Derby who, at eight years old, had also had his life disrupted by divorce, plus cancer, a bonus suicide, and now, a pandemic. I didn't want him to inherit my learned silence as a way of coping or to develop an automatic habit of smiling and nodding "yes" when he didn't really mean it. I leaned forward across the table and caught his eye. "Hey, we're going through a tough time, you and I, and I don't need you to be okay for *me*."

"Huh?" he said with a mouthful of toast and jam.

"Sometimes I get upset and it's not your job to fix it, to make me feel better. I can fix myself. Does that make sense?"

"I guess." He shrugged. "But I like it better when you're happy."

"I like it better when I'm happy too, but nobody's happy all the time and that's normal. Sometimes we're sad and sometimes we're mad. Sometimes I feel so mad that Mutti is gone and we're stuck in this house for God knows how long that I do stupid things like kick the chair across the room."

"That was funny." His mouth turned up in a grin.

"It was kind of silly." I smiled back. "But getting mad is okay. It's actually healthy, for both of us."

"How is it healthy, Mom? No one likes angry people."

"Well, yes, angry people can be hard to be around, but when we stuff down our feelings, especially the distasteful ones like anger and sadness, we can feel even worse. We can become even angrier and make ourselves sick with all that gunk inside. Feelings don't want to stay inside; they want to come out." I gagged for effect. "Get it?"

"So . . ." Derby arched his eyebrow. "Are you saying you want *me* to get mad and kick a chair?"

"I'm saying that sometimes Jack needs to rip the lid off the box."

I'm Not Okay

Later that week, I bicycled to my ex-husband's house to fetch Derby for our next several days together. I'd resurrected my old yellow cruiser from the back shed, clearing it of cobwebs and dusting off the seat with the idea that Derby and I could spend more time outside, and away from the house, by pedaling around our quiet town. I made my way across the West side, taking the neighborhood corners wide and inhaling the fragrant April air, and less than ten minutes later, I parked in front of a craftsman-style home. As I made my way to the front door, my right foot slipped between two flagstones in the walkway, causing my ankle to roll and pull me down.

"*Ow!* My ankle," I yelped in pain, drawing my ex out onto the front porch.

"Are you okay?" he looked down at me, crumpled on the sidewalk, pink polka-dot helmet still cinched under my chin, hot tears welling in my eyes.

Am I okay? *What kind of question is that?* I glared up at him as my mind ran through the list: recent suicide, finalizing our divorce, a rogue virus that might kill us all. "Okay" was not the word I'd have chosen to describe our current landscape, but because my ex-husband was not a mind reader, and probably because I was looking at him with an aggravated expression, he asked it again. "Are you okay?" And while I distinctly heard the real concern in his voice, I chose to ignore it and attack his words instead. "No!" I barked, and not unlike a terrier. "I AM NOT OKAY. DO I LOOK OKAY?" I rolled onto all fours and clumsily pushed myself into a one-legged, downward-facing dog. Attempting to regain some dignity in front of my son who'd now joined him on the porch, I slowly stood up to meet them at eye level, but when I attempted to put weight on my right foot, a current of pain shot up my leg and I stumbled. "OW!" I cried louder this time and grabbed for the branch of an ornamental pomegranate tree before I tumbled over.

"Mommy, stop moving," Derby ordered as he hurried down the front porch steps and took my arm to steady me.

"Do you think it's sprained?" my ex asked, eager to diagnose the problem.

"I don't know," I snapped. "Maybe, probably. Yes."

"Wow, it's really swelling up. Do you want some ice?"

My ankle was, as he'd keenly observed, doubling in size and turning the color of the pomegranate I'd just lunged for. It hurt badly and could likely benefit from some ice, but I stubbornly refused the help, turning instead to limp over to my bike. "Come on, honey," I instructed Derby, "get your bike, it's time to go."

I knew I shouldn't bicycle home, if I could even prop myself up onto the seat—and from there, I wasn't sure I could physically turn the pedals. But I couldn't stay there another minute. My rage was rushing upward toward the surface with unstoppable force—I could feel the lid coming off the metaphorical jack-in-the-box—and if I didn't make a quick exit, I would surely erupt and start screaming mean things, which I promised myself I wouldn't do. My personal rule: Don't yell at the ex in front of the kid. After Derby grabbed his own bike and pedaled down the street out of earshot, I turned to my ex-husband. "You know, you really ought to fix that. I'm surprised you haven't been sued already by the mailman, or," I sputtered, "by an elderly person. They wouldn't stand a chance."

On the ride home, I silently seethed. *Am I okay? Do I look okay?*

★ ★ ★

The next day when Rabbi B called, I picked up after the first ring, skipped over hello, and went straight to: "I am not okay. I am not fine. I am not doing well. And I am tired of people asking me if I'm okay, *okay*?"

"Okay," B agreed. "And who says you have to be okay?'

"Everyone. People. My ex-husband. I don't know, it's a strong vibe I'm getting."

"Do you have to react to it?"

I rolled my eyes, ignoring his comment.

"You know," he continued "there's a great book about this called *It's OK That You're NOT OK* by Megan Devine."

"Yeah, I have it," I said, dismissively. "Someone sent it to me. I don't remember who. Probably someone who secretly wants me to be okay."

"Well, don't blame me." B laughed. "I didn't send it to you, and anyway, what's so wrong with not being okay?"

"I'm afraid that if I give myself permission to 'flip the lid', so to speak, I'll become a scary rage monster. Not a contained, channeled fire, but the other kind you talked about—the runaway fire that burns down the neighborhood. And you know what scares me about that? I kind of want to burn it all down to the ground. To soot and sticks."

"And from the ashes the phoenix will rise," B added with dramatic flair.

"Am I supposed to be the phoenix?"

"That's what I was thinking."

I conjured an image of a majestic bird with expansive wings rising from the fiery depths. I hoped that, eventually, I could similarly rise above it all and be reborn into someone stronger. But maybe," I turned it over, "I need to sit in the rage for a while, in the 'not okay.'"

"I think that's perfectly okay," B said, pleased with his play on words.

"I worry, though, about how much is too much for Derby."

I gave him a brief summary of my flagstone meltdown. "I seem to be coming a bit unhinged and while I think that's okay for me, and it's understandable given the circumstances, I don't want to freak out my kid."

"Our job as parents is to help our kids feel loved and safe. That's number one, so I think your instinct is right to temper your temper around your son. Additionally, you—Sammy at the Jack in the Box—have another job, and that is to be real, to not sugarcoat and say everything's fine when it's not. When you were Derby's age, you weren't taught how to process pain; you were taught to stuff it down with a cheeseburger, to hold it together when maybe you wanted to fall apart, and now you're learning to do it differently, and just in time to teach your son a different way—to name the pain and break a pattern of bypassing, numbing out, and going through the motions of your life disconnected to how you feel. It's your turn to give Derby what you didn't get—a mom who invites him to feel it all and that you will be there for him either way."

"But really," I leveled, "there's got to be a line between being real and being *too* real, and I worry I don't know where the line is. Last week I gave Derby permission to kick a chair. What kind of parenting is that?"

"Your kind. Look, you're not going to get it right every time. You're learning as you teach him."

"This strikes me as one of those big developmental lessons I should have learned well before my fiftieth birthday."

"Delayed is better than permanently arrested," B cheered, then turned serious again. "Look, you've been cut open by your mom's suicide. It's an open wound and the work of digging around in there is difficult. It can be dark, devastating, but it's important to see what's in there. Look for patterns in your life when you've skipped over pain, ignored when you were hurting, said you were okay when you weren't."

"That's Mom's playbook," I said.

"Isn't it yours, too?"

Damn. This guy was good.

Slow Fade

For seven years, I told myself I was okay in my marriage when I wasn't. By the time we divorced, my husband and I had been married for fifteen years, and for the second half of them, I'd been unhappy, although I did all sorts of things to disguise this truth. First and foremost, I lied to myself. *I'm happy, I really am.* Then I made excuses that I repeated over and over. *We're just going through a tough time, we're different people, we love each other but nothing's perfect.* When that didn't work, I stuffed down my feelings of discontent with food, I numbed with alcohol, I overexercised, I disappeared in my work.

"You always look so happy on Facebook," Mom frequently chirped. This was back when I regularly posted family photos, and I'd simmer in the face of her upbeat commentary. She wants me to be happy, I'd think to myself, but I'm not. Sure, I put on a bright smile and pose for the camera. That's what we all do to create the great illusion, but she's not seeing us outside the frame, having the same tearful arguments that never resolve. She sees what she wants to see, but I know what this marriage really looks like, and it's not a happy one.

I stayed anyway.

I stayed because I wanted a good marriage story, one that

lasts and has one of those landmark anniversary parties with a big cake and a brass band. I stayed because on the day of our wedding, I took a vow I intended to keep, one I wholeheartedly wanted to keep. After the newlywed years wore off and our promises became difficult to hold, I stayed because I got pregnant, and I hoped that, maybe, becoming a mother would fill the loneliness in my marriage. It didn't, and still I stayed because I wanted a "normal" family for Derby, one with a mom and a dad living happily together. I stayed because I didn't want him to be a child of divorce like me, floating between two houses, never quite grounded in or belonging to one home. I stayed because divorce would mean separation from my son, and I didn't want to miss a single day seeing his sweet face.

For years, I prayed I could feel differently again. I prayed that if I had a bigger and more generous heart, I could forgive the hurtful things my husband and I said and did, and I could forget the awful fights we couldn't undo. I kept my deepest seeds of discontent hidden from plain sight, inwardly weighing the pros and cons of my marriage, negotiating my own happiness, justifying pain and rationalizing our bad behavior or excusing it because *we're so much better than this*. After holding it inside by sheer will, until I believed my heart might split in half or collapse from the heavy weight of it all, I spoke the unsaid truth out loud to my husband.

I'm hurting.

I'm scared.

I don't know how to fix this.

I feel alone.

He heard me. And it was then that we finally acknowledged what we'd been hiding in plain sight. We were trapped in our patterns. We'd adapted to a routine of discomfort that had created a great divide, a seismic rift of disconnection. Over the years, we'd both silently pulled away and retreated to our own corners, and because there were countless misunderstandings between us that we'd been unable to reconcile in a way that honored what we each needed, we'd stagnated in our unhappiness. We both knew this. We'd each felt it but speaking it out loud to each other made it all the more real. And because neither one of us were ready to endure the pain of walking away for good, we mutually agreed to work it out in couple's counseling, then group counseling, where we aired our hurts and disappointments in front of each other and to a group of witnesses. This could have been helpful, maybe it would have "fixed us" and saved our marriage, except, again, we didn't tell the whole truth. We left details out, we sidestepped the most jagged pieces in our marriage, the hidden hurts we ignored in our own home too. Too often, we'd leave our therapist's office and drive home in silence, and I'd return to my own inner dialogue: This marriage is a lie.

This endless rumination went on for so long that I was surprised when I finally hit my breaking point. When you think about leaving your marriage for years, when you feel paralyzed by inaction, too stuck in a loop of doubt and fear to do anything about it, there are many days—*many*—when you think, is this going to be the day we finally call it quits? Is this the day we finally have the inevitable conversation that leads to one of us moving out?

For me, my moment came while watching the DreamWorks animated movie *Trolls*. Derby and I were home alone, nesting together on the couch as we watched the movie's pivotal scene, where the enduringly optimistic Poppy, played by Anna Kendrick, slips into a deep depression in the face of impending doom. As the self-elected leader of the Trolls, she has been unable to save her friends from the hands of the miserable

Bergens, who have captured them and have imminent plans to eat them. Believing she has failed her family and friends, we watch as she dissolves from positively pink into a dismally gray version of herself. It's in this low-color moment when all seems lost for Poppy and the Trolls, until Branch, played by Justin Timberlake, comes to the rescue with a soul-piercing version of *True Colors.*

"You with the sad eyes,
don't be discouraged . . .
I see your true colors shining through . . .
Don't be afraid to let them show . . .
Your true colors are beautiful
like a rainbow . . ."

I listened, both transfixed and heartbroken, realizing with stark clarity that, like Poppy, I'd faded into a gray version of myself. For seven years, I'd slowly dimmed my own light for the sake of outward appearances, for my own convenience and because I thought wrongly that preserving the peace between me and my husband was more important than speaking the whole truth. At some point along the way, I'd convinced myself that my staying was a lesser offense than leaving—kinder and more generous, even, and that I could somehow protect us both from further hurt by dismissing my own needs, by fading away from myself. It hadn't worked and I'd become resentful and withdrawn—colorless—and I blamed him for dimming me, and I blamed myself for selfishly wanting out, for my cowardice for staying, for being a fake. As I sat on the couch, watching Poppy join Branch in a breathtaking duet that restores her to her brightest light, I resolved: This is the day I'm leaving this marriage. If I don't, I will fade away completely, and my son needs a mother who is colorful and alive. Derby deserves a rainbow. And so do I.

Of course, plenty of people can reconnect with their own light within their partnerships and marriages, but by the time I'd reached my breaking point, my insides and my outsides had become so misaligned and incompatible that I'd separated from my *self*. I wondered if I'd actually split into two people who could not reconcile, who were too oppositional to inhabit the same body. For me, I believed it was too late to become whole again, to right myself within the marriage. And even if I could, even if I could sloppily stitch both halves of myself back together, my husband was not willing to resolve his contradictory narrative either, the one he was inwardly telling himself alongside the story he was outwardly presenting to the world.

I couldn't lie anymore.

Our marriage was over.

There'd be no party with a brass band.

This was a heartbreaking reckoning, but hadn't we both suffered enough? I thought about this a lot over the course of our years together: Was there a limit to suffering? I believed there was, and we each had to decide for ourselves what we were willing to withstand and endure. My husband was brought up in a home with parents who'd stayed married for over fifty years and who'd instilled in him that couples stick it out, no matter what. My parents showed me another option, which is to leave if you're unhappy. I finally decided for myself that when my suffering was no longer teaching me something important, like the lesson of humility, patience, or resilience, or when my suffering was not helping our family but was only leading me deeper into despair, I had the right to stop the clock. My statute of limitations for suffering was seven years, and beyond that, I was unwilling to extend for more time.

Within a few short weeks of that fateful viewing of *Trolls*, my husband moved out and we had the conversation with Derby

I'd hoped we'd never have—sitting on the couch, all three of us, as my parents had done with me at eight years old, explaining that Mommy and Daddy were separating from each other, that we would always be a family, and that we would always love him. My therapist had suggested, on the occasion of this day ever arriving, that I read Derby a book called *Invisible String* that explains that people who love each other are always connected by love, and that even when we aren't in the presence of one other, we're connected, even if we're as far away as a high mountaintop or underwater in a submarine. Halfway through the reading of it, Derby kicked it off my lap with his foot and ran out of the room screaming.

"I'll go get him." His father stood up from the couch.

"No," I urged. "Let him go. He gets to be mad. This isn't what he wants, and he's allowed to show it. Think about it, we just totally fucked up his day, and tomorrow's not going to be much better."

I regretted that I was disrupting my child's life, his young sense of self, his safe routine. I'd created a complication, a snag in his seemingly seamless life. I'd made a choice he didn't agree with, one that felt threatening to him and was making me unpopular. I did it anyway, because I trusted it was the right thing to do. Not just for me, but eventually, for him too. I accepted that his adjustment period could take a long time—years, even—and I was relieved when my "eventually" happened much faster than that. With the prolonged burden of falsifying my story no longer draining me, I felt less gray, less diminished, not as shameful and small. This was a welcome shift, and still, it took me by surprise. I thought, perhaps this is what happens when you stop betraying yourself, when you stop pretending to be okay—you start feeling incrementally better right away.

There was promise in our decision to split, and relief, although I'd be lying again if I didn't admit there was fear, too. I was uncertain about what would happen next, how I'd support myself as a single mother, as a single woman fast approaching midlife. Divorce was a risk financially, and also it meant the loss of a support system, of a family structure and a reliable routine, the loss of our physical home. It meant the loss of a past lifestyle, of my social standing. Feeling different and outside the group was inevitable. I was no longer somebody's plus one; I could no longer count on dinner-party invites.

As a consolation, I could count on myself. I could look in the mirror again without shying away. I could stare into my own eyes with an unapologetic openness that radiated something I hadn't recognized in myself in years: self-respect. And I had to believe this gain was worth the risk.

Color Outside the Lines

Six months after my husband moved out, Klose died, and three months later, Mom followed, with the pandemic right on her heels. To say that lightning had struck my rainbow was not an exaggeration, yet despite all I'd lost in a short amount of time, I hadn't faded back to gray. I'd retained my color, although it could easily get stuck in one hue—blue for sad, red for rage, and, on more hopeful days, yellow for sunny-*ish*. When I explained my fixed color dial to B, he suggested an exercise called "Color Outside the Lines" that, he said, "might help you and Derby talk about how you're both feeling. Remember, you're modeling true emotion for him, the contrast between light and dark, and showing him how to be in control when we feel out of control." The idea was to take crayons or colored markers to a traditional coloring book, and intentionally color outside the lines. "By coloring outside the lines, you show him that grieving is messy and unpredictable. Our feelings don't always want to stay inside the lines, to be confined, and that's okay."

"There's that word again," I groaned.

"Oops, not *okay*," he caught himself. "Our feelings don't always want to stay inside the lines, and we should encourage them to cross the line. Better?"

"That works."

After Derby finished his homework, I asked him to join me at the dining room table with a box of crayons and some pages I'd ripped out of a Sea Creatures coloring book I'd found in the back of his closet. We each started working on our separate pages, and I intentionally scribbled outside the lines of a narwhal in bright pinks and greens to visually communicate B's point that we honor our grief by honoring all our feelings, not only the more acceptable ones that are easiest to contain, but also those that tend to be regarded as off-limits. I glanced over at Derby's drawing that, so far, was much less colorful than mine, but clearly communicating something. His starfish was nearly unrecognizable under a Jackson Pollack splattering of black crayon.

"Hey, buddy." I tried to sound light. "I like your black starfish."

He rolled his eyes. "Why are we doing this anyway?"

"To help us talk about how we're feeling." I paused and then edged cautiously: "So . . . how is your starfish feeling?"

He threw down his crayon. "My starfish, really, Mom? My starfish isn't feeling anything because it's a piece of paper."

I nodded in agreement. "My mistake, of course it is." I returned to my narwhal and allowed Derby to cool down. A minute later, I tried again. "So, never mind the starfish . . . how are *you* feeling?"

Derby looked at me with the same expression I'd perfected by his age. Klose used to call it "the look"—annoyance layered with mild contempt and tempered with enough patience to resist blurting something unkind. I was impressed with Derby's level of control, much more restrained than I'd been of late, but that wasn't the point of this exercise! He was supposed to let loose, to color outside the lines. "Don't hold back," I encouraged. "You can say it."

"Okay!" He erupted and crumpled the drawing in his tight little fist. "I'm sick of this! I'm sick of staying home. I miss my friends, I miss school, I hate *fucking* distance learning and going back and forth between you and Dad's house, and . . ." He sputtered "I'm too old to be coloring! I'm not a BABY!"

I allowed his outburst, his superb placement of profanity to underscore a point, and reached across the table and took his hand. He tried to shake me off, but I held it tightly. "You are not a baby. You're brave and I know this is hard and I'm sorry. And you have every right to be mad."

"I'm also bored," he cut in.

"You have every right to be bored."

He took a shaky breath and began to tear up.

"Are you also sad?" I asked gently.

"Yes, I'm sad!" he blurted. "I miss Mutti. She left me too, and no one sends me cards." He gestured to the yellow bowl on the table that held a stack of sympathy cards I'd received over the past few months, some I still hadn't had the courage to open and read.

"They're for you too," I said in consolation.

"None of them have my name on it."

I picked up the stack of envelopes and flipped through them. They were all addressed to me. He was right and I'd missed this subtlety. His relationship with Mom hadn't been acknowledged in the way mine had, but it was no less significant, no less important to him. I flashed back to the moment I'd told him she'd died, how he'd tried to hide his face, how he'd tried to understand what she'd done. He'd lost a grandmother he loved and with whom he had an active relationship. "Derby Fridays" had abruptly ended, and he felt the pain of her absence deeply, and no one had sent him a condolence card or directly reached out to him to offer their support. He wanted to be acknowledged, and I agreed he ought to be.

"I'm sorry, buddy. You should be getting cards too."

"It's okay, Mom. It's not your fault." He dropped his shoulders and sighed. "I'll just read yours."

"I can cross my name out and write yours instead?" I smiled. "Or better yet—*you* can cross my name out with that big black crayon."

He smiled back and softened. "Mom, you know I love being with you, but it's been a lot of you and me time and . . ." He paused. "I'm lonely."

"I get it." I squeezed his hand. "We have been together a lot. You don't have to apologize."

"Why can't you have another kid so I can have a brother?"

"Uh . . ." I stalled and considered my reasons for this: I'm perimenopausal, maybe even menopausal, I don't have a partner to impregnate me, I don't want another partner to impregnate me, if that was even possible. To Derby I simplified, "Honey, I'm probably too old to have another kid."

"Oh Mom, knock it off." He laughed. "You don't look a day older than seventeen, but if I can't have a brother, I'll take a corgi."

⋆ ⋆ ⋆

Less than a week later, an envelope arrived in the mail with Derby's name on it. I handed it to him, and he eyed me suspiciously.

"What's this?"

"It's for you."

He rolled his eyes. "Did you ask someone to do this?"

I shrugged, and he turned and walked to his room. Before closing the door, he looked back at me.

"I don't know anything about it." I said, pretending for the both of us.

Several minutes later, he reemerged and handed it back to

me. "That was nice, even if you did ask her to send it." He looked like he'd been crying, but when his lips turned up in a sheepish grin, I interpreted it as gratitude. His loss had been recognized, and that's what he'd needed. He left me in the kitchen and walked outside to play with the cats.

> *Dear Derby,*
>
> *You have experienced so much loss and sadness and it hurts my heart thinking of the weight you must feel at times. I hope you know how much you are loved by all of your family. Always know when things feel especially hard, or sad, or lonely, that you are not alone, and we are all here to help each other and hold each other up. I'm so sorry. So much love to you, Derby.*
>
> *XO, Auntie Gretta*

Shitty Sundays

Every Sunday, I sent Derby out the front door with a stuffed backpack and a heartfelt hug, assuring him, "I'll see you in a few days." Every week, I stood on the porch and watched him trudge down the stone path, slide into the passenger seat of his dad's car, and ride off, just as I had done when I was his age. Every week, before they turned the corner, I'd wave optimistically and force a smile, and once they were out of sight, my stomach would begin to twist and tighten as the invisible string between us stretched. As I visualized them driving farther away, one block, then another and another, the string extended and pulled harder until it was a taut line; as if we were in one of those action-adventure movies, standing on opposite sides of a deep ravine, the space between us growing more expansive and remote, and the rickety bamboo bridge held together by our fraying string unlikely to hold if I tried to cross over to him.

By the time I snapped back to the present, Derby was likely to be a few miles away, maybe even across town at Trader Joe's, far out of earshot and off my radar. I knew I could reach him on his father's cell phone and quickly reconnect, say hello while dropping a pin on his location, but Derby had asked repeatedly that I do not do this. "It's too hard," he pleaded. "When I'm with Dad, I'm with Dad, and when I'm with you, I'm with you." I understood this was his way of coping with our divorce, by compartmentalizing, and I tried hard to respect his boundary between Mom's and Dad's house by easing up on the string, by resisting the urge to pull him back across the bamboo bridge and into my arms.

Transition days—or, as I called them, Shitty Sundays—were my least favorite day of the week. They'd been hard from the start, but at least initially, when my husband and I first separated, the empty space created by Derby's absence was filled by a different parental duty: caretaking of my parents. In the early days of establishing our separate households, Derby and his dad would drive away, the invisible string would stretch, and before they made it to Trader Joe's, I was likely responding to a call from one of my sisters—"You'd better get up here"—and with cortisol pumping, I'd speed up the highway to tend to Klose, who was back in the ER, or to Mom, who needed a ride to her psychiatrist's office because she refused to go on her own. In the three months after Klose died, Mom and I kept each other company most Sundays. She'd come down to my place or I'd go up to hers and where we'd drink coffee and catch up on the news. Sometimes, if she were feeling up to it, we'd walk downtown for a sweet treat, and maybe pop into a consignment store. I'd naively thought our Sunday routine would continue indefinitely, and that even when our days were marked by loss, we had each other, and we'd get by.

Now, with Klose and Mom *and* Derby gone, my Sundays were quiet in a way they hadn't been before. The pandemic required they be uneventful too, and on this particular Sunday, I could scarcely hold my smile until my ex-husband's car turned the corner, and I hurried back inside and closed the door. It's only three days, I told myself. In three days, he will be back, his absence is only temporary. I slunk down in a nearby chair and confessed out loud: "I'm sorry, buddy. I didn't want this for you, schlepping between two houses, following in my footsteps, always packing and unpacking, never staying anywhere long enough to feel like you're home."

Last night, when Derby realized it was Saturday and tomorrow, he'd be leaving again, he cried: "I don't want to go, but I also miss Dad." Our divorce had created an internal conflict, a longing to be with us both, not one without the other, and I well understood his sense of loneliness and displacement, one he'd likely feel for the next ten years—at least, until he graduated from high school and went away to college and moved into the dorms; or off-campus with roommates, maybe a girlfriend; or transplanted himself to another place in the world entirely, somewhere he could finally claim a home, or at least a room of his own.

In the quiet, empty space of my own four walls, I held Derby's sadness, his cost for my freedom, and I let the tears come. I cried for him, I cried for me, and I cried for Mom. I cried for my before-loss life, and when I'd exhausted myself, I stood up and declared: Enough of this shit.

I'd learned the intensity of Shitty Sundays would diminish by sundown, at which point I'd reward myself for surviving this grueling day by drinking two glasses of wine and watching something R-rated. The trick was persevering from *now* until *then*, and so I strapped on a mask, and walked out the front door.

I kept my head down, hoping to avoid interactions with well-meaning neighbors with whom I'd have to decide—expose my sunken sad face or put on a happy one? After several blocks of avoidant behavior, I lifted my focus off the sidewalk—and that was when I saw her. The woman with the short silvery hair who wore a baseball hat and walked with a straight spine and a jaunty ease I well recognized. It was Mom's doppelganger. I'd seen this woman in town several times before Mom died and I'd marveled at their similarity—they even wore the same Costco puffy jacket in eggplant purple. I hadn't seen her in months and now, here she was, walking in my direction on the other side of the street, with a friend who must have said something to make her laugh. I stopped and stared. Damn, they really looked alike. We locked eyes and she smiled freely, just as Mom had greeted people on the street. As I watched them pass, I was struck with two discordant thoughts: this woman was a sign, a human masquerading as a message from beyond that my mother was still afoot in another dimension, and perhaps even saying hello; or this woman was only another human who looked nearly identical to my mother, passing by to serve as a hurtful reminder—unintentionally, of course—that my mother was dead. Because Shitty Sundays were not only synonymous with sadness, but also with self-pity, I opted for the latter explanation. Well, that's just rude, I nearly said out loud. Why does *she* still get to be here, while my version is gone?

I kicked my feet around the block like a scorned child until I nearly ran into a stop sign. Without realizing it, I'd walked into town. It was hardly hustling or bustling, but there were a scattering of people out. I walked past the bakery and the bookstore and stopped in front of an antique shop with the door propped open. "Come on in!" the shop owner enthusiastically called out from the front counter. She waved me forward. "We've got complimentary coffee." Why not? I thought. I could use the lift. I gratefully accepted the invitation, and strolled in.

Over the past few months, Derby and I had become regular customers of this shop. Antiquing was one of the few things to do in our small town that was predominantly shut for business. While many of the restaurants and retail stores had closed, at least temporarily, selling people's long forgotten and discarded remnants remained a lucrative business. On days when we tired of Old Maid and Uno and spraying each other with the hose, we'd walk into the shop and pick through the aisles. Based on what we'd seen on shows like *Antiques Roadshow*, we understood that one is most successful at this activity with a clear objective in mind, a singular item to search for and find. I'd landed on vintage gardening tools, while Derby was collecting an arsenal of medieval swords and turn-of-the-century coins that he believed would save us from capture and destitution. He frequently made the argument: "Mom, when this [the pandemic] is all over, we can retire."

Today, I carefully walked through the crowded aisles, running my fingers over hand-painted china and thin lace handkerchiefs until a rectangular mirror with piecrust beveled edges caught my eye. I stopped and stood in front of it, admiring its elegant design, when I caught my reflection. There I was in ball cap and fresh face, no makeup, noticeable circles under my eyes, and pale all over. I looked tired and worn but also—I looked like myself. I looked like Mom, yes, and I looked like me.

I stared into the mirror. Here I am, I thought. Here I AM. The survivor. Where I'd been catching glimpses of myself in mirrors for months and seeing *her,* I stared into my sunken eyes and wondered: what if I stopped looking for her, and started to look for me? This sounded like a riddle that might open a secret chamber, and I had the sense I was on the edge of understanding something profound, but unable to solve the mystery in the moment, I bought the mirror and carried it home.

Find a New Light Source

"What's your take on mirrors?" I asked B.

"You mean, beyond checking to see if you have egg on your face?"

"I was looking for something a little deeper. Underneath the egg."

"Well . . ." B performatively cleared his throat. "Mirrors are symbolic of self-reflection. They reveal shadows; they capture light. Mirrors reflect the truth, show us what's really there, on the surface and underneath. How's that?"

"I think Mom's death is revealing things about her I hadn't seen or fully recognized at the time and . . . I'm also beginning to see myself in a new light."

"Go on . . ." B encouraged.

"Well, as you know, I've been critical of Mom for not telling the truth, for presenting herself in a false way, and I'm realizing I'm no better. I did the same thing in my marriage. I hid from myself. I told a false story. And I can't pin that on her. That was my choice. My own cowardice."

"Now hold on," B cut in. "I'm going to challenge you here because you did, eventually, tell the truth about your marriage.

And it wasn't easy, and not without consequences. It cost you, and it cost your kid. Making that decision wasn't cowardice."

"It took me long enough to get there."

"Yes, maybe, but you did eventually step forward and I think your mother's death is calling you to step even further into the light. You dimmed yourself in your marriage, and you also lived in your mother's shadow your whole life."

"Did not," I said defensively.

"Are you sure? The way you talk about your mother, she shined like a brilliant sun, and you were her little Sammy, the moon that orbited around her."

What was he talking about? I sat back and crossed my arms over my chest, feeling like I'd just been outed by a group of mean girls in the locker room—*look, at her*, they pointed and laughed, *she's a MOON!* I disagreed with B's description of me, although he was right that Mom shined like the sun, the brightest light in my galaxy. She lit up every room she walked into, and the world gravitated toward her. It wasn't only me; most people wanted to be near Susan. Her energy was flirtatious, lovely and bright, and not the blinding version like floodlights on a stage but more like twinkle lights that make you feel warm and fuzzy inside. If I'd made a lifelong habit of soaking up her shine, if I'd become the moon to her sun, I did it with an unconscious willingness. Mom's light felt good, and it had always extended far enough to cover me, and that had been enough, hadn't it?

As if he'd heard my internal quandary, B said, "For most of your life, you depended on her to be the sun, to lift and light you up, and now that she's gone, you're being challenged to be your own light source. Think about what it means to be your own sun."

I laughed nervously. "Umm, I don't know how to be the sun."

"That's what I'm talking about. You've always been the moon."

I shifted in my chair uncomfortably. B was shining a

flashlight on parts of me I hadn't known I was hiding. I regretted introducing the mirror metaphor. Was it too late to turn this conversation back around to surface things? "I'm not really the sunny type," I said, attempting to deflect his analysis with a joke.

He didn't go for it.

"What I mean is that I've never been as bright as Mom. I've always been more brooding, more introverted and introspective. Prone to grumpy moods and catty judgment. I can turn myself down low in a way she never did, and this was our bit—she'd go high, I'd go low.

I thought back to an exchange that exemplified this—

"I don't want to," I'd groaned at thirty-nine, pregnant with my own child and still acting like one.

"Oh, quit your bellyaching." She elbowed me.

She'd flown to Austin to keep me company a month before my due date. It was triple-digit August heat, and I was crabby and uncomfortable, and she would not indulge me. "You're going to miss it," she called to me as she floated outside.

"Too hot," I called back.

"Oh, come on."

I pushed myself up off the couch and begrudgingly joined her on my back deck.

"What?"

"That." She pointed above the fence line. "Just look at that sunset. It's simply dazzling, is it not?" Not waiting for or needing an answer, she lifted her face to the sky, closed her eyes, and inhaled, as if she were metabolizing the light.

"We were different in that way," I returned to B. "I mean, we liked a lot of the same things—Edith Piaf and Elton John, thin-crust pizza, consignment cashmere—but I couldn't match her optimism, her ability to lift people up, to lift *herself* up."

"It's not either / or, turned up high or turned down low. A blinding sun or hiding in the shadows," B said. "You don't have to be as bright as her to shine, and you can still be your own source of light that isn't dependent on someone else. Does that make sense?"

I imagined myself as a singular light bulb on a dimmer switch.

B continued, "Your mom sounds like a beautiful soul, and I can feel her light every time you talk about her. She's also a cautionary tale because she didn't allow herself to dim. Even in her depression, she tried to maintain a brightness that people seemed to expect from her. I wonder if some of your anger toward her isn't really disappointment. You expected her to shine forever, and when her sun set, she let you down."

On the last day Mom and I were together, we sat in my sunny side yard, drinking white wine while Derby ran around in the uncut grass. She'd just returned from visiting her sister in Massachusetts. She seemed energized from her trip, chatty and demonstrative. She talked rapidly about the early-morning snowfall, the baked haddock, the crowded bar in New Hampshire where she'd watched the Democratic primary and cheered for Elizabeth Warren. Overall, her summary was upbeat, yet there was an unsettledness layered within her optimism. It was subtle, and still, I heard it. I listened to her, regarding her with quiet suspicion when she stopped mid-sentence and asked, "Is something wrong?" In the reflection of her sunglasses, I saw myself looking at her with questioning eyes.

"No." I shrugged it off, changed the subject.

When I replayed the memory now, it shifted into something

else. I'd thought this scene was about Mom—she saw herself through my eyes, silently scrutinizing her, and this unsettled her. Yet the scene more truly revealed my own unease. As I listened to her recount her trip back East, I thought, she's pretending to be okay. *Dammit, Mom, stop shining me on!* Her pretense annoyed me, and also I had a tickling of worry. Was she withholding something? My suspicion upset my childhood sense of safety. *Mommy, come back from behind the clouds. Shine, be my sun!*

"I wanted her to be both," I admitted to B. "A blazing sun that protects me, and also someone more like me, someone who can withstand the shadows."

"I know you'd give anything to have her back, but maybe," he suggested gently, "in her absence, you get to be more like you."

I was familiar with the idea that when you take something out of a room, you see what's left—but in my mind's eye, all I saw were unfinished hardwood floors and an empty glass of water.

"Remind me who am I again?"

"That's what we're trying to figure out."

The Move-On Crowd

Who am I?

I stared at myself in my new antique mirror. Shouldn't I have an answer for this? I considered B's questions: Who am I without Mom? Who am I in this world? Am I a moon? Can I be a sun? What kind of esoteric bullshit was this, anyway? I liked the coloring assignment much better. I didn't know how to answer these questions—how can I be a light source if I'm isolating in the dark?—and I was getting really tired of wandering around in my head looking for answers.

I plopped down on the couch, surveyed the empty room, and concluded: I need to be around people. While I knew how to isolate and had so far welcomed the global retreat indoors as an opportunity to grieve uninterrupted for more than the traditionally allotted two-point-five days, I was beginning to wonder if the extended alone time—seventy-five days, but who's counting?—was turning me too inward, making me too introspective. Without question, I had become more socially distant and withdrawn, and I knew I wasn't alone in this. Every day were news stories about the growing effects of social isolation—increased rate of heart disease, sleep disruption, anxiety, and depression—yet we were warned it wasn't safe to be around other people. The virus was spreading from continent to continent, country to country, and the death toll was rising at every stop along the way. Until a vaccine was available, we were encouraged to mask, keep a social distance, and, if possible, limit in-person interactions to a small handful of people. My sisters and I had heeded this advice; we'd closed our doors and hadn't seen each other beyond a Zoom screen in nearly three months. We'd kept to our own households, which meant, for me, interacting only with Derby and my ex-husband, and surely I wasn't expected to ride out the pandemic within this broken pod of three? Of course, if it were a matter of life and death, I'd do what I had to, but I wondered, would it be so bad to invite a friend over to sit in the backyard, at a distance, in masks, and just talk?

I called Miriam. "Don't tell my sisters, but if you want to come over, I'll break the rules and open the door."

"Oh, you're going to get in so much trouble. How much will you pay me to keep quiet?"

"You'd be breaking the rules, too, so nothing."

"Can I bring the dog?"

"As long as she wears a mask."

"Dogs don't need to wear masks," Miriam defended with a verbal eye roll.

"I'm kidding. You wear a mask, and she stays in your lap."

"I'm on my way."

When Miriam arrived, I was waiting for her on the patio, sitting in one of two lawn chairs I'd positioned facing each other in the sun, with at least six feet between them. "Let yourself in," I called. "The gate is open."

She held Annie, her Sheltie, in one arm and a travel coffee cup in the other hand. Her purple mask covered most of her face, but I could tell from her upturned eyes that she was smiling.

"Are we going to get arrested?" she teased.

There'd been recent reports of neighbors calling out other neighbors for not following social-distancing rules. "I think we're safe since we're under six people, but if I notice anyone peering out their windows and pointing at us, we'll shut it down before our transgression hits Nextdoor."

Miriam pulled down her mask to take a sip a coffee. "Hi, Sam."

I was happy to see her, relieved. It felt so long ago that she'd shown up at the house with bagels from Zabar's.

"How are you?" I pulled down my mask and smiled back at her.

"Oh, you know." She laughed ironically. "The world is fucked, and I miss my friend and I hate staring at their empty house every day."

This was why I called Miriam. She shared my loss as her own, and she wasn't afraid to talk openly about it. We'd spoken on the phone a few times since lockdown, and she'd been forthcoming with her messy feelings about Mom's death. I knew she was hurting deeply, wrestling with her own sense of guilt, and that living in such close proximity to former good times was taking a toll.

"I just can't get away from it," she said. "I go into the kitchen, and I can see into their living room. I take Annie for walks, and I have to pass by their front steps. The house is just standing there like a tomb. Have you and your sisters talked any more about what you're going to do? Will you sell it?"

"I don't know." I sighed. "We haven't been in it in weeks, and we can't really move forward until we feel safe being in there together."

"You and Derby could move in." She brightened.

"I've thought about it. We all agree it would be nice to keep the house in the family, but I worry that living there would make me miss Mom even more."

"I get that." Miriam's expression turned sober. "It used to be such a happy place, but it's a sad place now."

Miriam and Mom met at the *Press Democrat* in 1988 when they were both reporters assigned to a series called the "Ten Most Powerful People in Sonoma County." They would later remember that the best part of the assignment, beyond meeting each other, was meeting Nell Codding, wife of the highly recognized developer, Hugh Codding. Nell was no trophy wife; she was a political player in her own right, feisty and shrewd, and their favorite quote came from an unnamed female source who described Nell as "my kind of bitch." Mom and Miriam delighted in this, deeming it a high compliment and one they playfully used on each other for decades, emblazing *You're My Kind of Bitch* on T-shirts and coffee mugs that they exchanged at birthdays.

I met Miriam for the first time when she joined us for a Jazzercize aerobics class in downtown Santa Rosa. "My new friend from work is coming today," Mom had said to me and Gretta on the drive over to the dance studio. Miriam was younger than Mom by ten years and after giving her our best mean-girl glares in the full-length mirrors for an hour, we gave her a passing grade after class. "She seems cool," I said offhandedly to Mom on the drive home. "Yeah, I liked her sweatshirt," Gretta added. Miriam had always been Mom's young newspaper friend, then her neighbor, then her book club and dog-walking buddy, and even though I'd known her for thirty-five years as a regular guest at holiday meals and as the familiar who lived next door and frequently popped over for a glass of wine and to borrow staples for her own kitchen, we'd never known each other like this: as friends to each other. She'd made this distinction during one of our recent calls. "You know, you're only ten years younger than me, so it's not like we can't be friends too."

Miriam's friendship was becoming increasingly important to me as my other friends were moving on. I'd been graced with their loving attention in the early days of Mom's passing, and I knew they were there for me in spirit, but the pots of tulips and the frozen pizzas on the porch were far less frequent, if arriving at all. I understood that life continued to move forward and that my friends had lives of their own that demanded attention, and that the pandemic was making everyone more self-focused. I had friends separately dealing with their businesses closing or scrambling financially after being laid off. Other friends had sick relatives in faraway states; many others had strained marriages at home, and I didn't want to add on. I didn't want to be the friend who continues to bring up "my suicidal mom" when they were just trying to get through their own hard days.

Because Miriam was similarly shattered by Mom's death, she understood that even though time was passing, we were still knee-deep in grief every day, and outside of Rabbi B, she was my only friend whom I could talk to about my complicated feelings with regularity and without censoring to protect a squirmy audience.

"I have a confession." I leaned forward in my patio chair.

"Oh, God, do you have Covid?"

"Yes, and I've invited you here to spread it. No, it's something else. Before all this happened, I remember thinking my life had been pretty easy, adversity-free, and because I was one of the lucky ones who hadn't suffered for much, maybe I wasn't that interesting."

Miriam gave me a doubtful look. "I don't know about that. The interesting part."

"Let's be honest, no one's ever submitted a film to Sundance about my easy life."

Miriam laughed. "Okay, but—"

"But then," I interrupted, "tragedy struck—divorce, cancer, suicide—and now, I fear my friends think I'm too tragic. The turd in the party punch bowl."

"Well, be thankful there aren't many parties to attend these days."

"Do you ever feel that way? Like, here comes trouble, the bearer of more bad news. We'd better get out of her way before we catch what she's got."

She laughed. "I think more people are concerned about catching Covid than catching what you have."

"I'm not so sure. My hunch is they'd prefer I go back to being 'fun' and 'easy' and drop the griever act, already."

Miriam countered, "I think most people want to show up in hard times; they just don't know what to say or do, and"—she shrugged—"they have their own lives to worry about, especially now."

"I feel like my life is stuck in place. Do you think we'll ever move on?"

"I don't know, Sam. Not as long as I have to keep looking at that fucking house."

Purple Toes

On Wednesday, when the phone rang, I answered with an exaggerated groan.

"That bad, huh?"

"B, I'm sick of it."

"Define *it*."

"I'm sick of all this introspection, all these *feelings*. They won't let up. I'm sick of feeling mad, like when my ex-husband asks, 'What's up?' or 'Are you okay?' as if nothing's happened, as if we're just shooting the breeze on a summer day. I'm sick of sad, of missing Mom and Derby, of feeling hollow and lonely for them both. I'm sick of Shitty Sundays and all the bad news on TV and of feeling scared in this unpredictable world. And I understand it's my 'work' to do, to feel it all with courage and honesty and not shove it away or run from it like Mom did, but—" I paused and exhaled with exasperation. "I'm tired of it. The days are long and hard, and I worry I don't have enough light within me to be my own light source, as you suggest. Really, I get why Mom's sun finally burnt out. Life can feel like a big rolling ball of shit, and staying upbeat in the face of it is exhausting. So that's how I'm feeling today. I'm sick of it *all*."

"That's it?" B baited.

"I can keep going."

"I don't doubt it, but before you continue, remember that we're not talking about generating artificial light, turning on a smile when you feel like raging. We're talking about being real. Coming up to the edge of your grief by facing all aspects of it—the anger, the frustration and fatigue, the desperation, the resignation and apathy. You acknowledge your grief for what it is—a big ball of shit you cannot outrun—and since you can't get around it or ahead of it, let's talk about how you can harness your grief and channel it into something intentional, something meaningful. You have it within you to do this, and that's what makes you *resourceful*."

I considered this. What B said made sense. "It's just that I'm not sure how to practically apply it to the day to day."

"Okay, let's try this." He downshifted. "Tell me about something you're really sick of."

I looked around the room, searching for something I hadn't already mentioned, and settled on my bare feet.

"My toenail polish. I'm sick of this toenail polish, but I can't bring myself to take it off because . . ."

B waited and when I didn't offer to finish the sentence, he asked, "Because why?"

"Because it's been there since the day she died."

For the past three months, I'd been walking around in the spring lilac nail polish that had been applied to my toes within the final hours that Mom was still alive. She would have been pensively walking up and down the cliffside trail of Bodega Head, as reported by the women who last saw her, while I reclined in a salon chair with my feet submerged in bubbles, still grounded in the "before": before she jumped, before she left, before everything changed. In the three months since, I hadn't removed it because most salons were closed indefinitely; no one was getting pedicures in lockdown mode, and while I could have easily repainted them myself, I'd intentionally let them be.

To most anyone, it was just faded and chipped toenail polish, but I recognized it as a physical remnant from before I lost her, a lilac-colored time stamp from when she still walked on this Earth alongside me. The polish kept her near, and to remove it would mean That Day was truly in the past and irreversible, that those final moments when she was still here were gone to me forever, removed with a cotton ball and tossed away.

It's a way of holding on," I admitted to B. "A way of keeping her alive, still with me. It's my way of stopping the clock from moving forward. I know it's not rational, it's emotional, and I'm probably attaching too much meaning to chipped nail polish, but it's something tangible, something I can touch. It still exists in the present moment, in the physical world, on my physical body. The polish keeps her here somehow, not in the past tense, even though I know"—my voice dropped—"even though I know she's gone."

B sat quietly on the other end of the line, allowing the moment to breathe. He offered softly, "The polish keeps you rooted in your life before loss. Getting your toes painted was one of the last normal things you did before you found out what she'd done, so it makes sense you wouldn't want to remove it, because that means—"

"Time has passed, a full pedicure cycle," I croaked.

"Time *has* passed," he gently affirmed, "and it will continue to put distance between you and your mom, and there's a natural fear that can arise with the passing of time after someone you loved has died. That you'll forget. That you'll forget . . . her."

I looked down at my toes. The color had faded and chipped down to almost nothing more than speckled paint. The symbolism made my stomach tighten. *She's fading away.*

"You're not going to forget her," B assured, "and there can be ways to honor her, to keep her alive in a way that doesn't stop you from moving forward, from living your own life. What do you think about creating a ritual where you repaint them now for *her*? Make this ritual a connection point, something that bonds you, even though she's gone. Did she also like to get her toes painted?"

"Oh, yes," I said. "She had this one toe on her right foot that crept over on the others. She thought it was ugly but that it was less noticeable when all her toes were freshly painted. Mauve was her go-to color."

"Okay then, how about this—repaint them and dedicate one toe to her. Paint it a different color than the others. This can be your new ritual, a way to honor and remember her."

"Remove the paint with intention and create something meaningful."

"Now you're getting it."

⋆ ⋆ ⋆

The next week slumped along until I'd arrived at another Shitty Sunday that—bonus!—happened to be Mother's Day, the first of many first holidays to darken my doorstep. I quietly slipped out of bed at the sliver of sunrise, careful not to wake Derby, who lay diagonal across the bed, face down in his pillow. As the weekend had inched closer, I'd become increasingly anxious. I didn't want this day to arrive, my first Mother's Day without a mother. Throughout my life, Mother's Day had been a day of celebration that, depending on my age and geography, included cards and presents, sometimes cake, typically a visit or an outing together and always, at least, a phone call home. There hadn't been a year when I hadn't heard my mother's familiar voice on this day, always happy to hear from me. "*Bonjour,*" she'd coo, "how's my sweet daughter?"

I'd been out of bed for less than five minutes, and already this Mother's Day made no sense. It was no longer a day of celebration; it was a day of mourning, and I struggled with this inconsistency. It was incomprehensible to me that she was not here, that I would not hear her voice today, that I would not look into her animated eyes across a café table, that we wouldn't exchange our complimentary smiles, and I had no words to offer myself, no voice of reason that might explain this dramatic shift, that would put this day into context or provide consolation to me, the newly bereaved, a daughter denied her mother. I thought about the people all over the world who would be celebrating with their mothers today and how I was no longer one of them. I was still somebody's daughter, but I was on the outside now, not fitting in, not belonging. In one calendar year, I'd lost my membership to the Mother's Day Club and been admitted into another, the Missing Mom Club, where she and I wouldn't walk arm in arm, nor would we be snapping a selfie to post on socials with the inevitable, obnoxious caption reserved for mothers and daughters: *Aren't we cute?* No, we no longer shared this day, not in the way we always had. Again, I ruefully imagined the overflowing card stock for nearly all occasions in Target, minus the sentiments for people like me.

Happy Mother-less Day!

Orphan, thinking of you . . .

To the woman who has it all (except a mother) on this very special day . . .

I hadn't seen any cards like this on the shelves, except for those in the "blank" card section in which you can scribble in whatever sad sentiment you wish.

Blank. That's how I felt now.

Empty.

No words to describe this new loneliness. I'd received several lavish bouquets from friends and family that I'd crowded together on my mantel. My living room now had the look of a funeral home, which I guess was the point—that even with the unmistakable presence of primrose and the thick sweetness of purple hyacinth wandering into every room, the house still felt empty and breathless. The most aromatic flowers couldn't fill this new void.

A year ago, Mom was still here, and we were gearing up for a trip to Manhattan—she and the three daughters. A first. Mom and I had visited "The City" many times over the years; my maiden voyage at the moody and dispassionate age of fifteen when Mom suggested we go, "just the two of us," and I returned with my answer for most everything: "Sure, whatever." Six hours in the air followed by a sweltering cab ride into Midtown shook off my selfish funk. As we stepped into the rushing current of contrasting smells, deafening noise, and what felt like one hundred people crowded onto one square of sidewalk, I stared upward at the sixty-story high-rise that would be our home for the next five days and declared: "This is the coolest place on Earth."

"I thought you'd like it." Mom smiled smugly and tipped the driver.

Early into the spring of last year, I'd suggested we all go to New York for Mother's Day, share a single hotel room, and enjoy a few mother-daughter days *away*. As far as the scans were showing, Klose's cancer appeared to have settled into a manageable place—not gone, but not active—and he was the first to encourage her. "Go be a big shot in the big city."

"I don't know, babe. Are you sure?" she hedged.

"Yes, yes, yes." He waved her off with a grin. "Get out of here."

With his permission, Mom allowed herself to slip out of her caregiving role and reacquaint with her old self, the one who planned meticulously for trips, who made lists of museums and art galleries to visit, who decided she needed a new city bag to "hip-ify my outfits." She took a temporary break from her other lists, the ones that tracked medications and doctors' appointments, and she indulged herself in the excitement of upcoming travel. "Of course, we have to do Central Park, the Met, MoMA, shopping in SoHo, cafés in Little Italy, and wine bars in the West Village. Oh, and maybe an *off*-off-Broadway play," she said with a wry smile, "something controversial that pisses off the Republicans." I was encouraged by her spunk, her positive leaning toward the future, when Klose's cancer returned. Pesky black spots reemerged on the PET scan, and debilitating pain began to wrap around his spinal column. She called me after leaving the oncologist's office. "I can't leave him. I can't go anywhere right now."

Later that week, I sat with her at their dining-room table as we called to cancel our hotel in Midtown, two blocks from her favorite entrance to Central Park at 59th and 7th. She tried not to show it, but disappointment had welled beneath her eyes, and I could feel her fatigue; she was tired of life letting her down.

"I really, really wanted to have some fun," she attempted to say with cheer, but her voice cracked at "fun" and her eyes filled with tears. "Oh, Sammy." Her voice was pleading. "This is the pits."

I reached over and ran a hand down her back. "It's just on hold, okay? We'll go next year. I promise."

She dropped her head with resigned sadness. "Okay," she whispered.

Next year had come. Next year was now. It was Mother's Day, and she was gone. We had our chance, and we missed it. It was a conscious choice; we'd prioritized caring for Klose over shopping, and I am resolute that we made the best and right decision at the time. And still, we missed it, our last chance at Mother's Day in New York. It's not uncommon for people to slip into hindsight sentiment, to talk regrettably in post-mortem tones—*if only I'd known, I would have said yes. If only we'd known, we would have done it, thrown caution to the wind.*

The thing is, last-chance moments are rarely recognizable in the moment for what they are. When we decided not to go to New York last spring, I didn't know that meant we'd not go at all, ever again. I couldn't know this was it, our final opportunity to walk arm in arm down Fifth Avenue. Even if you're graced with intuitive foresight, there's no way to know these things, not really. Even when someone is sick, has cancer, or the person you love most seems to be coming undone, it's so easy, so naturally human, to think yourself into believing there will be more time, another season or another opportunity just around the corner to do whatever it is, and that the best thing to do today is the sensible thing, the rational, reasonable, and responsible thing—cancel the hotel and put the trip on hold.

I was tempted to break my fast with social media and post loudly in ALL CAPS: To all of you out there wavering, should we take the trip, should we do it now or wait until later? DON'T WAIT! Grab your special someone tight and drag them to Central Park. If you can, that is. If you can, I strongly suggest you do it before you can no longer get those moments back.

I poured myself a cup of coffee and padded out to the garden. It was a distant cry—three thousand miles, in fact, from the Olmsted Flower Bed in Central Park best known for its triumphant symphony of tulips, but my garden plot would have to do. I sat down on an old apple box as the sun creeped higher into the morning sky. Since I'd first scattered Mom's wildflower seeds, I'd watched, day by day, as little green faces popped through the soil, happily announcing their arrival, until the bed had become crowded with the undeniable sign of life. As the weeks wore on, I continued to slink outside in my pajama bottoms to water in the early-morning hours, as many sunrise walkers stopped to remark on my garden revival. "The last tenant didn't grow anything but weeds," one neighbor said.

"You're a natural gardener," said another. "It's so beautiful, gorgeous, cheerful," became the unsolicited and enthusiastic reaction from people strolling by. The older couple next door identified their favorite, the yellow lupine, and for everyone else there were the impossible-to-miss California poppies and native nasturtium that jockeyed for space, wrapping around each other and competing for brightest color. This morning, I recognized Brittany, the woman with the small white dog. As she approached and spotted me on the old apple box, she stopped and smiled widely. "Happy Mother's Day!" I felt struck by the words—hurt, actually—and as she waited for me to respond, a look of confusion replaced her enthusiasm, and that was when I realized she was addressing the greeting *to me*.

Of course! On this block, I am known as Derby's mother. I am not a motherless child. I am a mother to a child. Since moving in three months ago, I hadn't shared with my new neighbors that I'd lost my mother, so to them, I was the woman who lived on the corner, the one who tended her garden, the one with the young boy who ran around the yard and affectionately called me Mommy. In my early morning moments, I'd overlooked my role beyond being Susan's daughter. I was a mother too, and now, Mother's Day was for us, for me and my boy to exchange complimentary smiles, to walk arm and arm, to take silly photos. My heart ached for Mom. I longed desperately for her voice, for her laugh, for her to look at me with affection. I resented her absence, yet I wasn't on the outside like I'd earlier thought. I still belonged in this club, as mother to Derby. I was here after all. I was alive, and didn't I owe it to him—and to myself—to reclaim this day, to celebrate our relationship, to celebrate a brighter spring and summer?

Before this Mother's Day, I'd blindly assumed I'd have Mom forever—or, at least, that we'd have many more years together. Our time had run out much sooner than I'd anticipated, but Derby and I were still on the clock. We had time. We had each other. And if we were lucky, we'd walk in step for many years to come. "Thank you," I said to Brittany. "I'd better go wake him up."

* * *

As we sat at the dining room table both spreading jam on toast, Derby glanced over at the cascade of flowers on the mantel, blooms falling all over each other, trying their best to cheer me up.

"Why do you have so many flowers?" he asked.

"Because it's Mother's Day."

His eyes widened and his chewing came to a halt. "I don't have a present for you," he admitted with worry.

In years past and on the direction of his teacher, Derby would have made something for me at school. A beaded necklace. A ceramic heart. At the very least, a hand-drawn card. But Mother's Day crafts hadn't made it into the distance-learning curriculum. Teaching a full classroom of kids on a computer screen had its limitations, and second-grade teachers were simply trying to coach their students to sit still until lunch.

"That's okay." I smiled at Derby. "I don't need a present."

"Do you want me to make you coffee or something?

I raised my mug. "I already made it, but I appreciate that you appreciate the gift that is morning coffee."

"I actually think it's gross and you're addicted."

I laughed, "Where'd you hear that word? What does it mean to be *addicted*?"

"It means that you can't live without it even if it gives you bad breath. So, anyway," he pivoted, "what do you want to do today?"

"Well, you go back to your dad's later this morning, but what do you think about ditching this toast and stinky coffee and walking downtown for bagels?" We'd recently discovered, and with great elation, that our favorite bagel shop had reopened for takeout. "Let's go." He was up and out of his chair before I could set down my mug.

★ ★ ★

The great thing about young kids during a pandemic—or, I should say, the great thing about my eight-year-old during this particularly trying time, was that he lowered his expectations. Because there wasn't much to do or much of anywhere to go, going and doing anything outside our new and very limited routine felt special. Derby ate his pizza bagel with cream cheese and capers on a bench in front of the bagel shop like it was the best thing in the world and watching him lick his fingers in the dappled sunlight of our sleepy town was the best thing happening in my world, on this alternate version of Mother's Day. When Derby was a toddler, he had blond, almost translucent curls that framed his chunky little cherub face. When the sun hit him, he glowed like an angel. His hair had darkened incrementally each year, but as I looked at him now, eyes closed and lost in the moment, I thought, this child lassos me to the sun. He's not my light source. I'm mindful of assigning that role to others now, and still, there's no denying that Derby radiates from within, and it's my joy to bask in his glow.

★ ★ ★ ★

After his dad picked him up at noon and I closed the door and started to slide down the wall into my Sunday routine of self-pity, this one accentuated by the Motherless Mother's Day holiday, I reminded myself I'd specifically requested this pickup time so I could spend the second half of the day with my sisters. After Miriam's visit, I'd appealed to expand our collective pod so we could at least return to the house. Jenni and Gretta had agreed, and today we planned to meet in Sebastopol and split a bottle of Sancerre, or two, and talk about something other than the still-unchecked items on the whiteboard.

In the shower, which I'd intended to be short and without the regular deluge of tears, I focused again on my toes. The lilac paint was hardly hanging on, and the original color had turned a grayish purple. My feet looked like they were in mourning, and B was probably right that it was time for a fresh coat of paint. I hesitated. Was I ready to remove this reminder, this physical remnant of the last hours when Mom was alive? I understood the polish symbolically kept me grounded in my grief, stuck in a moment that had passed, and to remove it meant I was stepping forward. But what if I didn't want to step forward? What if I didn't want to move on? Once I took it off, there'd be no going back; there'd be no getting her back. Was it really so wrong to keep one foot stuck in the past?

"Not one foot, but two," I could hear B correcting me from the week before. "How about we compromise, and you keep one *toe* stuck in the past?"

Since he mentioned it, I'd warmed to the idea of painting one toe for Mom as a way to remember her, and I further rationalized that a spring jaunt to New York City would absolutely call for a fresh pedicure. If she were still here, Mom would be the first to goad me: "Darling, your feet look like they've just left the morgue. Give them some life, for Christ's sake."

"Okay, fine," I said out loud in the shower as if I were speaking directly to her. "In honor of the trip we didn't get to take, I will repaint them." The question was: What color? My in-home selection was limited, and I'd renamed them accordingly. Lonely Lemon, Pick-Yourself-Up Pink, Put-On-Some-Real-Pants Petunia, Get-a-Grip Gold, and, finally, the winner: Mother's Day Mauve. I joined Gretta and Jenni that afternoon in strappy sandals with fresh paint feeling as if I'd made a significant step forward, if only evident by one standout toe I'd painted a shade lighter than the others.

PART TWO

Release

Good Hair Day

Not long after I'd painted a toe in her honor, Mom walked into my dream as if she'd just left the salon herself. She floated into the foreground of my mind with silver hair that swept around her head like a celestial crown. "Do you like my hair?" she asked with unmasked pride. Before I could answer, her image faded, and I woke up alone in the dark.

My first thought: Well, at least in death, you finally got good hair.

Ask anyone who knew her—my mother's preoccupation with her hair was constant. It was either too thin, too flat, too frizzy, too gray, too short, too leggy, and, more frequently than not, "in *desperate* need of a haircut." Whether it was the latest mousse, gel, spray, serum, thickening shampoo, or volumizer, she was first in line to apply every new product on the market. "I feel good about this one," she'd say with eager optimism, only to conclude after wresting with her limp locks in the bathroom mirror: "Oh, I give up. It's just bad hair."

In 1988, the Oxford English Dictionary credited my mother for being the first to put into print the phrase, "bad hair day." Mom was an acclaimed journalist, a successful author, and a playwright who dug into serious issues, and she also loved that she'd be immortalized for bad hair because it pointed directly to her favorite obsession. After much trial and error—and by that, I mean decades—she insisted the only thing that returned her curls to the buoyant vitality of her younger years was muggy, East Coast salt air, an added incentive for visiting New England Nancy in the dog days of summer. "Feel that humidity?" she'd say as soon as we stepped foot outside of Logan Airport. "My hair's gonna look great for the next week."

During our last visit together, four days before she was gone forever, she asked the question I'd been posed hundreds of times over my lifetime. "So . . . should I get my hair cut or leave it?" Based on our long history, she'd likely already decided it was in desperate need of a haircut, so I volleyed back, "Up to you," and, as I suspected, the following afternoon she texted: *got my hair cut.* According to Jenni, who met her for a walk soon afterwards, "Her hair looked awesome. One of her best cuts."

I lay in the dark, mostly awake now, with a follow-up thought: You wasted a great haircut by jumping into the sea.

And now, mine was not cooperating. Over the past few months, mine had gone thin, flat, gray, and lifeless, and was in desperate need of something. I'd inherited Mom's bad hair—not fair!—and now she was gloating from another place, over the rainbow, the Other Side.

When I woke up the next morning, I could still clearly see Mom's silver sweep of heavenly hair and bright, beaming smile. The dream felt like a message, more than my mind making weird stuff up, because it was so *her*. Of course, she would want me to be the first to know she'd finally solved her hair problem. This was BIG news, I agreed, and worth transmitting across the divide. As I sipped my first cup of coffee, I played the mental movie back over and over. *Was that really you?* It seemed so absurdly believable. *Could it be?* I allowed myself to open up to the possibility because, why not? What more did I have to lose? She was gone, my hair was falling closely behind, and I'd been wandering around the house looking for her for months. *Bring it*, I dared. If that was you, if that was real, do it again. And next time, we need to talk about more than your hair.

Place the Call

For the next several nights, I asked her to return. I lay in bed whispering, "Mommy, please visit me. Mommy, please come." I'd drift off to sleep and—nothing. After five or six failed attempts, I chastised myself for being ridiculous. Desperate. A sad woman chasing after something that didn't exist, wanting and wishing for hocus-pocus magic to relieve my grief. Get a grip, Sam. At least, get some sleep.

She's gone.

Except I knew she wasn't *gone*, gone. That was what I'd been telling readers for most of my writing career, anyway. I hadn't caught the irony at the time, but my first ghostwriting project was writing for a psychic medium—that is, someone who communicates with *ghosts*—and I was hired to help ground my client's otherworldly craft in the tangible here and now and to appeal to readers who, like me, were both curious and skeptical of her unconventional profession. On our initial call, I'd admitted to the medium: I'm not *not* a believer, but I'm also not convinced it's real. "That's okay," she'd said. "It's not my job to convince you. I let the spirits speak for themselves."

And they did.

Countless hours of interviews and four best-selling book

collaborations later, I was convinced that Rebecca Rosen was not a magician performing an elaborate party trick; she was a bridge between this world and the next. Throughout the fifteen years we worked together, I witnessed her ability to channel spirits into large auditoriums packed with three hundred to five hundred people, many of whom insisted their dead loved ones were present in the room. I joined small group readings in her Denver office, where she identified details about the dead she couldn't have guessed or researched or known, and after years of observation and a careful study of her craft, I'd suspended my doubt; I believed in this other realm of possibility and connection, a realm Rebecca claimed was accessible to the living, and not only for mediums like herself. How many times had she told me, and I'd transcribed into the pages of her books: *Your loved ones are never truly gone. They exist in another form, in the unseen world, and they are on the ready to connect and communicate with you as soon as you place the call.* I'd witnessed this phenomenon, yet when it came to accessing this invisible phone line in my own life, I slipped back into my old skepticism because I'd been placing the call and no one was picking up. Maybe I'd been denied access to the Other Side, like an exclusive A-list club that slams the door on women over thirty?

"I think I'm the exception. Spirit communication isn't in my skill set. I should just stick to ghost*writing*." I'd called Rebecca to discuss another book collaboration when I drifted off script and shared my failed attempt at connecting with Mom.

"Sam, you, of all people, know how this works," Rebecca reprimanded me with her characteristic warmth. "You can connect with her any time, but I think your grief is getting in the way. You're focused on your hurt, on what you've lost, and your anger and resentment are working against you. I get the sense she's hesitant to meet you. If you can, get out of your head and into your heart. Think back to the good times when you were laughing together. Focus on how you loved each other, on what you meant to each other. Her physical body is gone, but your love for each other doesn't die, and that love is energy that can act like its own telephone line. As you're falling asleep, speak directly to her, and call her name three times. Choose the knowing that she is not gone and call her into your dreams."

That night, I tried again. I took a deep breath and closed my eyes. I whispered, "Mom, I'm inviting you in. Please come forward. I need you to show up. I need you to do this for me. I need *you*." I was pleading, I could hear it in my voice. I tried again. "Mom, I'm calling you in. Please show up for me and I will show up for you. Please." My voice edged toward insistent. "You owe me! Stop hiding!" There it was again, my red-hot rage, layered with the fear of rejection, of more abandonment. "Mom." I eased my tone. "I'm calling you in from wherever you are, from the hidden place. Come out of from behind the shadows and show yourself to me." I took another deep breath and focused on my heart; on how much love it held for her. "Susan, Susan, Susan," I whispered, "I love you. Susan, Susan, Susan, be with me. Susan, Susan, Susan, I am here, I am always right here. I will never leave you. Please join me." I opened my eyes and stared into the dark, feeling a rush of anticipation followed by worrisome dread. What if she doesn't show up? What if she does?

A Glimpse Through the Fog

I woke up in the dream, and I was standing barefoot on something coarse and cold. I wiggled my toes and immediately identified the texture: wet sand. I was on a beach, but I couldn't discern which one. I heard waves breaking not far from me and the smell of salt air blowing in from an open ocean, but my visibility was cloaked in fog. I wasn't sure in which direction to go, or if I should move at all, so I stood still and listened. Seagulls, waves, a fishing boat in the distance, and then, faintly, what sounded like the approach of footsteps. Goose bumps traveled up and down my arms as the steps continued, became louder, and grew closer. I squinted in the fog to see who or what was coming toward me.

Fog.

Footsteps.

Then, a figure walking out of the fog, moving with trepidation, head bowed and shoulders low. A woman wrapped in a white cotton sweater that engulfed her slender frame. I watched this vision in the fog, unmoving, until she stopped directly in front of me and lifted her face to mine, the face I knew almost better than my own, the one with the deep brown eyes and the arched eyebrows, the one I'd missed so much, the one that had abruptly vanished from my life *that day.*

I drew a sharp breath.

Mom.

I choked back tears as I looked into her tired, pleading eyes, rimmed with pain and remorse. She shook her head as her own tears spilled over.

"I'm sorry," she said in a low whisper.

My heart contracted at the sound of her voice, and I leaned forward with a longing to be held by her, to embrace her in return, but I stopped myself before getting too close. I stood firm in the sand, fighting my instinct to be flesh to flesh with my mother. I crossed my arms over my heart like an obstinate child, *her* obstinate child, and willed my anger forward.

"I'M SO MAD AT YOU!" I screamed. "HOW COULD YOU *DO* THAT?" I released months of grief in a single question.

I'd called her into my dream with the promise of love and now that she'd appeared, I'd turned on her. She flinched in the face of my outburst. I allowed the swelling current of my rage to rise again. "HOW COULD YOU DO THAT TO *ME*?"

She offered no answer and my anger—fueled by months of betrayal, a scorned child left alone on the edge of a cliff—began rushing through my body like a fire burning out of control and before I could harness it, I lost my footing and stumbled forward. Mom reached out her hand to steady me, a kindness and a gesture so familiar that I could only recognize it for what it was: a mother's love. All at once I was a toddler, a teenager, a young student heading off to college, a woman dressing on her wedding day with her mother by her side. I collapsed into her, and she held me as she had at every point of my life.

"Let it go," she whispered. "Let it all out."

I buried my face in the soft skin of her neck and sobbed. She held me until I felt wrung out, my rage vanquished. I was empty except for regret.

She spoke quietly into my ear. "I am so sorry I hurt you, that I hurt all of you."

"I'm so sorry too," I cried back.

"No, no, no," she whispered and pulled me tighter. "You have nothing to be sorry about."

I let her hold me and caress my hair until I had the courage to break from her embrace. I stared down at the sand, at our naked toes nearly touching. "I do." My lips quivered as I struggled to say the words I'd been ashamed to speak out loud, the words that had been caught in my throat for months. "I'm sorry I didn't stop you," I said, my voice cracking. "I'm sorry I wasn't there. I'm so sorry . . ." I gulped for air. "I'm sorry I couldn't save you—"

"Shhhh," Mom interrupted.

"No, I need to say this, please. I promised to keep you safe. I promised Klose, before he died, that I'd take care of you, that I'd be your person when he was gone, and . . ." I struggled to catch my breath. "I failed. I failed you."

"Sammy." She lifted my face. "Look at me."

I raised my wounded eyes.

"You did not fail me. You did everything you could. You all were all so kind, so loving and loyal. You all went above and beyond to help me, and I still did what I did. Please don't torment yourself. Saving me was not your job. Stopping me wasn't either." She put her hands on either side of my face, and suddenly she was Mom again, before she got so scared and sick, full of life and unconditional love. "Sweetie." She leaned in. "You did not fail me. None of you did. Please, please let that go."

I took a steadying breath and attempted to absorb her words when we were whipped from behind. The cold coastal wind pulled us apart. I reached for her, but she faded into the fog.

"No," I wailed. "Come back. I don't want to let go. I don't want to let *you* go."

But she was gone.

A Different Time Zone

The following afternoon, I took my habitual break from my ghostwriting project to walk outside and retrieve the mail. As usual, there were more pieces addressed to Mom than me. Today, renewal notices from the Southern Poverty Law Center and the National Organization for Women, the upcoming summer schedule for the Performing Arts Coalition, and a donation ask from Emily's List. I dutifully carried her bundle inside and dropped them on top of her growing stack as I asked myself the same question I did the day before and the day before that: Why am I saving her mail? Why don't I toss it? Why don't I cancel her forwarded mail altogether? My answer was the same as the day before and the day before that: I don't want to. Receiving Mom's mail was another one of those tricks I played on myself, like I'd done with the lilac toenail polish. Collecting Mom's mail tricked me into believing she was still around, as if she were only traveling abroad for an extended amount of time with no set return date, like when she and Klose decided to move from California to Germany in the early '90s for "a year or two, or maybe more." Gretta, Jenni and I, were attending college at the time, "so you three will be fine," they assured us. "We'll be back before anyone graduates." This was before cell phones and social media, so when they sold the family home we grew up in and left the country with only a few suitcases and the cat, they were gone, well beyond reach, far away in an unknown-to-us part of the world. And with no dedicated return date on the calendar, we had to trust they were out there somewhere, and that if we needed them, they could reach us from their German house phone or send us a fax.

And maybe, I thought, that was how it was again now.

After my second vivid dream, this time with Mom speaking directly to me and appearing in a white knit sweater as if she still existed somewhere, out there in the fog, I looked at her stack of mail on the dining room table with quick clarity. That's it—you're just in a different time zone! One that exists outside our standard thirty-eight and is far harder to pinpoint or track because it's elusive and timeless. In the zone of the afterlife, I imagined Mom traveled easily. No missed or cancelled flights. No bulky oversized bag to drag around that threatens to throw your back out when you haul it up a set of narrow stairs. Rather, in her time zone, she could easily lift off, free of baggage and physical tethers, allowing her to fly high and free with her arms outstretched and the wind in her silver hair.

And wouldn't she love that? To be the child in *The Snowman*, her favorite winter movie, the British animated short film we watched together as a family every Thanksgiving once the dinner dishes were cleared. Mom's favorite scene, set to the ethereal lyrics "walking in the air," tracks the young boy and his come-to-life snowman as they take flight and soar high above the ground, hand in hand, crossing the world's oceans and flying low over villages, through tangled forests, and beyond the Northern Lights, all in the course of one wintry, moonlit night. My mother loved the snow. Snow angels, snowflakes, snowstorms, the dance of the Snow Queen. She insisted its icy magic made everything more beautiful. Yes, I'd like to believe you exist there, in the wintry beyond, at least some of the time, and that your new travel pass allows you short layovers in this world, if only in the dreams of the living, where we can connect and catch up before you take flight again.

As I gazed at her stack of mail, I smiled hopefully. So maybe she's not here, but she is somewhere.

★ ★ ★ ★

"Do you think I'm nuts?" I asked B after recounting my latest dream with Mom.

"Was it a spirit visitation, an inspired dream from another time zone, or was it only wishful thinking?" B responded. "I'm not to say. Whatever *it* was, I think you're beginning to explore the possibility that you can still have a relationship with her, even in death. Even though she's physically gone, on a cellular level she's not gone, because you share the same DNA."

"I get that I embody her genetic information and that we're still 'in relationship' because I carry parts of her within me, but aside from the science, about this other thing—having a conversation *with* her—do you think my mind is making it up?"

"The mind is a master at logical thinking, for processing, for organizing and creating structure. But trust and knowing come from our intuition, our hearts. So, what does your heart say? Are you making it up?"

"No." I answered without thinking about it. "My heart says that my mother and I spoke to each other. How we did this and from where, I don't know, but the heart of what we exchanged felt real."

"Maybe don't question it so much and allow it to guide you if that's what it's doing. Did the dream feel clarifying?"

"It was a start. I still have many unanswered questions."

"The mind has many unanswered questions," B corrected with a smile. "What does your heart want to know?"

"My heart wants to know why. Okay, maybe my mind wants to know why. Does it matter who's asking? I want to know why she did it. My heart needs this to heal. At least, I think it does."

"You're stuck in your head," B said. "Trying to explain. And I understand you want answers. I did too, after my dad died. But what if there aren't any?"

"No," I rejected. "I don't accept that. And Mom wouldn't either. She'd ask questions. She'd go after the story."

"Okay," he said, giving in. "Then ask questions, and if there is an answer, are you prepared for it?"

The Why

It had been several weeks since the dream in the fog, and every night since, I had invited her to return.

Nothing.

My wishful thinking that Mom was flying around in another time zone seemed silly now, and during the days, I was back to where I'd been, wandering around the house without resolve.

One overcast morning, I pulled on a sweater I'd found at a local boutique soon after my separation from my husband. It was a gift to myself that spoke to how I felt at the time. In white cursive stitching over black cotton: *Free as a Bird*. When I'd bought it, Derby wasn't yet reading, and now, over a year later, he stared up at my chest and mouthed the words.

"I like your sweater." He smiled, pleased with himself for understanding the script.

"Thanks." I smiled back, withholding its personal meaning.

He read it again, more thoughtfully this time. He looked at me with seriousness. "At least, that's what Mutti is now."

My breath caught in my throat. My son had derived his own meaning that matched my snowy image of Mom flying unencumbered in her own time zone, wind in her hair, a smile that sparkled like winter diamonds. So maybe it wasn't silly, after all? Maybe Mom was trying to connect from somewhere out there, and Derby was her little messenger, reminding me to answer the trans-international call.

That night, I did my best to tamper my bossy insistence that she reveal herself. I closed my eyes in the dark and quietly asked, "Mom, please come forward. Meet me in the middle. Meet me in the in-between. Meet me wherever you are and help me understand. Please help me know why."

* * *

I woke up in the dream and this time, I knew exactly where I was—the fateful spot, Bodega Head. I gazed out toward the horizon and spotted her sitting on one of the concrete block benches that faced west toward the sea, not far from where she'd last been seen. She was wearing the same white sweater from before, and as the wind blew off the bluff, the fabric fluttered like the high grass on the winding trail above. I slowly walked up from behind her and sat down, interrupting her expression of deep contemplation.

"You came back," she said softly without breaking her gaze on the water.

"So did you," I returned with disbelief.

She faced me and searched my eyes. "I understand you have questions."

"You do? How'd you know that?"

"I can hear you." She smiled. "The walls between here and there are thinner than you think."

I flashed back to a scene of her pounding on my locked bedroom door in the mid-'80s. I was around fifteen, obsessed with The Violent Femmes, Doc Martens, and thick black eyeliner. On this particular night, I'd sneaked my best friend, LeLe, in through my window after curfew. We'd been careless and loud, laughing and playing music like no one would hear us.

"Samantha, open the door!" she warned. "I know there's more than one of you in there." I cracked the door open as my friend hid in the closet. "Yeah?" I lowered my black eyelids.

"Tell your friend she's going home. And you're grounded."

I hadn't been allowed to leave the house for two weeks, outside of school, and now, in our dream space, my mother had caught me again and there was no point denying it. She was right; I did have questions, so many, and one that continued to dominate.

"Why'd you do it?"

"Oh, sweetie," she sighed. "That's complicated. There is no one answer, I'm afraid. It's layered."

"Start at the top layer, then."

She closed her eyes and took a deep meditative breath, as I'd seen her do countless times before thoughtfully answering a hard question. When she opened her eyes, she began. "I suppose at the top layer was hope; or, rather, the absence of hope. Throughout that long, hard year of Klose battling cancer, I willed myself to have hope that he'd survive—that we'd survive—but after he died, my hope went with him."

"Have hope, don't be a dope. Remember how he used to say that?" I smiled at the memory.

Mom smiled too, but it was cracked with sadness. "He was always such a funny, clever guy, and far smarter than me. I think he did have hope until the end, but it was different for me. After he died, I didn't see a future for myself."

"But you had so much to be hopeful for," I pressed gently, "and so much worth living for. You had all of us, your family and friends, your writing, all the causes you were involved in. Even without Klose, your life was still full; enviable, even. Wasn't that enough? Weren't *we* enough?"

She tightened. "I had a lot to keep me going, you're right . . . but I couldn't see it."

"It was all right there, right in front of you."

"Yes, but I couldn't *see* it. I'd lost focus. I know now that I'd slipped into a depression, and maybe something deeper, something invisible I didn't understand. As Klose became more and more sick, I couldn't shake the increasingly awful feeling of dread, of darkness closing in. I tried ignoring it, avoiding it with distractions, staying busy. I tried to will it away, pray it away, push it away, but it would always return. Looking back, I see that I should have stayed on the pills; I should have listened to the doctors. I should have engaged more in therapy."

Her admission finally diffused some of my hurt, some of my confusion, although not entirely. "You were surrounded by so many people who loved you, who wanted to help you, who would have done anything had you asked, and you wouldn't let us. Why did you reject it?"

"I didn't entirely dismiss it." She raised an eyebrow. "I went to all those appointments with you at Kaiser."

"Not very willingly," I muttered.

It was months after our first visit to the psychiatric department, when she'd declared, "I'm not depressed, and I don't want to take any more pills," that I'd eventually found her a doctor she liked well enough, and who successfully convinced her to try an antidepressant to help with her escalating overwhelm and worry, only for her to conclude after five days of taking them, "they aren't working." Mom said the pills made her feel "jangly" and "jumpy" and even though she'd been told that antidepressants work slowly and that most people won't experience any benefit for the first ten to fourteen days and she'd been advised to stick it out at least that long, she was insistent after five. "I'm going off them."

"There are others we can try," her doctor suggested at the following appointment. Given only my limited understanding of depression and anxiety, I knew both were highly treatable, and medication could significantly help, so I encouraged her too. "Mom, I think that's a good idea. Try something else."

Lexapro, Wellbutrin, Remeron, Trazodone, Ativan, Zoloft, Doxepin, Cymbalta. She tried them all for four or five days, sometimes fewer, until she grew impatient, insisted they weren't working, and stopped taking them without her doctor's permission. I became increasingly concerned that an overlap of powerful drugs in rapid succession might exacerbate her symptoms and potentially create new ones, and I was frustrated by the medical directive provided to us, that the only way to test the effectiveness of these medications was by trial and error because they affected individuals differently, to varying degrees and at an unpredictable rate. This willy-nilly approach annoyed my mother, who was looking for a magic pill and there wasn't one; there were many, and it was anyone's guess how many you had to try until finding the right one, the magic one, if it even existed.

One afternoon, as I drove us to her appointment and where she hoped, again, that her doctor could prescribe something "better" or agree to let her forego medication entirely, I repeated the point. "Mom, these medicines take time to get into your system, to take effect. Why don't you stay on this one for a little longer? You've tried so many now."

"It's *not* working," she seethed. "It's making me forgetful and foggy, and do you know what happens, darling, when you're no longer clever and smart, when people no longer want to hear what you think or what you have to say? It's worse than losing your looks. Much worse. Without your mind, you're irrelevant. You become invisible, unnecessary. You might as well be dead."

Whoa. Who was this stranger in my car? And where were those words coming from? They were cruel and unforgiving, and she was directing them at herself. I'd never heard my mother use that tone before, not toward others present or not. She hadn't used it on me, and she wasn't ever hateful toward herself. She sat in the passenger seat as if carved from ice, and I inwardly reeled and said nothing more.

"Do you remember that car ride?" I asked her now in the dream.

"Oh, yes." She shook her head. "That drive was not my finest moment."

"What was going on there? I'd never heard you speak that way."

After a long pause, she said, "Well, I suppose that was my ageism talking."

"*Ageism*? Come on. You wrote, like, a thousand columns and more than a few books on aging. What was your decree? Age with daring, humor, and grace. You celebrated getting older."

"Yes, but I hadn't intended to age the way I did. I hadn't accounted for the unwanted snag in my mind that reared its head that fateful year, and I feared it was only the beginning. What would happen if I unraveled to the point I couldn't be fixed? Where would that leave me? Where would I *fit*? Where would I fit in our family? Where would I fit in the world?" She faced me with weary eyes. "Who would want a wretch like me?"

"Oh, Mom." I reached over and took her hand. "That's where you were wrong. You always fit in everywhere and with everyone. And as your daughter, I wanted you any way I could have you, and I always wanted more of you, even the complicated version at the end."

"Are you sure about that?" She eyed me with doubt.

"Okay, I admit that monologue in the car took me by surprise. It didn't sound like you."

"That was the changed Susan," she said, her disdain from the car ride returning.

"I admit, you were different. Your moods were less predictable."

"I hated that version of myself."

I squeezed her hand. "I didn't. To be honest, I welcomed a different version of you. Not the struggling version, of course, but a change from your trademark happy, happy, happy, sunny, sunny, sunny, all the time. Remember when I told you that your new eccentricity was only making you more interesting?"

"I recall not finding much comfort in that assessment."

I elbowed her gently. "That's because you'd lost your sense of humor by then."

"Aha!" She turned to me, finally giving in to a grin. "If I could no longer take a joke, I was clearly unwell."

"I agree, that should have been the tell, but seriously—we have to address your resistance to receiving help. You acted like you were above it."

"I did not act above it," she defended.

"Oh, yeah, you did, and it surprised me because you were always doing for others. Volunteering at the Food Bank and the local library, donating to hospice. You made time for friends who were struggling with their marriages, with money, with immobility or whatever it was, but when it came to receiving help for yourself, you wouldn't accept it. I don't get it."

"Sammy, you have to understand that when I started to spiral, I was afraid to admit the truth that I needed help, even to myself. I was trying not to show it, but I was becoming more and more panicked and . . ." She held back for a moment. "I was also proud. I wanted to believe I could handle it, whatever *it* was. That I could beat it. And I wanted other people to believe that too, that I was the strong and confident woman I'd always been. That I was still *me*, even if that meant I was only acting."

Okay, now we were starting to get somewhere.

Mom grew up in Meadville, Pennsylvania, where my grandfather, Paul Frey, ran the zipper factory, the town's single largest employer, and where his wife Helen dutifully stayed home and ran their household. It was the 1940s and '50s, and this was the model for most girls and boys growing up in our country, but by the time Mom entered adulthood as an Ohio University college graduate and a young bride in 1965, the expectations and opportunities were shifting for women—and many men, like my progressive-leaning father, were changing their minds too. When he suggested they shake off provincial tradition and move to San Diego, where they could both pursue careers and barbeque on the beach, Mom liberated herself—goodbye, good girl!—and packed up her winter wool sweaters and hit the open road, daring to become something more than a homemaker and a wife. By 1970, Mom was working as a full-time reporter for the *San Diego Evening Tribune*, covering the coveted Women's Page and New York fashion week while her baby girl was sucking on a pacifier at home. Feminism had gone mainstream, and Mom was reaping the benefits.

I grew up in a house with two full-time working parents and where Mom's side of the bookshelf was cluttered with issues of *Ms.* magazine and stacks of books by Betty Friedan, Shirley Chisholm, and Gloria Steinem. In the early years, Mom's on-screen heroes were Barbara Walters and Jane Fonda, and years later, when Mom became more politically active, she aligned with the views of Hillary Clinton, Michelle Obama, and Ruth Bader Ginsberg. Mom's feminist ideals of equity, opportunity, empowerment, and individual choice weren't cloaked, nor were they bumper-sticker slogans she easily threw around. For as long as I could remember, she lived her beliefs out loud. She involved herself in the National Women's History Project, wrote frequently about women's rights in her syndicated column for *The New York Times*, marched for equal pay through the streets of San Francisco, mailed pro-choice postcards to Congress, and hosted suffragette parties in our backyard, where she and her girlfriends donned white linen and debated every controversial topic they could think of until the wine was gone. Mom's position as an ardent supporter of the Women's Movement, along with her resolute dedication to raise women up and give them a voice, was a dynamic current that energized our home, and she empowered me and my sisters with her rallying call: *I am strong, I am invincible, I am woman!* Be an unwavering force of Oh Yes You Can. There's nothing stopping you.

Her words had worked to inspired us forward, and she had marched proudly in the front of the line. And now, I recognized her blanket directive had a few frayed ends. What happens when you retire and become less visible and less professionally relevant, and your partner gets sick? What happens when you become a full-time caretaker who then also needs caretaking? What happens when life pokes holes in your impenetrable persona and you realize you can no longer do everything you set your mind to? When life eventually gets in the way and you need help, what do you do then?

"This was where your '70s brand of feminism needed an upgrade," I said to Mom in the dream. "Instead of encouraging women to do it all, how about encouraging women to be it all?"

"*Be* it all? Explain."

"Meaning, we can be imperfect women. We can be in pain, in fear. We can ask for help when we need it and receive it without judgment. We're allowed to struggle, Mom, and not be ashamed of it, or black-marked for needing it. This is textbook Brené Brown—it's when we courageously show up as our real selves with our insides hanging out. That's true strength."

"Yes, yes." Mom nodded. "I was blind and now I see."

I sensed a hint of impatience, and I knew I ought to ease up on my lecture tone before she vanished on me, but something was clicking into place. I turned the key another notch. "Is that also how you felt about *me*? That I should suck it up and silently soldier through hard times, even if I needed help? Even if I was unhappy in my marriage or struggling professionally or feeling insecure about my own stability? Because asking for help is weak? A personal failing?"

"No." Her answer was swift. "I never thought you were weak. I've always been proud of all three of you, all of you daughters, and all my grandkids."

"Then why didn't you afford yourself the same grace?"

She shrugged. "Because I wanted to be better."

"Better than what?"

"I wanted to be the person I'd always tried to be for myself, for you daughters, for Klose, for everyone who knew me: a capable woman, and I feared what people would think when they found out I was no longer as capable as I'd once presented myself to be."

"Mom . . ." I shook my head. "I needed you to be an example for both of us that even when we're feeling defeated, we're still worthy, we're still enough. We don't have to hide. We don't have to pretend. We get to tell the truth, even if it's scary to us. Even if it's scary to other people."

"I'm sorry, sweetie. I kind of messed that lesson up. In this department, I think you need to be the example I wasn't."

Writing Practice

I woke up startled and wide-eyed from the dream, from talking with Mom again as if she were sitting right next to me. I clumsily reached for my notebook and pen, the one I kept on my nightstand for middle-of-the-night moments like this, where reality and dreaming blur and something emerges, a thought or an idea worth writing down in the dark. I scribbled a few things and fell back asleep.

The next morning, before diving into my ghostwriting project, I opened a new document and saved it as: *The Why*. I spent the next hour transferring my handwritten notes onto the digital page, filling in with what more I could remember from the dream. When I was done, I had a rambling run-on sentence that filled several pages. It was a mess, but there was something there that felt true. Something that felt guided and not manufactured by me. I returned to it the following morning and the one after that, diving back in for twenty to thirty stolen minutes before the start of my paid writing day. I continued to rearrange and revise *The Why* until it sounded like I'd heard her in the dream, a complete back-and-forth dialogue between the two of us.

I wrote Mom's side of the conversation the way in which I approach all first-person narratives: I get inside another person's head by getting out of my own. This isn't a technique I've studied, if it even is one; it's how I unconsciously trained myself to ghostwrite over the years and somehow, miraculously, it works. Other ghostwriters I know write to loud music. Some write in crowded cafés and coworking spaces where dogs sit underfoot. I've tried this, I have, and I cannot do it. I am too easily distracted by noise and will easily be lured into the conversations around me, and not as an interesting contributor to the subject matter being discussed but as an unapologetic eavesdropper. And if you add a loud espresso machine steaming oat milk or the complete anthology of the Beatles playing overhead, forget it. An abundance of auditory stimulation will stop me before I can start. I once abandoned a WeWork membership because of one man who slurped his midday soup. Even when I positioned myself in a private cubby desk on the other side of the break-room wall, the slow intake of broth was all I could hear for the full seventeen minutes—yep, I clocked it—that it took him to slowly savor each spoonful, and even after he finished, my focus was lost for the remainder of the day. My inability to tolerate external noise is my impediment, and I own it. Soup ought to be enjoyed—slurped, even—without a side-eye by me, which is why I eventually removed myself from the collaborative workspace I now refer to as WeSlurp.

I learned that because I work best in controlled silence, I require a home office, one where I can close the windows to external sound, stash my phone in another room, and silence all email and news alerts on my laptop. And still, I wear noise-cancelling headphones and kick the cats out the front door to further minimize distractions and constant pleas for food.

Once I have external noise under control, I turn down my internal voice like they encourage you to do in meditation or in yoga class, and then I listen for the voice of the person I'm translating onto the page. Listening is key because it allows me to *hear* them. This might sound obvious; except I don't use transcription software. I don't record my interviews or conversations with people, I never have, so when I hear another person's voice, it's because I'm recalling from memory their words, their cadence and inflection, as well as their unspoken intention as I hear it in my mind. I do take notes when I interview people, either over the phone or in person, and I type or scribble as they talk, so it's not that I'm completely writing blind. My notes create a base outline, and I expand their voice from there. Other "ghosts" have suggested I could save myself a lot of time and trouble by recording and translating my client's words verbatim, but a literal translation isn't enough for me. It's missing something. The spirit of the person. The only time I used a service like this, it didn't work; the pages I turned out lacked depth and heart. I ended up scrapping the scripted translation and reverting to my mental dictation to rewrite the chapter, recalling my client's voice as I heard it in my head. It's not everyone's way, but it's the only way for me. I just cannot get another person's words right until I can hear them in real time as my own, at which point I can go beyond the words spoken and intuitively translate their thoughts, feelings, and reactions onto the page.

"If you don't transcribe, how do you know you aren't getting it wrong and writing a bunch of stuff they never said?" a fellow ghostwriter asked me once. A fair question, and if I hadn't been validated over and over again by clients who exclaim, "Wow, it sounds just like me," and editors who similarly remark, "You nailed their voice!" I would have abandoned my practice years ago.

"The way you describe how you ghostwrite is similar to how I channel spirits," noted my client, the medium, after we completed our first book together.

"I hadn't thought of it that way," I said, "but yes, that tracks. And when I write in your voice, I'm channeling the channeler."

I knew Mom's voice as well as my own, probably because it was the first voice I heard while floating in my warm embryonic bubble, the same voice that whispered "hello" as soon as I entered this bright world, the same voice that guided me through childhood and continued to coach me into adulthood. Throughout my life, Mom's voice was always there, engraving itself into my mind like a well-worn track on a record, one that with repetition and over time, I learned to play back at will. I could recall Mom's voice in an instant, choosing from a lifetime of conversations, and since she'd died, I had frequently conjured her voice to comfort me. Recollection of the past was easy, but what I'd heard in the dream was something else. It was a voice that felt present, as if she were whispering things in my ear I hadn't known before. While I didn't want to put words in my mother's mouth—after all, she was no longer here to correct or edit me—I hadn't wanted to lose the thread of our dream dialogue, so I did what she'd instructed me to do all my life: When you hear a great line or a thread of interesting conversation in passing, when you see something you don't want to forget, like moonlight on the Seine or a new restaurant you want to try or a book title that catches your eye, pull out your notebook or find the nearest scrap of paper, and write it down. Mom may have been famously credited for Bad Hair Day but if there were three words that guided her more than any others and which she strongly encouraged others to adopt and follow, they were, without question: Write It Down.

And so, I did.

Once I finished *The Why*, I wrote about the dream of her heavenly hair. I reconstructed our dialogue from the dream in which she appeared, walking out of the fog. I revised her words until they sounded exactly as I'd heard her, then I began to initiate new conversations by calling her forward onto the page. Since *The Why*, Mom hadn't returned to my dreams except to play a cameo role, fading out of the scene as soon as she entered, and I still had many burning questions to ask her, so I decided to try my hand at automatic writing, the process of writing without the conscious mind to bring forth messages of truth from deeper sources. In woo-woo circles like the ones to which the medium belongs, this practice is referred to more formally as psychography and it's used to channel spirits. While this skill is far outside my realm of expertise and far above my pay grade, a quick Google search on "how to" automatic write didn't sound altogether different from how I began all my writing assignments, especially on days when I felt stuck and the words weren't coming without a fight: Close your eyes and breathe deeply in through your nose and out through your mouth. Once your mind is quiet and clear, ask a question and let the answer come. Write it down.

I reasoned that I could do this because the automatic writing process was akin to how I channeled the living, but channeling my dead mother? This was a next-level writing assignment, and I could already hear the criticism. You did *what*? You wrote in your dead mother's voice? That's impossible, flagrant. And you're likely to bring a curse on yourself. Also, it disrespects your mother, who would want to speak for herself.

I agreed with the last part. She would want to speak for herself, and she always had without reservation. Unfortunately, she no longer had that luxury, and I felt strongly that Susan still had important things to say. In a weird way, inviting her to converse with me on the page felt natural and right, exactly the thing she and I would do, writer to writer, mother to daughter. Also, I wasn't bound by an NDA. What could she do to stop me?

I opened up a new document and titled it *Mom How*. I closed my eyes, took a deep breath and asked my next question.

I sat in the quiet.

I listened.

I waited.

I listened some more.

And rather than write down what I thought she would say or what I wanted her to say, I wrote down what I heard her saying.

Mom How

"Mom, people are really struggling with how you left. They're pretty pissed at how you did it, actually. A few of your friends even said you ruined beaches for them, and some others have sworn off Bodega Head and this part of the coastline, like *forever.* They won't even drive out here for crab sandwiches anymore."

"No! The crab sandwiches at Spud Point?" She shook her head with true regret.

I'd met her again on the cliffs of Bodega Head, and this time we meandered along the winding path that traveled south, in the direction of Point Reyes.

"I've struggled with it too, given your lifelong fear of heights. For months now, I've wandered around the house in a daze. My mother jumped three hundred feet into the Pacific? Who does that? And why would you, of all people, do that?"

"You do remember what I always said about my fear of heights? My fear wasn't that I'd fall, but that I'd jump."

"I do remember you saying that, although I never thought you'd actually *do* it. I thought you were just being dramatic."

As the wind picked up, she paused along the path, waiting for me to catch up.

"I did finally arrive at an understanding, though, one that at least makes some sense to me."

She turned a curious eye. "Do tell."

"Well, for starters, you loved it here. You loved everything about it. The smell of the salt air, the endless expanse of blue, the powerful crash of the waves, and whether it was the Pacific or the Atlantic, you were always drawn to the ocean's edge. Wherever you were, it was your respite, your home away from home, your place to just be, where all was truly well."

"Very astute, my smart daughter." She deeply inhaled the air and started back along the trail.

Encouraged, I pressed on. "So, it makes sense to me that you'd come here as your last place to be. You knew that she, the ocean, would be here as she always was, your steady and dependable friend, your familiar. And she'd recognize you even if you no longer recognized yourself. She'd welcome you without judgment. She'd hold space for you, no questions asked."

"'*When I went back to the sea it wasn't waiting. Neither had it gone away.*' Mary Oliver was the best at capturing her details."

"Then, am I right?"

Mom stopped again and turned her gaze toward the water. "After Klose died, I frequently went out to the beach, as you know. I'd walk for hours on Doran and Dillon. Sometimes I'd sink into the sand and scream into the wind and chastise him for dying, for leaving me alone, uncertain of what came next for *me*. I missed him so much and I hated that he was gone. I couldn't fathom it. How could he be dead? The open-endedness of life without him scared me, and when I was out here, the crashing waves provided me some relief. Some. For a fleeting time, it would drown out my fearful mind and the darkness I couldn't shake."

I interjected, "That day, when we talked on the phone, you told me you were going to the beach, and I didn't question it for all those reasons."

"You weren't meant to stop me," she said, picking up on my residual guilt. "I'd made up my mind."

"I understood that afterward. That day was different. You had no intention of coming back."

Mom took my hand. "Come, let's sit down." A clustering of boulders covered in flowering ice plant provided us a safe place to sit at a distance from the edge.

"I drove out here that day and I prayed, please take me far away from my suffering, relieve me of this awfulness, this pain. Take me somewhere else. Save *me* from myself."

"And did she? Save you?"

"Yes and no," Mom answered softly. "I can finally breathe again. The dark ogre of fear doesn't have me by the neck like it did, but I have a new suffering, the pain I've left behind." She caught my eye. "I hadn't considered the devastation I would cause or what it would really mean to leave my life."

"Suicide is selfish," I hissed, not hiding my resentment.

"I understand why you see it that way. But you were always on my mind. All of you were. I *was* thinking about you, but I wasn't thinking clearly. I wasn't in my right mind. I was already somewhere else, convinced you would all be better off without me."

I shook my head. "That's not true."

"You've all spent many painful hours turning this around in your own heads, chasing the timeline, digging into the details and asking the right questions, and Sammy, there are pieces of this story that cannot be fully understood or explained, and it'll make you crazy if you keep trying to figure it out."

"What I'm still trying to figure out is when you made the decision to jump, because after Los Angeles, you promised me you would never try anything like that again."

She turned away. "I don't want to talk about that place."

"We have to. It's time."

"Next time," she pushed back and faded from the page.

Missing Something

"It's been brought to my attention that I may have missed something," I said to B on our regular call.

"What's that?"

"Did I tell you that about nine months before my mom died, she'd attempted something?"

"Attempted *what*?"

"Well, she cut herself."

"She did?" he said, surprised. "Yes, I missed that. Or you missed it, because I'd remember that detail."

"I didn't mention it because, if you'll believe me, I honestly thought it was irrelevant."

"Feels relevant."

"Yeah, that's what Clara said."

"Who's Clara?"

"Clara is one of Mom's oldest friends. They went to elementary school together in Meadville, and she's having a really hard time with this. I mean, we all are, and she's really struggling to understand what happened. She called me the other night, and as we were going through the timeline, the 'cut' came up."

"And . . ." B said eagerly.

"And she was shocked. She had no idea it had happened, and

then she became mad that she hadn't known. Actually, I think she was directly mad at *me*."

"How many people knew about this?"

"Not many. Klose. My sisters. Miriam."

"And is there a reason you kept it from others?"

"I wasn't intentionally leaving it out," I said defensively. "It wasn't a conscious withholding, although—" I stopped and drifted back into memory. "It's true that Mom didn't want anyone to know."

"Okay, back up. Tell me what happened."

★ ★ ★

The summer before Klose passed away, I was in the Las Vegas airport, waiting for my plane to board. I'd gone for a quick weekend away, and as I was sitting at the gate, Gretta called. I saw her name light up my screen, and as had become my habit over the past several months with Klose in and out of hospitals, I answered promptly and braced for bad news.

"Is everything okay?"

"Sam . . ." Her voice was tentative. "Something has happened."

I covered my ears to mask the sound of a nearby row of ringing slot machines. "What is it?"

Silence, then, "Susan tried to hurt herself."

Gretta shared what she knew: earlier that morning when Klose was in the shower, Mom said, "Oh, shit, Klose, I just did something stupid." When he peeked his head around the curtain, she was standing at the bathroom sink, where she'd taken a plastic disposable razor to her wrist and made a small cut, not deep enough to cause any blood loss, but still enough to create alarm. He'd dressed quickly, called my sisters, and drove Mom to the hospital, where they'd admitted her to the emergency room.

"We're all here now," Gretta said.

"I'll be there as soon as I can."

After the endless ninety-minute flight from Nevada, I'd driven directly from the Oakland airport to the Santa Rosa hospital. I walked through the ER until I found the room where the four of them sat in a cluster, and as soon as Mom saw me, she dropped her head and began to cry. I hurried over and sat down next to her, taking her hand and gently nudging up the hospital gown to see her slender wrist wrapped in tape. "It was really stupid." She shook her head. "I don't know why I did it."

I didn't know what to say, what to ask or do, and so I held her hand until the doctor appeared in the doorway.

"Hi, Ms. Swartz," said a man in a white coat and a trim beard. "I'm Dr. Karnicky and I understand you had an incident this morning."

"Yes," she said with reluctance. "I suppose I did."

I stood up and allowed the doctor to sit on the stool next to her. He pulled the tape back to inspect her wrist. "Not much harm done, but it is cause for concern."

Mom averted her eyes.

"I'm going to ask you a series of questions and I need you to do your best to answer them truthfully, okay?"

Mom slowly turned toward the doctor and steadied her gaze.

"Has anything like this happened before?"

"No."

"Have you had thoughts of ending your life?"

"No."

"Have you made plans for ending your life?"

"No.

"Is there a history of suicide in your family?'

"No."

"Is there a history of depression in your family?'

She shrugged. "Not that I know of."

"Have you been diagnosed or treated for depression or for any mental-health condition?"

She didn't answer.

"Mom?" I interjected from across the room.

"I'm not sure that I have depression," she said dryly. "I think I'm just a little overwhelmed . . ."

The four of us jumped in, jockeying for the doctor's attention.

"But she's been treated for circumstantial depression . . ."

"Her husband has cancer . . ."

"She's been prescribed several different medications . . ."

"She's been anxious, not sleeping . . ."

Mom interrupted, "I don't think that has anything to do with it. I don't know why I did it," she said to the roomful of us. "It was just really stupid, okay?"

"Can I talk to Susan alone?" the doctor asked.

We were directed to a private waiting room and over an hour later, Dr. Karnicky entered and sat down. "Thanks for waiting," he said. "These things sometimes take time, and it's not always a clear case, which is why I wanted to speak with Susan alone, and after talking with her, I believe she engaged in what is often referred to as a 'suicidal gesture' which is generally defined as self-injury that is typically not meant to end life, but to mimic suicide and communicate distress." He paused and looked at the roomful of us to gauge our understanding. We nodded and he continued. "She insists she's not suicidal, nor that she has suicidal ideation. She also insists she's not clinically depressed, despite the medications prescribed to her over the past several months. She very much wants to go home, and after assessing her, I don't detect any signs of cognitive decline, of mental illness. She's very smart, very articulate, and very stubborn. I see no physical reason to keep her in the emergency room for any longer. She's not presenting as a danger to herself, *but* given the stressors described to me as the primary caregiver at home, and because she did inflict self-harm, if even only superficially, I'm going to recommend a 5150 hold at our affiliated behavioral health-care facility."

"A hold?" Klose leaned forward. "Can you explain what that is, doc?"

"Specifically, Susan will not go home today. Instead, she'll spend seventy-two hours at an offsite facility—"

"For further assessment?" Klose asked.

"And to keep her safe. While the gesture was minimal, the probability of a person who has attempted, expressed intent, or even suggested suicide to later die by suicide is higher than someone who hasn't. So, until your family can create a safety plan at home and build support for Susan to promote her ongoing protection, this will be an intermediary step for a few days. She'll be in good hands, receive counseling. They'll review and update her medications, allow her some rest."

The four of us looked at each other. A behavioral health-care facility? Was this just a friendly term for: mental institution? This felt like a serious move, and premature, but then again, Mom currently had tape wrapped around her wrist. Dr. Karnicky left us to consider this option, although we'd later learn that a 5150 isn't voluntary; it's a legal action that cannot be revoked by the individual once it's in place, but Dr. Karnicky allowed us to deliberate as a family, leading us to believe we were in control of the situation; at least, momentarily.

Klose was the first to ask out loud, "What do we do?"

If only there were an easy answer. Mom was insisting she was fit to go home, and while we wanted that to be true, there was no pretending she hadn't deviated far off script. Of course, we all knew she was overwhelmed with caretaking and that she'd become more frequently agitated and irritable, and that she was fickle about taking her prescribed medication, but—a razor to the wrist? This gesture contradicted everything she'd been telling us for months. *I'm fine. I can do this. I don't need any more pills. And, for God's sake, I'm not depressed.* And hadn't she also told us all, countless times, to "please stop treating *me* like the patient"? Yet here we were in the emergency room, where she'd been fitted for green scrubs.

When Dr. Karnicky returned with his clipboard, Klose spoke for the group when he admitted she'd probably be safer at the facility than at home. While Klose was on an upswing—his cancer had miraculously retreated for the summer months, alleviating him of critical pain and allowing him to reengage in daily life again—managing his disease still required his primary focus. And my sisters and I had full-time jobs, kids, partners, and dogs. We could make ourselves available frequently, and we had, but we couldn't be at their house and on watch around the clock unless we took turns, which was a scenario we agreed to figure out while Mom was "on hold."

Later that afternoon, my mother was prepped to be transferred to an acute facility, a move she didn't ultimately resist. In fact, as the ER staff got her paperwork in order, she made light of it, asking Jenni to take a picture of her "in my hospital gear before I head to the nut house." She posed with her hand on her hip and forced a flirtatious smile, as if to say *Isn't this all so ridiculous?* Was it? Or was she downplaying the seriousness of what she'd done? When a hospital guard was called to wheel her out to an ambulance with the four of us trailing behind, she lowered her voice and finally leveled with me: "Don't tell anyone about this. Especially my sister. She'll never forgive me."

I did as she told me. I didn't tell anyone where she was going because she'd asked me not to, and also I didn't say anything because I could hardly make sense of it myself. The morning after the ER visit that landed her with a 5150 hold, I sat in my home office, staring at my computer screen. I was on deadline to finish a book proposal about a global vegan revolution while my mother was two towns over, sharing a secured room with *Girl, Interrupted*. I called her at noon to check in, and she'd answered the main line at our designated call time like a punctual inmate.

"Hi, Mom, how are you?" My guilt was audible. "Is it awful in there?"

"Not so bad." Her tone was subdued. "Although the coffee leaves something to be desired. I have a roommate, a young woman named Cecily who's quite the character. Breaks curfew, walks around topless, curses like a sailor."

"Oh, my God."

"I have group therapy today," she said without enthusiasm, changing the subject.

"And you're going to go, *right?*"

"Yes, yes, yes, I'll go, although I'm not sure how they can help me."

"Let them help you," I implored. "Maybe there's something with your medication that they can adjust. Or someone you can talk to about what happened."

"We'll see."

For the next seventy-two hours that Mom was in treatment, the four of us attempted to make a safety plan. "Once she comes home," Dr. Karnicky had said, "in addition to encouraging her to commit to taking her medication as prescribed and seeking out a therapist with whom she will engage willingly, I also advise you to consider 'triggers' in the house and remove them."

"What did he mean by triggers?" I asked out loud and to no one in particular.

"Things that stress her out," Gretta answered.

We'd met at the house so Klose could comfortably recline in

his favorite chair with a thermos full of coffee while the three of us assessed the house directly.

"Well, then, we have to get rid of the lists," Jenni said. "That's first and foremost."

"Exactly," Gretta called from the kitchen. "She has Post-its all over the place, plus this big paper calendar on the kitchen table and that running list of medications over there on the legal pad."

"Hey, what's wrong with a legal pad?" Klose mumbled as he jotted down something on the one in his lap.

"She needs one primary calendar and one ongoing list that is centrally located," Jenni suggested, "so the surfaces aren't so cluttered."

"And we should probably have the house cleaned," I added as I circled the living room, picking up empty water glasses and organizing helter-skelter magazines into one orderly stack. "She's always complaining about what a mess it is."

"And we should see about hiring someone to help out around the house and run errands," Jenni called from the bathroom.

"And what about a food service to help her with cooking?" Gretta suggested. "She's always complaining about that too, even though she used to love to cook."

"Oh, she won't like that," I warned.

"Maybe she won't," Jenni said, "but I think we should have someone here to help out and keep an eye on things."

We all three walked into the living room and plopped down on the couch. "We can take turns being here in the evenings, but what about during the day?" Gretta asked.

"Maybe Miriam can come over," Jenni suggested.

"I might be able to do a few remote writing days here, until school gets out at three," I offered.

"I'm here." Klose cleared his throat.

We stopped talking and turned in his direction.

"I'm here," he said again, calmly, but with authority. "And I can keep an eye on her."

Gretta leaned forward. "Daddy," she treaded softly, "you were in the shower when . . . you were here when she cut herself. You were here and she did it anyway. I know this is uncomfortable and confusing and some of it seems unnecessary, but I think we need to put some backup in place until we can figure out what's going on with her. You should be able to take a shower without worrying."

He soft-pedaled, "Oh, I don't think that will happen again."

"I'm not so sure," Gretta pressed gently. "I think we need some extra help until we can make sure she's safe."

Klose took a measured breath and considered this. He crossed his legs and took a long drink of his coffee. "Okay," he said, eventually. "Maybe you're right."

"And on the point of safety," Jenni suggested, "we should probably remove triggering objects from the house."

I joked, "Hide your razor, Klose. You'll have to shave after she goes to bed."

"Not just razors. Other things, too." Jenni shot me a disapproving look.

"Sorry." I pushed back against the couch cushions. "Too soon."

Klose directly addressed Jenni and winked at me. "Like what other things, kid? As you girls like to point out at every family dinner, our kitchen knives are dull as dirt. I wouldn't worry."

* * *

I wasn't making light of it; none of us were. Sure, I inserted humor here and there as a coping mechanism during a highly confusing and unstable time. We thought we'd understood the landscape—Klose was battling cancer and Mom had become agitated and very likely depressed, even though she wouldn't admit it. Now, she'd been loosely institutionalized and we were all shaking our heads, *What the hell?* We were uncertain how to respond, but we didn't have a lot of time to ruminate; we had to act.

While she was at the facility, my sisters and I stepped into action, meeting daily at the house to clean and declutter and to check in on Klose, while also maintaining our day jobs and attending to our own households before visiting hours began at five o'clock, at which time when we'd meet in the facility's lobby, check in at the front desk, and wait for our names to be called. Once cleared, we were allowed to enter just two at a time through a set of heavy double doors with a flashing security alarm and where we were escorted by a large guard who walked us down a long, colorless hallway to a break room with scattered metal tables and chairs and a few vending machines in the corner.

On the first night, Gretta and I went first, and Mom was waiting when we walked in. She greeted us with a timid smile and invited us to sit down. As we assembled ourselves around the tiny table, she nervously fiddled with her hair. I hated seeing her in there, a mismatch for this scene, being treated like a criminal, a security risk.

"How are you doing?" I struggled to make conversation. "How's therapy?" Do you feel like it's helping?"

She shrugged and sidestepped our questions about treatment and new medications, steering the dialogue in the direction of a more pressing question: "When do I get to leave?"

I wondered about this too. From what I'd observed so far, the facility primarily served as a holding tank, a place for her to temporarily be under watch. Additionally, she was attending group therapy and she'd already received a psychiatric evaluation where they'd switched her medication to Latuda, an antipsychotic drug that Mom said was "making me forget my words" and that she'd refused to continue taking until they came up with an alternative. As Dr. Karnicky had promised us, she was receiving medical attention—but was it helping? How much was it helping? And in another forty-eight short hours, would she be ready to go home?

Despite my own apprehensions, I answered her question. "Probably in a couple more days."

She looked around the room and back at us. "I've played along long enough. Get me out of here."

⋆ ⋆ ⋆

On the second day, we were told, "She doesn't present as a high risk, although she's not really engaging in therapy, and she's refusing to take medication."

"Then what happens next?"

"This is a place to be safe," her attending doctor advised us over the phone. "It's not a place to get better. We're preparing her discharge paperwork with a recommendation to continue outpatient treatment."

I wanted her to come home. We all did. But the question loomed: Would she be ready? After considering her stubbornness to accept professional help even under a 5150 hold, we weren't so sure. We were not clinicians, we had no expertise in this gray field, but we maintained we knew Mom better than anyone on staff, and the woman who sat across from me in the break room needed some talk therapy, at least. She might have convinced the staff she wasn't a risk, and we weren't so sure. Did we fear she'd try and cut herself again? Maybe she would, maybe she wouldn't, and anyway, we weren't convinced she'd actually attempted to harm herself in the first place. She'd suggested it, Dr. Karnicky had said, with a *gesture*. This delineation of self-injury was different than a clear suicide attempt. It didn't fall under the category of "intent," either. It communicated *distress*, he'd said, and had forty eight hours alleviated her distress?

"Mom, talk to me," I said on the second night of visitation.

"I've told you; I didn't mean to actually *do* anything."

I wasn't used to this, her shutting me out, and I didn't recognize her in this new role: a woman hospitalized. As we sat facing each other in metal chairs, I was tempted to say, *can you please cut the shit so we can all go home?* Instead, I said, "What do you need?"

"What I need"—she dropped her voice—"is to be back in my own bed."

I suspected that something more was required, something beyond the seventy-two-hour hold, and I worried that we—four educated, informed, self-advocating, and very engaged adults who were not afraid to intervene on Mom's behalf—were still not equipped to respond to her needs, whatever those were, so when Jenni suggested an inpatient facility she'd located in Southern California, I said, "Tell me more."

With the help of a licensed psychologist friend, Jenni had searched Sonoma County, the greater Northern California area, then enlarged the map to include the entire state before she'd found a viable psychiatric-care facility staffed with trained clinicians and therapists, and where there was an available bed and no waitlist.

"The inpatient facilities in this area are primarily focused on substance abuse and addiction," Jenni said. "And those facilities are the only ones covered by private insurance because mental health isn't recognized in the same way, not by the medical community or the community at large. I located only seven facilities for people with mental-health struggles in the *country*, and only one in California. It may be our only option."

Our only option was expensive, ten thousand dollars a week, and it was a seven-hour drive away.

"They have a room, but we have to act fast. And we have to send them a deposit before she arrives."

The clock was ticking. Her seventy-two hours were almost up, and she'd been given the green light to go home. We were tired and desperate and out of good ideas. What should we do? What do you do with someone who is clearly in some kind of crisis, but who isn't considered a clear and present danger, who isn't presenting as mentally ill, who is physically healthy and able-bodied and can clearly articulate her preferences, and who is insisting she knows her own mind? What do you do with this person who may or may not be a future risk to themselves, and who does not qualify or meet the criteria for an extended hold? What do you do when this person is the one you love most, when this person is your mother and you want to respect her position in the family, and when you want to preserve her dignity, her personal agency, and also protect her from harm?

"It would be far easier to bring her home," Jenni said. "And cheaper. And a lot of people would do exactly that because they don't have a choice; they don't have the accessibility or the resources to pay for treatment at a residential facility. We're fortunate that we can get the money together and get her there, so I think we should do it."

We left it to Klose to make the decision, and with his vote, it was unanimous.

* * *

Elevation Heights sounded more like an exclusive rehab facility or a boutique spa retreat, which is how we sold it.

"It's in a beautiful two-story home in a safe neighborhood in the hills just north of Los Angeles. You'll have your own room, and only six of you stay at a time," explained Jenni. "All your meals will be prepared by an in-house chef, and you'll get one-on-one therapy every day."

We'd arrived the morning of her discharge with a change in plans. We were seated at a metal table in their private meeting room, and Mom eyed us with suspicion. "This feels like a mutiny," she said, and I couldn't blame her for feeling deceived.

"It looks like a nice place," I tried. "Much nicer than this." My eyes crawled along the beige, lifeless walls. "Really, nothing like this."

"No," she quickly snapped. "I'm not going."

"Mom . . ." I appealed.

"No, I can't go to Los Angeles." She yanked at her gray sweatpants. "I can't go to LA looking like *this.*" She stared at me without blinking. "I won't do it."

"We think it will be helpful," Gretta attempted to soothe her.

"And how are we going to pay for it?" Mom challenged. "I'm sure it's outrageously expensive."

"We've got it covered." Jenni gestured to Gretta and me.

"No, no, no." She leaned back in her chair and crossed her arms in protest. "I don't want you daughters paying for this." She turned to Klose. "Babe, I want to go home. I don't want to go somewhere else. I need to be home with you. I need to take care of you. *Please.*" Her tone had turned from defiant to pleading, and my heart broke. I was sickened by the idea of sending my mother someplace far from home, where she wouldn't be with family, but with people we'd only seen pictures of on a website. Klose took her hand and smiled sadly. I knew this was equally devastating for him. "I know you want to come home, but sweetie, you're having a hard time, and you can do this. It'll be good for you. And I'll be just fine, I will."

"You'll forget to take your meds and remove your compression socks," she warned weakly, attempting to regain some ground.

"I'll remember." He laughed lightly. "I'll be okay." And he baited, "Rumor has it that this place has a swimming pool."

We discussed ahead of time that Klose would be the only one of us who could convince her to go. We couldn't force the decision on her; she had to agree, and after making her case several times—"I cannot go to Los Angeles, it's too far away"—and pleading with us all—"I don't want to do this"—she finally relented with tears in her eyes. "Okay, if you all think I should go, I'll go." She lifted her head and smoothed her gray turtleneck. "But I need some new clothes."

In the two hours before her late-morning release, Gretta and I tore off to the nearest Target with Mom's handwritten list, running up and down the aisles and searching for her must-have items: sandals, size nine; yoga clothes, swimsuit, jammies (nice); sun hat, tweezers. We returned at noon as she was signing papers to leave, when a young man in an Oakland A's baseball hat and an oversized hoodie charged through the lobby.

"Yo, Susan, you out?" he hollered as if he were in a packed stadium.

She looked up at him and smiled, a flash of her old confidence returning. "Bye, Gabe."

As we walked out the front doors, she whispered to me, "Gabe works here. Says I'm the coolest 'older chick' he's ever met."

With her vanity intact and a suitcase packed with new clothes from Target, Mom slid into the back seat of Jenni's car, and with Klose in the passenger seat programming the GPS, they pulled away from the nut house and headed down south for the day spa.

⋆ ⋆ ⋆

Mom spent three weeks at Elevation Heights, where, according to her primary therapist, the clinical director and the on-site psychiatrist, she was making "great progress!" An "ideal patient" is what they called her when we dialed in as a group to check in at the end of the first week. "She's been reinforcing her coping skills, learning how to accept help and trust, and integrating in her peer group." They further explained that she was following a daily schedule of breakfast, group therapy, private therapy, and a daily visit from the psychiatrist who changed her medication, again—this time to Risperidone and Seroquel, both heavy-duty antipsychotic drugs that he believed would help with her anxiety. In addition to regular call-ins to her new team of professionals, we were allowed to speak to Mom privately. Some days she was cryptic and terse, on other days she acted bored and distant. After the first week turned into a second, we agreed that she sounded more earnest and engaged. The resistance she'd presented initially seemed to have softened, and by week three, she was reporting, "I'm following the program. I'm being good, doing what they tell me to do."

For the three weeks she was at Elevation, I continued to keep my promise not to tell anyone where she was, including her own sister, and to deflect any pointed questions about her whereabouts with vague answers: *She's doing well, busy with Klose, I hardly see her myself.* For three weeks, I kept her secret, and in exchange, I prayed she was getting the professional help she needed, that she was finally opening up about the impulse that drove her to nick her wrist. I wrestled with guilt that she was away from us, and I was also relieved, not only because I was hopeful about her treatment, but because I needed the break. We were all exhausted. Making the rushed and difficult decision to admit her, plus scrambling to pull together the funds to pay for it, had depleted us. The first day of her admission, a physical weight lifted off of me. I hated to admit this, but knowing I wouldn't have to drive to a hospital or meet face to face with a doctor allowed me to return to some sense of normalcy in my own life. I could finally catch up on work and refocus my energy on Derby while stepping away, temporarily, from Mom's immediate needs.

On the day of her scheduled release that had been enthusiastically green-lit by her care team—"She's ready!"—Gretta and I, who'd made the seven-hour drive to Los Angeles the day before, rang the doorbell of a contemporary Mexican-style home in Agoura Hills, an upscale suburban neighborhood with picturesque views. Mom answered the door with a disguised hesitation I'd come to recognize, and that she attempted to mask by hugging us both. She felt thin, but not fragile, and she'd made the effort, I noticed, to put on a cheerful turquoise top.

"I'm so happy to see you." She smiled and looked back and forth between us. "Come in." She stepped aside and waved us through the door and into the foyer.

The house was brightened by floor-to-ceiling windows and decorated with brightly colored stock art, oversized furniture, and throw blankets. She led us through room after room, and after introducing us to Patty, the head chef, and Jill—"my yoga buddy"—and grabbing her packed bags from her upstairs room with a handsome view of the hills, she turned and said, "Okay, let's go."

"That's it?" I asked. "You can just walk out the door? Don't you have to sign out or something?"

"I've already done all that."

Gretta and I looked at each other and shrugged, and without anyone holding us back, we made our exit. Departing Elevation Heights was a non-event compared to leaving the acute facility, and after a quick stop through the Starbucks drive-through for iced lattes and scones, we were headed north up the I-5 without delay. The drive would take us seven hours, possibly nine if we hit traffic, and my mother, who had a history of easily filling that amount of extended time with nonstop observations and lively conversation, was quiet at the start. She retreated to the back seat and gazed out the window. Shit, I thought, what if, after all this, she isn't better? I had so many questions, but I didn't want to press; I didn't want to overstep or overwhelm her with an interview. She sat quietly while Gretta and I made superficial conversation, and as the minutes ticked forward, my disappointment swelled. I wanted her to be better for her own sake, and also I wanted her to be better for us. I wanted her to show us she hadn't wasted her time and our money by shining it on for the doctors in sunny Southern California. For the first hour, I was apprehensive, but after she finished her latte and announced—"Finally, coffee with a pulse"—and when she began to hum along to Elton John's "Rocket Man", I was encouraged. Then, when she began asking us what we were reading for pleasure and watching on Netflix, I thought: Okay, maybe she is better. Maybe the time away helped. Maybe she's figured some things out and she's making her way back to who she was before she spiraled. I badly wanted this, and for the duration of the trip, it seemed possible, and when we finally pulled up to their house in Sebastopol, I hoped we were past the worst of it, that we could move forward. As Gretta and I unpacked her suitcase, she paused in the backseat until she spotted Klose at the top of the stairs on the front porch, reading the newspaper in the late-afternoon sun.

"There she is," he called down.

"Hi, babe." Mom smiled upward.

"Well, don't just sit there. Get on up here."

We hugged her goodbye and watched as she ascended the steps into the arms of her man.

* * *

After her return from Elevation Heights, Mom followed the safety plan we'd put into place when she was at the acute facility. She started seeing a new therapist and attending a series of outpatient wellness classes sponsored by the local hospital. She appeared to be engaging willingly in the available care, which signaled progress—a breakthrough, really—and still, my sisters and I exercised caution. We rotated evening visits and checked in regularly over the phone, calling each other afterward to compare notes: "How do things seem?" "How does he sound?" "How does *she* sound?" We were still actively involved, keeping watch and standing guard, while also working hard not to hover and communicate our apprehension. I knew it was important to Mom that we trust her to be left alone, to respect her as the smart and competent adult who raised us, and as the weeks wore on, she allayed some doubt. She reorganized the house, started to cook again, returned to her water aerobics class, and bought new clothes and makeup for the first time since Klose had gotten sick. She'd even made the fifty-minute drive into San Francisco to have dinner with a friend at her favorite French restaurant, leading us to believe we could slowly back off and allow them the space to live their lives more independently, as they always had, as Bob and Susan.

We all wanted to move past that summer, Mom especially. She rarely brought it up except for in cloaked terms like "my bad patch" or "my trip down south." She maintained that no one needed to know about her August absence and the event that preceded it, and given her visible signs of resiliency, I didn't push it. If she didn't want her sister or her friends to know about this blip in the timeline, I supposed that was her business. I intervened only to insist her doctors and therapist be privy to what happened, including the new medications and treatment she'd been prescribed throughout the summer. "They can't effectively support you going forward," I reasoned, "if they don't have all the information."

"Fine, if you think so," Mom acquiesced, and allowed me to pay the fifty-dollar transfer fee to have her records officially released from the private facility down south to the health-care chain up north. And when those records arrived and were reviewed by her primary care doctor without question, and when her psychiatrist approved her medication change without correction or alarm, we sighed relief. And when her new therapist didn't raise any red flags of imminent danger, we relaxed a little bit more. And when Klose, who was sharing the same bed with her every night, pulled me aside and said, "Hey, Sam, she's going to be all right," I interpreted this as another layer of assurance that Mom was no longer a threat to herself. We'd finally arrived in a safe zone.

⋆ ⋆ ⋆

I broke from the memory and returned to B. "So, when Mom's friend, Clara, said to me the other night, 'If you'd known she'd done *that*, then you must have known what she'd *do*,' I still say no. I did not know that eight months later, Mom would go far beyond the initial gesture and take her life for good. Even though we'd been told there exists a higher probability of someone dying by suicide if they have previously attempted, it's not definitive. It's not a foregone conclusion. A higher probability does not mean an inevitability, especially with someone who doesn't express ideation or intent or make a clear attempt."

I was getting heated.

"It's not definitive," B agreed. "Point A doesn't always lead to Point B. If only it were that simple, that predictable, that *logical*. Suicide is none of those, but that's what people want to hear. They want to be able to say, 'Oh, now I get it, now I understand how this could happen, now it makes sense.' Because the alternative is to reckon with the fact that some things cannot be predicted, explained, reasoned with, rationalized, or prevented. Sometimes, horrible and unexpected things happen to the people we love and there is nothing we can do about it, or ever fully understand. This makes people like Clara very uncomfortable. It makes them feel uncertain, suspicious, and fearful of life. If Susan, the always bright and blazing sun, can slip into darkness, what does that mean for the rest of us? If she can become suicidal, then maybe I can, too."

"The thing is," I said, "most people don't become suicidal. It is human nature to *live*, to endure. Plenty of people do things that compromise their health and safety, and it doesn't mean they want to die. If everyone who ever overate, overworked, drank too much, drove too fast, and occasionally did 'something stupid' were candidates for suicide, we'd all be next in line."

"This is a terrifying thought, which is why they're looking to you to give them evidence that Susan was mentally ill and suicidal all along. If they can put her in a box, then her death can make sense and they can relax their fears about their own mortality."

"I will not put my mother in a box," I rebutted. "And does suicide ever make sense?"

"That's a good question and be honest here. Isn't that what you've been doing, too? Trying to make sense of it?"

"Yes," I had to admit. I'd been trying to understand and reconcile her death since it happened, and maybe that was why Clara's comment was agitating me. Her implication was I'd missed something obvious or, worse, I'd left something out of the story or failed to make a connection that was relevant. And now I questioned myself: Why hadn't I thought Mom's "gesture" had relevance?

* * *

My memory drifted back to a Friday in late September, a full six weeks after Mom had returned from Los Angeles. After she'd picked Derby up from school and I'd finished writing for the day, she and I sat in my living room drinking wine. Perhaps due to the influence of the Sauvignon Blanc that blurred our boundaries, I broached the subject that had become a non-issue since the summer months.

"Mom, I need to ask you something."

"Mm-hmm," she said with an air of suspicion.

"Why did you do it?"

She set down her wine glass and eyed me. "I figured you'd ask me this at some point. That you'd want an explanation."

"Do you have one?"

She shifted in her chair. "Well, I don't know . . ." She paused as if she'd never thought about it before now. "I think I was just experimenting. Seeing what it would feel like." Her tone was noncommittal, aloof.

Feel like? A razor to the wrist? Her answer unsettled me, but I didn't contradict her.

"I should have never done it," she continued with a hint of impatience. "It was a dumb mistake, a weak moment, one I wish we could all erase."

This felt like an opening. It was more than she'd ever admitted out loud. "Do you ever think about doing it . . . again?"

"No," she said swiftly. "No, I don't."

"You know, your ER doctor told us that after someone has done something like that, there's a higher probability of . . ."

Mom raised an eyebrow. "Of what?"

"Of trying to hurt yourself again."

"Phht," Mom dismissed with a wave of her hand. "That's not going to happen, and," she said smugly, "I'm not a statistic."

She wanted me to drop it, and I didn't want to ruin our afternoon together, but I also felt a sense of responsibility to hold her accountable.

"Mom . . ." I inched forward and caught her eye. "You have to promise to tell me if you're ever thinking about doing something like that again."

"I will." She held my gaze.

"Promise me."

"I promise you."

I pushed, "I can't help you if you're not being honest with me."

"I know, *Sammy*," she pushed back. "I will be honest. I promise." She lifted her glass and took a sip, and without another word, we moved on to something else.

* * *

Again, I returned to B: "I can understand why Clara may have felt misled by not having known this part of the story, and in my defense, we all felt misled. We all felt duped. Mom masterfully convinced not only me and my sisters and Klose and Miriam, but also her highly regarded therapist and every medical worker who treated her that the 'gesture' was irrelevant moving forward, nothing to dwell on beyond her return from Los Angeles. Do you know what the Elevation team sent her home with? A gratitude journal with writing prompts and bubbles to fill in. It might as well have been a coloring book. And do you know what their primary directive was? 'Continue putting your health first.' That isn't the directive you give to someone you suspect is suicidal. Everyone ought to put their health first, that's a given."

"And . . ." B leaned into conjecture. "It sounds like after Los Angeles, she doubled down on presenting a false front because she didn't want anyone to think she'd dare do it again."

"She wanted us to believe it was irrelevant, but it meant something. I see that now. It was an important detail, and it's not that I missed it. It's that I took her on her word."

"Of course you did. Your mother told you she'd never try it again, and you wanted to believe her. That doesn't make you negligent. It makes you her daughter. It makes you any child with blind loyalty and love."

"I don't know. I think it makes me her fool."

Blindsided

With this new insight in mind, I opened up a document and titled it *Blindsided*. I closed my eyes, took a deep breath, and called my mother to the page. "Next time is now," I said out loud. "We need to talk about this." I slipped deeper into the blank page of my mind and after a few minutes, she stepped forward from the in-between with the sea reflecting in the background.

"You promised me," I said right away. "You promised you'd tell me if you ever thought about doing something like that again."

"I know I did." Her face fell. "I'm sorry."

"I believed you."

"I wanted to believe me too," she said sadly. "I wanted to believe I could get better."

Her vulnerability deescalated the fight in me, and still I pushed, "After you died, people asked me: "Did you know? Did you have any warning signs or indications that she was suicidal?" You cannot imagine how many smart people have asked this dumb question: *Did I know*? What did they expect me to say? Yep, I knew, but I was busy getting a pedicure that day. There was *no knowing*, even knowing the full backstory. So, in talking about your death, I skipped over this part because you asked me to keep it between us and I honored your privacy. I knew you were ashamed of your time away, so I protected you from what you'd done. I left the 'cut' out of the telling, and not only because you asked me to, but also because you convinced me it was a fluke, a one-off that should have never happened, a stupid mistake that would never be repeated, and not a foreshadowing or a predictor of what was to come. I went along with you on this because making a nick on your wrist was harmless, juvenile, even. The surface scratch healed within days. It was forgettable. But what you did eight months later? Incomprehensible. An act you cannot heal from or return. And I guess I'm feeling defensive towards comments suggesting that we *should have known.* Because of the ER visit and Elevation Heights, we must have known you would eventually do this. We should have seen it coming, as if we'd recklessly looked the other way or weren't paying attention. We were paying attention. Hyper attention. But the interior landscape of mental decline isn't clear in the way that people on the outside might believe it is. For us, it was far from obvious, and that was by your design. You went to great lengths to make us believe you were better, or better enough, and that you were not someone to be stuffed in a box and conveniently labeled a suicidal woman."

"I'm a good actress when I want to be." She said regretfully. "I wanted everyone to forget that ever happened. I wanted the whole memory to go away."

I paced back and forth on the page, attempting to connect the dots. "But at some point, you knew what you would do."

"Yes."

"When did you know?"

"Oh, I don't know when exactly. It's a blur. But at some point, I knew something had gone wrong with my head. I became compromised, as you say, and all the well-intentioned doctors and mental-health care professionals who worked with me floated a number of things—clinical depression, manic depression, bipolar disorder, a psychotic break. These were offered as potential explanations for my behavior, but I was never diagnosed, no condition was ever definitive, only suggested and treated with pill after pill after pill. So, I don't know, maybe I was suffering from one of those things, or maybe I'd simply mixed too much medication in a short window of time? Maybe it was my mother's Alzheimer's coming to get me? Perhaps the culmination of stress and sleep deprivation from caretaking changed the chemicals in my mind? Maybe there were deeper demons, or a condition unidentified that went undiagnosed for years, long before Klose got sick. We'll never know for sure, where it came from or what 'it' was exactly. What I can tell you is that after Klose died, I believed I was suffering from something incurable that I couldn't hide anymore, that I couldn't fake or fix. I no longer knew my fragile mind, and I was becoming more and more detached from the old me, and I didn't want to burden you all with the pain of watching me lose *me,* the version I loved, that everyone loved. I wanted to spare you the pain of watching me forget myself and become somebody else, someone nobody knows, as I'd witnessed with my own mother. I didn't want you or anyone I loved to suffer my suffering, and when I did what I did, I was seeking freedom for everyone."

I felt her earnestness, her loving intention, and I understood how this made sense to her. I felt her selflessness, her spirit of generosity, the protective mother who makes a hard choice from a place of deep love, hoping and praying it is the best choice for everyone involved. I felt her heart, and still I wished for a different outcome because I wasn't free. Not at all.

* * *

For days after my calls with Clara and B, my head spun in delayed confusion. Had I done something wrong, leaving out this piece of Mom's story until now? Had I been disingenuous to those who'd asked, "Was there any indication?" I'd kept it quiet that summer and then, given all we'd endured since Klose's initial cancer diagnosis, I'd put the gesture in a container, separate and apart from the full chronology of events. Was this a form of denial? Self-selective memory? A survival skill some therapists referred to as compartmentalization, or simply a facet of grief? I wasn't sure what was driving me and I wondered if there was more to the story that I'd unconsciously buried. I rewound into the past and started digging.

Klose's memorial was held in late January, five full months after Mom's return from Elevation Hills, and on the morning of his service, she basked in the bright lights illuminating the podium at the Unitarian Church. She delivered a heartfelt and humorous tribute to a crowd of nearly three hundred people who recognized her trademark vibrancy and confident energy. There she was, the Susan we all knew and loved, a revered pillar of our community, my hero. As she fearlessly stood before us, I remarked inwardly: There she is. She is not gone. She is not lost to us! She's back, returned from whatever dark place she'd slipped to. While it was unquestionably a sad time—her husband of nearly forty years had just died and she was grieving, as expected, and she'd had a rough year, to put it mildly—there she was, commanding the spotlight, holding the attention of the room. My mother, my brilliant sun.

After the service, she and I walked out of the church with linked arms, and she held her head high as we passed the full aisles, flashing her assuring smile, a beacon of triumph and resilience that attendees followed into the reception hall. For two hours she engaged with guests, sipped wine, and let her laugh carry throughout the room, and when the reception was over, she invited my sisters and I, along with several of her friends, back to her house for an after-party, and where at least twelve of us squeezed in around Klose's dining-room table, drinking more wine until very late into the evening.

When everyone finally began to take their leave, Mom asked me to sleep over, and after changing into our flannel pajamas, we huddled together on the couch with steaming mugs of tea to unpack the details of the day.

"I'm afraid about what happens tomorrow." Her party face turned somber.

"I'll be here," I said in an attempt to cheer her. "What do you want to do?"

"It's not only what happens tomorrow, I'm afraid. It's what happens the day after and the day after that."

"Now that's he gone, you mean?"

She nodded. "And there's no party to plan."

I interpreted her comment as a reflection of grief and a widow's uncertainty. "It will be important to make new plans," I suggested. "To have something to look forward to doing next. Why don't you take a trip back East to visit Nancy? You could ride out the winter there."

"I do love the snow," she said wistfully and sipped her tea.

Less than two weeks later, Mom was Boston bound, and this time, she'd slept at my house, and I'd gotten up at four in the morning to drive her to the airport shuttle parking lot. I was bleary-eyed and noncommunicative, and she was excited and chatty, talking the entire car ride over about what she was looking forward to eating—lobster and haddock—and drinking—Cape Codders, a tart combination of cranberry juice, vodka, and fresh lime—and what she couldn't wait to do—lace up her snow boots and take icy walks along the Ipswich River. As we waited in the dark and watched the Airporter pull into the lot, she turned to me and beamed. "Sammy, I woke up feeling happy today. I feel the old me returning." She hugged me deeply and bounded onto the bus.

For the nearly three weeks that she was in Ipswich, I felt similar relief to when she'd been at Elevation Heights—her absence afforded me time to focus in on my own life, specifically moving into a new house across town. While I took care of me, I hoped that New England Nancy would lift Mom's spirits and give her renewed energy for when she returned home. Every few days, Mom called to check in, and from what I gleaned from her voice, it was working. She and Nancy were spending their evenings in front of the fire, binge-watching *Grace and Frankie*, and spending their days driving up and down Cape Ann to consignment shops, and as far north as New Hampshire to snowshoe in the woods. The uptick in her voice sounded genuine, so when she called one afternoon to tell me she'd booked her return flight home, I said, "Are you sure? Already? Nancy said you could stay as long as you want, and there's no rush to leave."

"I know, but I'm ready to come home." Her answer wasn't sentimental; it was assured. "I have things I want to do. I've been thinking about rearranging the house a bit, painting a wall a bright color, taking a class to learn how to use my new iPhone, and maybe"—her voice turned up a notch—"I'll soon be ready for a new puppy."

I wondered if she shouldn't stay longer since the eastern low temps seemed to be reviving her, but because everything she talked about felt positive and forward-thinking, I said, "Okay, send me your flight info."

She'd flown home on a Wednesday night and by Friday afternoon, she was sitting in my sunny side yard drinking white wine while Derby ran around in the uncut grass. She appeared energized and demonstrative, yet there was that unsettledness I noticed, remember? As I listened to her recount her trip back East, I thought, she's pretending to be okay, but she's withholding something. I sensed she was shining me on and this annoyed me. No, that's wrong. It wasn't annoyance. It was something else. It was, as B had earlier suggested, the stab of disappointment. I sensed that she was shining me on when what I really wanted from her was to shine even brighter. *Please, Mommy, don't drift back behind the clouds. Stay out here in the light, don't dip below the horizon, don't disappear again.* I didn't want her complexity, as I'd earlier told myself, or to join me on the other side of the moon. I wanted her to shine forever, to remain my dependable sun, and I wanted her to follow through on her promise to get better. In my side yard that day, I wanted to believe she was already better and would only continue to brighten into the spring. I wanted her to be the exception to what we'd learned—that after an attempt, there exists a higher possibility of a repeat effort—and I believed she would prove this statistic wrong because if anyone could outsmart mental illness and overcome the odds, it was my exceptional mother. Descending into darkness was not my mother's story. Or, at least, it wasn't the story I wanted to tell.

When she died four short days later, I was shocked, because you can never be prepared for or expecting something like that. Suicide is unthinkable. And when she did what she did, I couldn't believe it. How could it be that my mother, who'd loved life so fully, chose to leave it? How could it be true that my irrepressible mother had taken a turn she couldn't turn back from? I couldn't accept that suicide happened to her, because it didn't fit with my version of who I knew her to be. And still, when she surprised us and went spiraling into those awful summer months, I did my best to help her navigate the unexpected changes in her behavior. I moved in as close as she'd let me, her loyal daughter, unwavering in my commitment to stand alongside her through it all, for whatever came next. I would have done that, absolutely and indefinitely. Except when I looked at it now, I saw a thread of the story I hadn't noticed before—all my life, I'd unconsciously held her to the same impossibly high standard to which she held herself. *I am strong, I am unshakeable, I am Susan!* And it was inconceivable to me that my mother, whom I'd elevated to such great heights, was so close to the edge and about to fall.

Should I have known better? That's a good question. I thought I understood what was happening, and I was wrong. I thought we were back in a safe zone, and we weren't.

I didn't know the unknowable.

I didn't see what was coming next.

And that is because you cannot know someone else's thoughts, not fully, not even when it is the person closest to you. You cannot comprehend when someone's mind has become as thin as seashells, not absolutely, and you also cannot control what your loved ones will do. I was shocked by what I didn't predict and couldn't prevent. I hadn't missed anything. It's just that there's a limit to what we allow ourselves to see, and what others are willing to show us.

Dip into Darkness

"My mom kept journals throughout her life," I said to B on our next call, "including one written the year before her death. I have them all and . . ." I paused, unsure. "Do you think I should read them?"

"I'm surprised you haven't already," he said without any hesitation. "I know that if my dad had kept a journal leading up to his suicide, I would definitely have read it. He left nothing like that behind. You have access to your mom in a way most people do not."

"I've thought about reading it many times, but I think I'm scared it will reveal things about her that I haven't been ready to see. At the same time, I'm curious. Maybe reading it will help me to understand her more, or validate what I already suspect, what I've come to believe on my own?"

"You don't know what's in there, so you have to be prepared for whatever you find. Reading it won't change what she did—you have to be clear on that point—but it may shed some light. Or it may not. If you do decide to read it, just be careful not to lose yourself in it. Following her into her fear will be seductive, and you risk your ability to differentiate between her fear and your own. It's okay to go in, to poke around in the dark, as long as you're mindful that that's what you're doing."

"Okay, so how do I do that? Be mindful?"

"Name it and frame it. I'm reading my mom's journal. I'm intentionally setting a time limit for how long I will read it. And before you dive in," B emphasized, "remind yourself *why* you're doing it. I am not here to absorb her pain and suffering. I am here as her witness, no more. This holds true for reading any of her journals, writing about her suicide, walking into her bedroom, going out to Bodega Head. When you venture into the darkness, name it and frame it every time. This is very important. Don't just dive in or you may get lost in the deep end of the pool."

* * *

My next free night alone, I settled into the safety of my bed and placed Mom's journal on my lap. I planned to read for one hour, and I looked at the clock to intentionally set the start time.

Nine o'clock.

I am here as your witness, I said aloud and opened her journal with the John Steinbeck quote on the cover: *I nearly always write, just as I nearly always breathe.*

The first page was dated January 2, 2019, just over one year before she died. Below the date, her words, right there, in front of me. The familiarity of her handwriting took my breath away, abridged cursive in ballpoint pen. I'd recognize her longhand anywhere, as I'd seen it all my life, scrolled in birthday cards, lined notebooks, on lists, and on countless Post-its, index cards, and scraps of paper. I slowly read the first line. *Today I will go to Spirit Rock and learn how to keep my mind clear and calm. My ongoing challenge. Breathing in, I calm myself, Breathing out, I smile.*

I stopped abruptly, feeling wrong to be doing this, as if it were a breach of her privacy, an intrusion of her inner thoughts, her secrets revealed. I considered closing the journal and hiding it again in my dresser drawer, but my curiosity, along with my desire to be in her presence again, won out. I continued to read without her consent.

February 16: *Last night I was on the couch for two hours. How much sleep can I lose?*
March 20: *Hope. Love. Faith. Go above the fear. Push through the fog.*
April 13: *I am a prisoner in my own house.*
May 10: *Klose is afraid of dying and I, too, am afraid of his dying and living in pain and confusion, unable to rejoin the world.*
May 11: *Please sleep. Please be clear. Please get strong. Please be you.*
June 24: *I woke up feeling scared that I was losing it, in a cyclone, riding a wave about to crash, every metaphor I could think of.*

As I turned the pages, ingesting every word, feeling their weight land heavy on my heart, I tried to heed B's warning: Don't follow her fear and make it your own. I paused before turning the page. Should I stop now?

9:42
I hesitated.
9:43
I turned the page and allowed her words to pull me forward.
July 4: *Saw psychiatrist and he changed Zoloft to*

Lexapro and back to Trazadone after explaining to me that it wasn't addicting or a dementia worry.

July 19: *This madness, I now believe, is situational. My response is to push it away.*

August 4: *Elevation Hills. I feel anxious, alone, removed though worried over, but there is no rescue, no fix.*

August 6: *When did my crazy begin? Officially? Could it be traced back? I miss being unafraid of life.*

Her isolation was there in fragmented bits and pieces, a throughline that became increasingly despondent the deeper I went.

August 10: *Every day is worse. And there is no end to worse.*

August 13: *How can I get past this? Where was the missed detour? Where is Susan? I can't fake happiness, hope any longer.*

August 15: *I so wish I could fix myself for them but there is no magic glue stick to put my good parts back together.*

Her entries spoke increasingly of a longing for her old life, a lonely missing of what was, a searching for "*the old me, the fine and happy me*".

August 31: *My head hurts, trying to reassure everyone. How long until someone sees the fear and blankness?*

September 2: *Oh, for innocent, hope-filled sunny poached eggs on buttered toast mornings. With endless coffee and bright, meaningful conversation. Happy people, happy days. I remember those days before no catastrophes on the horizon.*

Then, a break in the timeline. Pages torn out and very few entries between September and late November, where she picked up again.

> November 28: *Thanksgiving. My sweet man is gone and there is one empty place at the table.*
> December 1: *Be bold, strong, gutsy. Stay on the upside. Be the woman Klose believed in and others do, too. Do not crash. Do not disappoint.*

Much of what I'd intuited was there, like corroborating evidence, written in her own hand. *I am dismal, disparate, desperate . . . I am very much loved, even celebrated, but I am my own burden.*

> On January 31: *I wish I could explain but I can't. I just know I can't keep doing this. As much as I love you all and don't want to leave you in pain, stop trying to save me, the unsavable.*

On February twenty-fifth, the day she died, there was no journal entry, but she'd written a separate note, a suicide note, the one I'd rejected during the shocking early hours of discovery. I'd tucked it into the back of the journal, and I read it slowly now, recognizing language that was echoed throughout her entries: *I tried to be me, but I can't find me. I have no idea what caused this, and I have no hope it will ever go away. I am sorry, everyone. I love you.*

When I finished, it was past midnight. I had been reading for three hours, longer than I'd intended, consuming every word to the last page. I carefully closed the journal and folded the note.

I slipped out of bed and opened the dresser drawer that kept all the sad things and pushed the journal to the back like it was a bewitched book of spells. I returned to bed and sat with what I'd learned.

My mother was in distress, desperately wanting to be better, to feel different, to return to the Susan she thought we all wanted her to be. She had separated from and lost herself and she could not find her way back, as much as she tried, as much as she also wanted to believe she could "find me" again. Her pain was so palpable, so raw, right there: *I cannot endure this awfulness, this torment anymore*, she'd written in her final note.

As I digested her words, a wave of shock returned, followed by aching sadness. It had been nearly six months since her death, and I finally saw my mother. I'd had a series of what I believed to be revelatory dreams and I'd summoned her to the page for inspired conversation to help me remember and broaden my understanding of what happened That Day, yet I hadn't fully appreciated her internal battle because I'd been hyper-focused on how I felt. On my own torment. On my own unanswered pain. On what I'd lost. On how I'd been duped and deceived and left behind. I'd made her death so personal to *me*, and now I saw her struggle outside of myself, through her eyes, through her own pen.

For over a year, she'd chronicled her teetering mind. She hadn't shared the darkest details with us, but she had dared to be honest with herself, illustrating her tightrope walk toward the edge with a recurring sketch in the corner of the page. I hadn't recognized the doodle at first, dismissing it until it reappeared again and again. On closer look, its significance was impossible to mistake—a stick figure at the top of a straight-lined cliff, arms outstretched, and the clumsy curve of a wave below. On the next page another drawing—a clock with its hands striking midnight. This one had a title. In her own scribbled handwriting: *Time has run out.*

Return to Bodega

From one day to the next, they appeared, dancing from the side of the road and from every street corner, blowing their cotton-candy trumpets and teetering in high heels. The naked ladies were out on full parade. The amaryllis belladonna, Mom's splashy birthday flower, had returned, which meant it was August.

I'm not sure when Mom began drawing a parallel to the arrival of the distinctly pink and showy flower and her late-summer birthday, but the two had become irreversibly intwined after she began writing about them in her syndicated column on an annual basis.

As the naked ladies continued to stretch tall and unabashedly wave at every passerby happening down the country roads connecting Petaluma to Tomales and Graton to Healdsburg, more and more mail arrived. In between the L.L. Bean catalogs and calls to renew her annual membership to the local NPR station were birthday cards with notes written to me from Mom's best friends, honoring her on this day, and honoring me too. "It can only get better," wrote Aunt Nancy.

Beyond marking it on the calendar, I considered how I wanted to honor her this year, her first birthday she'd ever miss.

Last year, we'd gathered at their house, not more than a week after she'd returned from Elevation Hills. Miriam was there. The mood was a little forced, but altogether festive, and we'd feasted on red wine and spaghetti aglio e olio, a simple combination of fresh olive oil, garlic and parmesan revered by our family, but that I had no taste for this year. Finally, I arrived at what felt right, and I texted Gretta and Jenni: *As you both know, Mom's birthday is this week and I'm feeling called to go to Bodega Head. You are both welcome to join me, but only if you want to go. I'm fine to go alone—really—and I'll go either way. I've been putting it off and it's finally time.*

Of course, I'd dreamt about Bodega Head. I'd returned to its edge countless times in my mind, but I had yet to physically go there. I remembered it briefly making an appearance on the whiteboard as something my sisters and I intended to brave together, and then once we retreated indoors, we erased it from the list. Now, as her August birthday approached, it felt appropriate—necessary, even—to see it with my own eyes, to be there in the flesh, not only in my head, but really there, as she had been in those final moments. I believed I needed this to move forward.

My sisters didn't equally share my visceral tug to the coastline but agreed to go with me anyway, and three days later, we piled into Gretta's Subaru and headed west from Sebastopol toward the coast, following the curvy two-lane road past apple orchards and farm stands, cows grazing along fence lines tangled in blackberry bushes. I'd made this drive countless times throughout my life, but never in this way.

"I'm going to stop here," Gretta said as we crossed over Salmon Creek and passed the A-frame schoolhouse featured in Albert Hitchcock's 1963 thriller, *The Birds*. She pulled over to the side of the road and jumped out of the driver's seat with a pair of gardening scissors she pulled from her bag. "I brought them in case we found some," she explained. "I'll be quick." She kneeled close to a large cluster of naked ladies and sliced them at the base. "For her birthday bouquet," she said as she slid back into the car and handed the flowers to me.

Back on the road, we rounded through the small town of Bodega, past the white steepled church on the hill, the small Calvary cemetery on an adjacent hill, and through a tunnel of eucalyptus trees. Jenni broke the silence as we turned right onto Bodega Highway. "This isn't an impulsive destination. It takes a solid forty-five minutes to get out here from Sebastopol, and it would have taken her an hour from my house 'that' morning. Meaning, she would have had over an hour to change her mind and turn around."

She could have and she hadn't, I thought. Her mind was set. She'd already written her note and left the house, putting her plan into motion.

As we finally made the turn off Westshore Road in Bodega Bay and made the back-and-forth climb to the ocean overlook at the top of the hill, I recalled B's cautious advice: "Whether it's reading her journals or going out to the coast, be mindful of why you're doing it. It's not to absorb her pain and suffering. It's to gain clarity, maybe, and to release some of your grief. Always remember, when you go into the darkness, name it, frame it. Give yourself parameters or you risk getting lost."

When the car crested over the hill, my stomach turned over at the sight of the ocean beyond the cliffside parking lot, an expansive body of water that stretches down the Northern California coastline. Gretta pulled into a spot and cut the engine. All three of us took a collective breath and hesitated before opening the car's doors. We were welcomed by a mild temperature, mid-50s was my guess, and a bright and clear sky, and still I zipped up my hoodie and held myself tight. As we walked in the direction of the water, I noted how dramatically different it felt to be here, in real space and time, beyond what my mind had envisioned these past several months. I quickened my pace, suddenly eager to reach the trail head, to retrace her footsteps, to find the spot from where she'd jumped, to look down at the rocks below and feel the spit of ocean air on my skin.

"I'm going to stay here," Jenni said, falling back. She was recovering from a knee surgery, and I'd wondered how mobile she'd be in this terrain. "My knee's hurting today so I'm not going to walk up the trail." She pointed to the far corner of the parking lot where several people had set up beach chairs and tripods, likely to catch a glimpse of passing gray and blue whales. "I brought my own chair. I'll meet you over there."

"Okay. We won't be long."

As Gretta and I hiked up the trail, I remembered why people made the drive out here, why Bodega Head made it into so many of the travel magazines and online guides. Especially on a day like this when the typically thick fog was absent, and the overhead light was an almost piercing bright blue, it was stunning, and also perilous. Without a guardrail or a fence, the sheer drop from where we stood to the jagged rocks below was the difference of only a few missteps, which makes the experience exhilarating and also challenging. In the early days after Mom's suicide, Gretta had described this stretch of the coastline as "taking," and as we continued our climb, I had to agree. The churning water below appeared cold and unforgiving.

And still, as we hiked up the trail and from every angle, the symbolism of the scene wasn't lost on me, why Mom chose this particular vista to escape from her pain. There was hopeful beauty here, a sense of something bigger, greater. Squinting toward the horizon, I flashed back to the condolence card we'd found in her car after it had been towed from the lot we'd just parked. It was of an iconic beach scene, with a well-worn path and high grass on either side, leading downward to the ocean's edge. Inside was a note from a friend written to Mom after Klose's passing, and it had been straddling the emergency brake between the two seats, along with her purse, her phone, and a copy of her durable power of attorney. "Look at this," I'd remarked to Jenni and Gretta when I found it. "Coincidence or a clue?" They shrugged it off, but I believed the card served as a visual map, directing her to the water, to her pathway home.

"I think this is it," Gretta said, interrupting my memory and bringing me back to the moment. She'd stopped at the base of the Fisherman's Memorial, a series of concrete benches arranged in the shape of a ship's hull to honor the men who'd died in this sea, and where a couple onlookers were seated, cuddled next to each other and taking selfies.

"Do you want to look over?" I tilted my head toward the water.

"I don't know," Gretta wavered.

"Come on." I took her hand. "We'll be careful." I led her off the trail in the direction of the spot described to us by the sheriff who'd been first on the scene.

"Okay, but not too close." Gretta gently pulled me back. "Really, Sam, we don't need any more of us going over."

I slowed my pace. "He said near the ice plant, although there's ice plant everywhere." It followed the trail north and south. "Maybe right there?" I pointed to a curve in the edge. We walked slowly, hand in hand, until we were nearly looking over and I instinctively sank down to all fours. The drop was less than a foot away.

"Sam," Gretta warned. "Be careful." She got down on the ground with me.

I inched forward until I could lean over the edge. "Jesus Christ," I said, as a wave broke and crashed on the rocks hundreds of feet below. "This is higher than I remembered." I leaned back, suddenly dizzy, fearful that if the ground gave just a little, we'd both roll off the edge.

"I can't do it." Gretta moved back. "We're too close."

I scooted backward and leaned against her. We sat quietly as the wind picked up and seagulls flew overhead.

"It's a dramatic way to go," I finally said. "You gotta give her that."

Gretta smiled sadly. "I guess."

"Really, stepping off that edge takes some kind of crazy conviction."

Gretta exhaled. "Or just some kind of crazy."

I shifted my weight, moved to stand. "Do you want to walk some more down the trail?"

"Sure, and I want to find somewhere we can leave the naked ladies."

"Keep your voice low when you say things like that."

We walked until we found another elbow further down the trail, and where we sat down at an outcropping of more ice plant. As Gretta placed the flowers near the edge, but not too close, I said, "I brought something too." I dug through my bag until I found them. I slid Mom's silver hoops out of a jewelry pouch.

"Remember how they were in the bathroom?"

Gretta nodded slowly. "I'd forgotten."

"I still don't understand why she didn't wear them that day, and I think it must have been intentional, because she wore them always."

"Always," Gretta agreed.

"Maybe she wanted us to have them, like a memento to remember her, but I feel like they belong with her. What do you think?"

Gretta looked at the tarnished hoops in my outstretched hand and touched them with her own. "They should be with her."

"Should we throw them in?"

"With the flowers," Gretta said, scooping up the bundle of naked ladies.

We leaned out again, as far to the edge as we could without fear of falling, where the red rooted tips of the ice plant began to travel downward toward the sea, and we tossed them into the air. *Take them back. They belong with you.* As I imagined Mom's earrings and her favorite flowers landing in a pocket of water that would eventually be pulled out to sea and free her from this trapped place, I closed my eyes and offered a silent prayer to be carried with the salt air:

It is your birthday and I miss you, here, with us now. I miss you every minute, every hour, and every day that you're not here, and I am sorry that fear drove you to this edge, that you felt separate and alone, and that you died here, without me holding your hand, without me here to say, please hold on for one minute more. Hold on while we get help. It's not too late for you. Don't give up, don't let go. Stay.

* * *

On our drive back inland, I thought about how my mother had not sought help; she'd sought escape, and that she had her own reasons for believing that seeking help for herself was beyond or beneath her. And that whether I'd learned it directly from her, absorbed it from our prevalent culture of self-sufficiency, or if I'd simply adopted it as my own feminist leaning, there had been times in my life when I hadn't asked for help either, times when I needed it, and I chose to stay silent, to hide and pretend. At nine years old, new to divorce and the routine of splitting my life between two homes, there were many days when I unlocked the front door after school, let myself into a quiet, empty house, and didn't speak to anyone for hours. I didn't ask for a parent to come home early to keep me company, or even to call to check in. Instead, I learned how to wait out the afternoon, to keep my own company and befriend the setting sun. At fifteen, I rebelled against solitude by becoming sexually active and, almost immediately, pregnant. I didn't ask for help then, either. I kept my condition a secret, made an appointment at Planned Parenthood, took the city bus downtown, and took care of it. Later, at age twenty, overwhelmed by the immensity of a university campus, I dropped out of college "for just a year," I promised, and when people asked, Mom pointedly—"If you don't finish school, what will you *do* with your life?" I said, "Don't worry about me, I'll figure it out." I bartended for two years, made enough money to travel through Europe, and when I returned to college as I'd promised, I was fortunate to land an internship and then a full-time job at a respected broadcast outlet. By then, I'd learned how to take care of myself, to be an independent, strong, successful woman who, instead of asking for help, works her way around needing it. And when my marriage to the man I met at that broadcast outlet became untenable, I worked around that too. I faked it for cameras and asked for no one to save me, until finally, I stepped in to save myself.

Did I also think I was above receiving help? That I could absorb every blow in my life without personal injury? That I could "go it alone" indefinitely? That I could survive without needing anyone? Or maybe, I thought now, maybe I wasn't above receiving help. I was afraid to ask for it, either because I didn't believe I'd receive it, or I'd be criticized or, worse, rejected for needing it. Wasn't that the secret Mom and I had both tucked away—that if we were found out, we'd be thrown out for appearing needy and weak? While I wished more than anything that Mom would have accepted the preventive care she needed before getting to the point she did—the literal point where land meets sea—who was I to judge her reasons for withholding support when I wasn't exactly the poster child for vulnerability, either? Wasn't I just as guilty of dismissing an outstretched hand, assuming I'd ever asked for one? As we turned down the winding road that led back toward Bodega, I detected a shift in my internal tide: This cycle of silently suffering has to end. Help is not a four-letter word.

★ ★ ★

On Wednesday, when B answered, I said, "Before we get started, I want to say I'm grateful for you, and I'm also grateful to me for calling you when I did, for knowing right away that Mom's death would be too much for me to hold alone, that I would need help."

"You're welcome," B said warmly, and then teased, "You just feeling extra sentimental today, or did something bring this on?"

"I finally went out to Bodega Head."

"Ahhh," he said slowly. "And what did you find out there?"

"Gretta and I walked up and down the bluff, searching for the spot from where she jumped, and as I sat there, looking over the edge, at the sheer, violent drop to rocks and water below, I thought what she did was really, really messed up, and also what she did was daring."

"Interesting word choice. Not a description that frequently comes up with suicide. Say more."

"I think I've told you my mom was afraid of heights. She got nervous on a single Ferris wheel, and it has perplexed everyone who knew this about her. Why would Susan, who was squeamish on bridges and anything above a second story, jump off a cliff? And I don't think it's without meaning. That's what hit me when I was out there. My mother was terrified about her mental health, of suffering the same fate as her own mother. And remember that none of her doctors or therapists believed she was suffering from cognitive decline. Never was there a mention of early dementia or Alzheimer's disease. In fact, at every turn, they confirmed her mental competence. But she thought differently. She was certain she was losing a grip on her mind, and there was no way back for her, and I wonder if in that single act of jumping, she faced her two biggest fears."

"Faced them or gave into them?" B challenged.

"Can it be both? I'm sure a lot of people would disagree with me that she'd thought through her death in any conscious way, but I believe she did. She chose Bodega Head, and not only because it was a favorite spot of hers; we found multiple photos of it in her iPad search history just days before she died. She'd been doing her homework, making a plan, writing a note. I mean, she wasn't thinking like a clear-headed person, I won't argue that, but she was thinking to some degree. And again, I'm sure this is an unpopular position, but I think she deserves acknowledgement for doing the scariest, most outrageous thing, for taking control of her life when she thought she was losing control. For exercising her right to choose. Mom believed strongly in the right-to-die movement, and over her journalism career, she wrote countless columns on the topics of "death cafés" and "death doulas." Not only did she believe that one should live life on their own terms, but also this extended to dying, and when Mom did what she did, I think she was asserting her personal freedom to die on her terms. Don't mistake me—I'm not congratulating or condoning what she did. I hate the choice she made, and I wish she would have chosen differently. I wish she would have called me and said, "Come get me, I'm on the edge, I'm about to do something *really* stupid." I would have much rather she made that choice, but she didn't, and I respect that she asserted herself while she still could. No one pushed her. She jumped. And maybe she thought it was the only choice she had left—to which I strongly disagree—and still, it was hers to make. Does that make sense or is my mind playing tricks on me?"

"We all have free will, and that extends to suicide," B said.

"Okay," I exhaled. "At least, now I know that when critics gather outside my house, they'll also be making a stop at yours."

B laughed. "I'm used to being unpopular. You get used to it. And look, I've said this before: you honor your mom by honoring her death. Also, you honor your mom by holding her accountable. This is different than judging or condemning her. It means you're holding her accountable for her choice. It's not a choice you like, but it's the choice she made. Was it a conscious choice? That's debatable. Planning to end your life by committing an act of violence against yourself, and by extension, causing pain and suffering for many others, indicates compromised thinking, without a doubt. But I think what you're saying is that even under the influence of mental instability, you still want to honor your mom in those final moments. You want to honor her final act of free will, rather than dismissing her and her actions outright as unconscious or completely beyond or outside of her control."

"I want to honor *her.* She would hate to be remembered only as a 'mental illness' or labeled as a 'diagnosis,' as if that's all that was left of her, that she'd been stripped completely of her*self.* I'm certain she'd want to be remembered for her mind, which was beautiful and kind and quick and clever. Even at the end, when her mind was deceiving her, when it was telling her there was no better way, her last act was symbolic."

"I tend to agree with you, and—" B emphasized, "life has a way of pushing all of us to the edge, and we each choose our response. I respect that you want to honor your mother's choice, misguided as it was, and at the same time, I think her death is challenging you to make a different one."

We Have to Stop Meeting Like This

On Labor Day, the majority of the workforce wasn't working, but they weren't kicking back at the communal parks and pools, either. Even though we were experiencing unusually high, triple-digit record heat in our area, most people I knew were staying in or, at least, safely distancing from the world at large by enjoying chilled white wine in the privacy of their backyards. Derby was with his dad, so I decided to take a much-needed break from my deadline writing and spend a couple of hours automatic writing. I hadn't invited Mom to the page since reading her journal and returning to Bodega Head, and I asked myself, why? Was I afraid of uncovering something more about her, about myself? This process of dialoguing with Mom on the page had become a refuge, a way for me to be with her again, and at the same time, it was painful to go there, and I supposed that was why I was resisting to write. I mean, how much deeper did we need to go? Maybe we were done digging into the past? Although, I knew about myself that when I'd rather do anything other than change the litter box or start my taxes seven months early, when everything sounds better than sitting down at my computer, the only solution is the writing itself. Relief is found on the other side of the words, and avoiding it was just postponing it.

Today, my resistance was minimal. I'd reheated my coffee only twice and changed out of my sweatpants only once. I sat down and opened a new document. I closed my eyes, concentrated on my breath, and focused in on the stillness of the room. I encouraged myself: Write forward, write through. And I asked a new question: What do you want me to see? What do you want me to know? When I opened my eyes, I began describing the scene and typing the back-and-forth dialogue that came through.

I found Mom back at Bodega Head with her eyes closed, face lifted to the sun, sitting cross-legged at the Fisherman's Memorial where Gretta and I had recently been. I made my way up the trail and as I approached, she opened her eyes and smiled warmly. "We have to stop meeting like this."

I sat down next to her.

"But, really"—she poked me lightly—"we have to stop meeting *here*."

"Why?" I looked around. "Has someone followed us?"

"You've followed *me*," she said kindly. "Back here."

"I'm not following."

"I understand why you return to this spot. It makes perfect sense that you'd continue to return to where I last *was*, but I'm not here anymore."

"Then where are you, if not here?"

"I'm here with you now, but I don't *reside* here, is what I mean. Nor am I lost at sea. I've moved on to another place, and . . ." she hesitated, "maybe you should, too."

"I can come here if I want to." I crossed my arms like a disobedient teenager.

"Of course, you can," she said, indulging me. "I can't stop you, or anyone else, for that matter. I've seen plenty of my friends out here since it happened, leaving flowers and sweet notes, walking the trails, searching for me, in a way. Some, like you, walk to the edge. Others try to retrace my footsteps. They look down at the rocks and the crashing surf like you've done, as if they might catch a part of me that hasn't yet fallen."

"Jumped," I clarified.

"Yes, jumped," she repeated softly and waited for a series of waves to break before continuing. "Sammy, I want you to understand something. The me on these cliffs was me in one moment in time. This final moment of my life was only one moment in my life. One awful and tragic moment, but one I'm no longer in. I'm no longer on the edge, thank God, and I don't want you to come back here, again and again, and suffer on my behalf. I feel your sadness in this place, and I worry you're suffering *for* me. Feeling my pain *as your own*."

This was exactly what B had cautioned against. She leaned into me. "It may take some time still, but I want you to try to move past this one moment, okay? Remember me in other moments."

I considered this, and admitted, "It's not only this moment. I read your journal from the last year."

"I wondered if you would." Her eyes darkened. "Did you find what you were looking for?"

I stared out at the endless horizon. "You wrote some scary stuff in there. What you'd been hiding, how alone in your mind you'd become. It hurt to read it, but I couldn't put it down."

She sighed. "I don't doubt it was difficult for you to read what I'd written there, but the woman who wrote in that journal is no different than the woman who wandered to the edge of these cliffs; she represents a snapshot in time, the last hard year of my life that I hope, I pray, doesn't ultimately define *me*. I trust you found all my journals, that date back to before you were born. I had a full box of them, and they tell a different story, a much happier one, of a wonderful life. The pages I wrote leading up to this moment, are only one piece of my story, they're only one piece of *me*, the confused and fearful one. I understand your curiosity and I'm not upset you read it, but my motherly advice is to see what you need to see, then get out. Really, Sammy, don't dwell inside my sick head any longer, and don't trick yourself into thinking you must return to this place to be with me."

I considered this. "I think it was defiant, what you did."

Mom turned a questioning eye. "What?"

"I hate what you did, but it wasn't until I'd read your journal and came out here that I understood you'd left on your own terms."

Mom groaned uncomfortably. "Oh, I don't know about that. I think it was more desperate than anything else." Mom took my hand in hers. "Sweetie, I appreciate your loyalty to me, and trying so hard to understand me, but . . ." Her expression turned serious. "I believe the more defiant thing for me to have done would have been to stay alive. Don't make me the hero of this story."

I returned my gaze to the water and allowed her words to sink in. "I know it wasn't your choice to get sick. You would never have chosen that. Still, I wish you would have allowed yourself to receive care, to have admitted you needed it, to believe you deserved it. That might have made a difference. It might have changed the ending." We sat quietly for a moment. "It would have been your seventy-seventh birthday had you stuck around."

"We both missed our birthdays this year, didn't we? Me and Klose. And what he would have given to have had another birthday. Do you remember what he said in the hospital just hours before he died?"

I shook my head, not able to recall the memory, his final hours had all blended together.

"He turned to the attending nurse, that lovely woman who

had been so kind and patient with him. He turned to her and said, "Save my life." Mom's voice choked. "He held on as long as he could. He would have never given up." A bird flew overhead, the waves crashed and we sat in stillness for another minute more until she pivoted. "You know what I want for my birthday this year?"

"I'm not sure you still get to make birthday requests," I said with obvious sarcasm. "You may have forfeited that right."

She raised a playful eyebrow. "Well, if you're feeling generous, honor me this year by remembering how I lived more than how I died. That's what I want. Release me from this moment and remember me away from this place."

I inhaled the coastal air. "It is beautiful here," I finally said, "but if I'm being honest, it's not my favorite part of our coastline. Too many tourists, and nearly always windy and cold."

She laughed. "You *do* know that people travel from all over the world for this view?"

I shrugged. "The whale watchers can have it."

"Well, now that that's settled . . ."

"So, if we aren't going to meet here, where do I find you next?"

"Oh, goody." She clapped her hands together "This is the fun part. We can meet *anywhere*."

Time Travel

The trick to meeting Mom somewhere other than the fateful cliffs of Bodega Head was to release her from that moment in space and time and remember our whole life together and focus on what we had versus what I'd lost.

Remember how I lived more than how I died.
Remember back to happy times.
Remember all of me.

Once I allowed myself to expand backward and reach into my memories from before That Day, there were many alternatives to choose from and to play back with delight. I could easily recall us laughing together over everything and nothing in particular. I could instantly imagine us deep in conversation, sitting knee to knee on a sofa or leaning forward over a café table. Once I established a setting, I'd will my mind to *go there,* and then—I'd invite her to join me.

Mom, Mutti, Susan . . .

Join me here.

The first time I did this, I remembered a photo I'd taken of Mom during a summer trip to New York in the mid-'90s. We sat on a park bench in Central Park's Tunnel of Trees, and in one hand she held a coffee cup and in the other, a cherry jelly doughnut that spilled powdered sugar down the front of her black T-shirt. I recreated this specific moment in my mind, and then I envisioned it anew:

"How's this meeting place?"

"Classic," she said and licked sugar from her fingers.

"This scene is kind of overdone, but we did always love to come here."

"Oh, sure, it may be in every rom-com, but it never goes out of style." A woman passed by in a siren-red beret, followed by a young couple holding hands, speaking rapidly in Italian. "I just love the energy of this city, don't you?"

"What's it like where you are now, wherever that is when you're not here with me?"

She licked another finger free of sugar. "Well, I don't want to spoil the surprise, but"—she lowered her voice to a conspiring whisper—"you won't be disappointed."

"Are you okay? And . . ." I leveled, "don't bullshit me this time."

"I'm in good hands." She looked upward. "Getting the help I need."

"Is he there?"

"Who, Klose?" She feigned innocence.

"Yes, who else? Was he waiting for you in a pair of Wranglers and his hiking boots?"

She laughed. "His uniform. That never went out of style, either. Yes, he was there, although not at first. He was pretty mad at me too, for leaving you all. He couldn't understand why I would have given up when he would have given anything to stay. But you know Klose. He could never be mad for long."

"So, you're together?"

Her face lit up.

"That makes me happy, although I hope you're not having *too* much fun," I said, "while the rest of us are stuck here."

She set down her coffee cup and faced me with concern. "Do you feel stuck?"

I looked at her and shrugged. "I'm not sure how to live with you gone. I'm trying."

"Oh, sweetie, don't stop living because of what I did. There's so much to love about life." She fixed her focus on the city beyond the park. "Just look at it, smell it, hear it, taste it. I want you and your sisters, and my grandkids, to live full and beautiful lives. That is my greatest hope for you."

I followed her eyeline beyond the park, at the current of people moving up and down the street, at the palpable swell of energy, of life. It was right there, I saw it, but I didn't feel a part of it. I was somewhere else. Looking in on the world, not *in it*. Disconnected.

"Sammy, take it." She held out her half-eaten doughnut with cherry filling oozing out from one side. "Finish it for me?"

I took the gooey mess.

"And finish this." She gestured at the scene in front us. "Being in the world doesn't last forever. Eat it up."

Throughout the early fall, I met Mom at our favorite bookstores and cafés in San Francisco, Point Reyes, and Provincetown. I imagined us stretching out poolside at Lake Austin Spa, one of our favorite springtime retreats, and walking along Crane's Beach in Massachusetts, our preferred stretch of white sand in the summer.

I restarted conversations from memory, and at other times, I introduced new material.

"Menopause, what's your take?" I positioned us side by side in chaise lounge chairs, dipping our toes in a pool.

"You do know that I wrote two books about menopause,"

she chided. "The do's and don'ts with hormones. Go back and read them."

"Outdated. Hormone replacement therapy is trending right now."

She waved me off. "Oh, that topic is ever-changing. The one constant is that you need to take care of your thinning bones. Lift weights, just like RBG. Take your vitamin D." She squinted in the sunlight. "And if you're getting it from a natural source like this one, don't forget to wear your sunscreen."

On another day, while perusing the sale stack on the sidewalk outside Copperfield's Books, I imagined her flipping pages next to me.

"Remember *The Time Traveler's Wife*?" she asked. "What was that great line, something about travel as a metaphor for memory?"

"'We are all time travelers in our minds, if not in our bodies,'" I quoted.

"Kind of like what we're doing now." She elbowed me and smiled.

In the middle of an outdoor yoga class, I reimagined us side by side on pink and purple mats.

"For all my effort to 'be still now,' it was a constant challenge for me," she whispered, lifting her right foot into tree pose and stretching her arms toward the sky. "I was afraid of the inner stillness, afraid of what I'd find there. That's why I kept so busy, constantly doing, surrounding myself with people. All the activity kept me out of my head."

"I sometimes resented how busy you were," I whispered back, "because I always wanted more time with you. And also, because I couldn't keep up with you."

"Being busy is not a good life goal," Mom returned. "I always envied *you* for being better than me at being alone, probably because you were an only child, at least for the first nine years of your life. I never learned how to be alone. I grew up with a sister, then I had a college roommate. I got married after that, and then I had you, my career, lots of friends. I always had people around. After Klose died, I felt alone in a way I never had. At night, I'd lie with my grief, with my escalating fear and uncertainty of what would happen next. I hated the stillness, the haunting quiet. As much as I tried to embrace it, like my hero Sylvia Boorstein, I really didn't like to go there. I applaud you for sitting in yours."

"The world is still in semi-forced isolation mode." I reminded her. "I don't really have a choice but to sit in it."

Mom shook her head. "Not true. We always have a choice."

Were we truly having these conversations? I believe we were. Was she truly there, in spirit, speaking to me from a different time zone? I heard her as if she were in the room. I felt her near, the lightness of her touch on my shoulder, the caress of her gaze on my check. I sensed her presence like a warm cashmere sweater or a cup of Sleepytime tea.

Can I prove it?

No.

Do I need to?

I believe we each are permitted to have our own unique relationship with our dead loved ones, just as we did when they were alive, and the nature of that relationship is not for others to dictate or decide. When Mom was alive, we talked nearly every day. Why should that change now? Why should we end the conversation when there was so much more to say? And especially because of the way she died, there were things we had to address, difficult conversations I insisted we have in order for me to make peace with her and with myself. Regardless of where she was now, *we had to talk*. I wasn't letting her off the hook.

The other compelling reason for continuing our conversation had to do with remembering. I hadn't anticipated what it would mean to lose the person who remembers with you because they share your history, they share your same stories, the beginning, middle, and the end. I couldn't predict what it would mean to lose the person who can recall the other side of the debate, the punchline of the joke, the one person who can fill in the details of a scene in a way that no one else can because they alone were there with you, as your witness. Mom and I spent forty-nine years together. We had a lifetime of memories that belonged solely to us, and if I didn't continue to refresh those memories, I worried I'd lose them. At some point, without her there to remind me, to retell her side of the story, I feared I'd forget the story altogether, so I started having those conversations too, as a way of remembering for us both.

ME: Remember when we tried pasta carbonara for the first time?

MOM: Yes! We were in New York in January, and it started snowing so hard. Remember how we got caught in the middle of it?

ME: Yes, and we didn't know what to do because we weren't wearing the right clothes. We'd packed like idiot Californians.

MOM LAUGHING: That's right! We were wearing light jackets, so we ducked into that tiny Italian restaurant in SoHo to warm up.

ME: And when the waiter asked us what we wanted to order . . .

BOTH OF US: We said we didn't care! He could order for us, as long as it was something hot.

ME: I'd never heard of pasta carbonara, and oh, my God, I'd never tasted anything so good in my life.

MOM (FAKING AN ITALIAN ACCENT): The salty prosciutto, the heavy cream, the parmigiana.

ME: And remember, we sat there for hours, eating and drinking red wine because we didn't want to go back outside.

MOM: Oh, yes, we had that little table in the window and the snowy scene from inside was so beautiful. I love that memory.

ME: Me, too.

Throughout the early fall, we dialogued like this—less often in my dreams, more frequently on the page, and I also began to converse with her during my early-morning walks around the neighborhood, and afterward, in the shower. On many days, I'd be in the middle of rinsing my hair and suddenly, a single line, a familiar phrase, back-and-forth banter would arrive without warning, and I'd jump out of the shower dripping wet and run through the house, looking for a pen to write it down before I forgot the whisperings in my ear. And whether I conjured forth these conversations from somewhere unconscious and unseen, between magic and absolutes, or created them in the intersection of memory, longing, and imagination, they felt real to me, and that was all the proof I needed. Proof that I was finally beginning to heal.

A Different Shade of Grief

"I don't feel mad anymore," I said to B, surprising myself with this admission. "Maybe it's the change in seasons. Does cooler air help to cool the rage?"

"It's a decent theory."

"Don't get me wrong, I can still get mad, but I almost have to stir it up. It's not immediately there, sitting in the chair next to me like one of my cats, ready to scratch up the armrest."

"Well, then, *mazel tov*. It sounds like you're graduating from your angry stage."

"I thought you encouraged anger."

"Not indefinitely."

"That's a relief," I audibly exhaled. "Because explosive anger isn't really my style."

"No, you prefer to stuff it down with a cheeseburger."

"Funny, but really, I'm not trying to stuff it down or put a fake smile on it. I don't feel angry like I did before. Maybe I'm just tired of being mad all the time. Or maybe I'm worn out by it."

"Perhaps both. Or maybe it's run its course. And the question is: If you aren't angry, what are you?"

I thought about this in the context of the last month,

dialoguing with Mom on a walk, on the page. Whenever I was with her, I felt uplifted, my heart full, but as soon as I returned to my time zone, to the one where she was undeniably absent, a longing curled around me like a coastal fog.

"When I take away the anger, what's left is simply missing *her.* I miss her in the world. I miss who she was, how she lived her life. I miss us together as we were. I miss being seen by her. Being witnessed. I miss being loved by a mom."

"With death by suicide, the first stage of grief is often consumed by the 'how' of the death, the final moment that cannot be turned back, the final act that can be impossible to reconcile. The suicide story keeps the mind busy, scattered, and distracted by questions that rarely, if ever, have a clear conclusion. These questions create their own grief. The haunting is in the 'how' and it can last a long time."

This resonated, but I needed him to say more. "Go on."

"How your mom died was shocking, dramatic, and violent," he said. "None of you saw it coming, not really; unlike with your stepdad, who was sick with cancer for over a year. You all hoped he'd get better, and he did for a while, but I think you all knew that eventually, his cancer would kill him. With your mom, the 'how' and the 'why' took everyone by surprise, and so *reacting* to her suicide has taken the front seat in your grieving process. It's dominated the other shades of grief."

He was right. Still, to date, whenever I talked about Mom with Miriam or Aunt Nancy or, really, with anyone who knew her, we focused on the details of her death. We didn't do this with Klose. We didn't ruminate on his cancer or question his cause of death. How he died was no longer a discussion. In fact, it hadn't been a discussion since the morning we lost him at Memorial Hospital.

"For a long time after my dad took his life, I was angry, really angry," B said. "Like you, I felt betrayed, robbed, abandoned, and I wanted him to explain himself, to justify his actions. After he died, it was like I became the acting prosecutor in a criminal case, and day after day, I'd march Dad into court and try him for his crime even though the outcome was always the same: He was guilty of taking his life. And I finally realized this exercise of punishing him wasn't going to change what happened. It wasn't going to bring him back or make me feel any better about what he did. In fact, it was only serving to hurt *me*. Releasing some of your anger doesn't mean you're done grieving," B clarified. "It just means you're done trying her for the crime. And once the courtroom is empty, there's more room for compassion and empathy. There's more room to grieve your relationship, a full lifetime together, and those memories are more important than the details of her death."

Spaghetti carbonara over Bodega Head.

"Of course, you couldn't do this in the beginning," he said, "but it sounds like you're at a turning point. You're ready to move forward."

"How's your relationship with your dad now?" I asked. "Now that you're not angry with him?"

"Better than ever."

Give Up the Ghost

Was it Monday, Tuesday, or Wednesday? It didn't matter. Every day, I was pushing closer to my deadline. The manuscript I was ghostwriting was due by the end of the year, and even though it was only early October, I knew from years of experience that the next few months of working hours would be interrupted by holiday schedules—mine, my client's, and the publisher's. I was beginning to fret that I wouldn't finish in time while also juggling *life*. Derby's elementary school had finally reopened, but only for an abbreviated three-hour day, and where he sat masked and at long tables in small groupings of four. The shortened schedule allowed the kids to resocialize and receive some much-needed academic instruction after many months of isolating at home, and while I appreciated the return to campus, for his sake and mine, the school bell snuck up quickly.

I held my writing work alongside my parenting responsibilities, and in my other hand, I held my evolving grief. On the morning that was either Monday, Tuesday, or Wednesday, I broke focus from the manuscript and checked the clock. I had ninety minutes before my time was up. I sat back in my chair, knowing better that I ought to sit up and push forward.

I resisted. I was tired of pushing. Where was the relief? Was it truly coming, as B had suggested? I let my eyes wander away from my monitor to travel outside my office window, landing on the skeleton of a twelve-foot-tall sunflower I hadn't yet cut down. It had become a meeting spot for the neighborhood birds that liked to perch and sway atop its lopsided head and nibble its sun-kissed face for seeds.

"I've been thinking about something." Mom entered my reflective moment, sitting down in the swayback leather chair opposite my desk.

"What's that?" I responded, indulging this unexpected break in time and space.

"It's not enough for you to be the 'ghost' anymore." She pointed to herself. "I'm the ghost now. It's time for you to be something else."

"Do you have something in mind?"

"I do. I think it's time for you to tell your own story."

Nervous apprehension traveled up my spine and lodged itself in my throat. I'd been ghostwriting for fifteen years, and I'd honed my craft by learning how to quiet my own voice and speak for others. At intermittent times, during the darkest days of my marriage, I'd wondered if I'd trained myself too well and lost my voice completely. After all, a good ghost is neither seen nor heard, and over the years, it had become easier to speak for others—more natural, even—to tell other people's stories than to tell my own. I knew a handful of ghostwriters, colleagues who'd become friends, who were opiniated and outspoken, so I couldn't blame the craft for silencing me. Rather, it had enabled me to fade. It had encouraged my introverted, invisible side, the child who learned to quietly observe and disappear in plain sight.

In the last year that Mom was alive, we'd typically end "Derby Fridays" by having a glass of wine and catching up for thirty minutes before she left my house for hers. One afternoon, while we were sipping Sauvignon Blanc and talking about nothing in particular, Derby interrupted with nothing in particular, and, without missing a beat, Mom warned: "Derby, let the grown-ups talk."

Tiny hairs stood up on the back of my neck. I hadn't heard the phrase in years—decades, even—and there it was. I instantly recognized my childhood reaction in Derby: head bowed, suddenly quiet, retreating within himself. How many times had I also been instructed to silence myself as a kid? I'd forgotten all about it until now when the memory came rushing back—Mom socializing with friends. Drinks on the coffee table. Mom relaxing back on our living-room couch while I played on the floor beside her. As she and her friends talked and laughed and carried on, I sat quietly, listening until an opening presented itself for me to jump into the conversation with something irrelevant, as kids do.

Sammy, *shhhh,* let the grown-ups talk.

When I traced the memory back, I was four or five years old, and I easily recalled the feeling of being hushed: embarrassed, shamed for the dumb thing I said, wishing I could shove the words back down my throat and disappear into the fabric of the couch. Above all things, I wanted to please my mother and I learned early on that when she was talking, I ought to quietly listen, play small, and speak only when invited. This was the same girl, a few years later at Jack in the Box, who understood that the best way to survive divorce was to nod my head in agreement and shove my words down with a cheeseburger.

This was a curious revelation.

Because this wasn't my experience with Mom as an adult. We spoke frequently and freely with each other, she welcomed and encouraged my opinions, and my quips and candor easily made her laugh. As an adult, Mom was the one I loved conversing with the most—she was the first person I called—but on that Friday afternoon, when she said to Derby, "Let the grown-ups talk," something unconscious rattled within me, a belief I'd formed about myself that had informed much of my life. As a kid, I learned my value was my silence, in making room for others to be seen and heard, and to maximize my value, please my mother, and be *loved*, I learned to lie low, to listen and observe, to enter a room unnoticed, to dim and fade into the background like an invisible new moon. This was my superpower, like Violet in *The Incredibles*. Without realizing it, I'd leaned on invisibility, not only in childhood and throughout my young life, but also as an adult by channeling my superpower into a successful career.

As a ghost.

For fifteen years, I'd been invited into people's homes all over the country, where I utilized my skills as an empathetic listener and observer to gather the details and untold secrets of their lives. I considered this a privilege, and also my pleasure. There had been the year I'd spent the week before Christmas in a beautifully appointed apartment above snowy Central Park, drinking French press coffee with a client who shared with me the most colorful stories of her life. A different year and with a different client, I was invited to a traditional Italian Sunday-night dinner on Staten Island. For hours, I passed homemade ravioli, chicken piccata, and multiple bottles of Chianti back and forth across the family table with people I would have never met or known otherwise, had I not been the ghostwriter. There were many aspects of the job I loved—the access and the intimacy ranked high on my list—but the trade-off was that my role as the ghost could impede my real life, like the time I attended a book-release party at a Barnes & Noble in Connecticut and my breasts started leaking milk. I'd left my still-nursing eight-month-old on the other side of the country to attend the launch, and I hadn't anticipated this unwelcome lactose moment. I buttoned up my blazer and stepped away from the signing table.

"What's wrong?" my client mouthed as I inched further away.

"Oh, it's nothing. Will you excuse me?"

I'd managed to write nearly the full manuscript without disclosing to my client or our editor that I was pregnant and then, right before submitting the last chapter to the publisher, I'd had an emergency cesarean section and delivered a baby boy. Still, I'd cranked out the final pages a week later, no one the wiser. As a ghostwriter, I omitted this milestone moment from my work life because I hadn't wanted to cause concern. How can a pregnant woman deliver a book and a baby within the same month? I believed it was my job to do both, to tell my client's story even if it meant burying my own. So, on the night my client was signing stacks of their instant *New York Times* bestseller, I quietly excused myself from the event and sat in the dark parking lot of Barnes & Noble, pumping breast milk into tiny plastic bags that I concealed at the bottom of my purse.

Many years had taught me how to successfully play a ghost, and now Mom was suggesting I retire the role.

"What story do I tell?" I asked her.

"Yours. Leave me out of it."

"You're a big part of my story, and let's be honest, you left me with pretty compelling material to work with."

"That may be true, but I think it's time for you to step forward and for me to step aside. I've talked enough, don't you agree?"

I rolled it over, not entirely comfortable with the idea. "I'd always hoped we'd write together, like Sue Monk Kidd and her daughter Ann."

Mom smiled. "*Traveling With Pomegranates*. That was a sweet book."

* * *

For years before she died, I'd had a recurring fantasy where the two of us sat across from each other with our separate laptops. Our writers' table would be covered with paper drafts of our working manuscript, along with red editor's pencils and bowls of snacks and bubbly water. Wouldn't that be so fun, I'd mused, to free up some time to write together? Once I met my current deadline and got past the next ghostwriting project, we could do that, I promised myself, except for that the current deadline always became a new deadline and the next project was always followed by another, and now the opportunity was gone.

The closest we'd gotten to collaborating was when she'd visited Austin for a week to edit my first book, a memoir titled *The Package Deal*, that I'd written under a pen name. The first morning of her visit, she roused herself at six o'clock and started marking pages in her pajamas. "I can do this until lunchtime," she said, "as long as you keep bringing me coffee." I hadn't asked her to fly halfway across the country to help me out, but she'd offered and I was touched, especially since I knew her standard policy about editing other people's work, especially friends and family: "I'm no good at editing because I just want to change it to sound like how I'd write it." But when she learned that I was rushing to complete the final draft of my book for submission, she said, "For you, my darling, I will make an exception."

Every morning of her stay, she edited pages in bed, and in the afternoon, we reviewed them in the front room over cheese and wine. She'd gone line by line and page by page, making smart suggestions and funny word swaps that she scribbled into the margins. By the end of the week, she and I had reviewed the entire book, and I wished she'd never leave.

"Oh, I've got it!" Her enthusiasm interrupted my memory, bringing me back to the dreamy in-between. "Let me be *your* ghostwriter. Get it? Because I'm the ghost now?"

"Clever."

"I thought so."

"Just one thing. Given your ghostlike, nonphysical state, I will still have to do all the writing."

"Right, technically, you will. But, this time, instead of you being the ghost, I'll be the one in the shadows. Your silent scribe."

"But you like center stage."

"Once upon a time, I did."

"People aren't going to like it," I warned her. "The story I want to tell is heavy on the dark stuff."

She shrugged. "What does your friend B say? If you aren't offending or challenging people, then you're not speaking up enough."

"Fair point, but I'm not sure where to start."

"Well, that's up to you. Just promise me one thing."

"Anything."

"Tell the truth."

PART THREE

Rise Up

I've Been Ghosted

"My mom's ghosting me," I said to B on Wednesday.

"Sounds appropriate."

"What if I told you that my mother, in ghost form, was encouraging me not to be a ghost anymore?"

"I wouldn't ask too many questions, and I'd say it's about time."

"What's wrong with being a ghost?"

"I think it worked for you for a long time, and now it sounds like she, you, whoever's doing the talking, is telling you that you've outgrown the role."

"I've been the voice for other people for over fifteen years. What am I supposed to do instead? My skill set is fairly niche."

"This is about more than ghost*writing*, though, isn't it?"

He was doing it again, challenging me to go deeper.

"Is it?" I backpedaled.

"*Is it?*" he mocked. "Okay, don't say I didn't warn you. This is about becoming a ghost to yourself: disappearing in your work, your marriage, playing the moon to your mom's sun. At different times in your life, playing the 'ghost' has served you, but you're too good at it. You excel at disappearing, at fading into the wallpaper. Throughout the pandemic, even, you've said you're perfectly fine retreating indoors."

"It's a relief, is it not?"

"For some, for *you*. Not for everybody. And especially not after eight months of it."

"Well," I defended, "I told you that a big part of my job is to be silent and selfless."

"Selfless is very different than self-*lost*, and again, we're talking about more than your job. What has served you professionally is no longer serving you personally. No one should be a ghost in their own life."

"Ouch."

"You were warned. Look," B eased, "your mom told a story about her own mental health that wasn't true. You withhold the truth in a different way, by hiding behind other people's stories. Neither is healthy nor honest. What if the truth was your new tool, and not your invisibility? What if your strength was no longer disappearing in the shadows, or being a mirror to others? What if your strength is being you?"

"Feels a bit indulgent."

"Growth needs to be indulged, and anyway, I think this is what you writers call advancing the narrative."

Go Big

"Tell a new story about visibility on the cusp of your fiftieth birthday. And, think about it, what better time to be called out of the shadows?"

This was how B had enthusiastically ended our call, and I'd worked hard to stifle a sarcastic retort. I wasn't opposed to personal growth, *okay?* My resistance was in direct response to my birthday. He'd remembered it when this year, I wanted to skip it, kind of like a leap year for special cases because, really, this was not the year to turn fifty. Not during an ongoing pandemic. Not when I was still wandering around the house in isolation sweatpants. Fifty is a milestone, a BIG moment, and for my fiftieth, I'd intended to be in Hawaii, sipping Mai Tais as I floated in tropical ocean water alongside sea turtles and my son, whose birthday lands two days before mine. Last year, his father and I treated him to a weekend at The Wizarding World of Harry Potter in Universal City, and where he ran around the theme park with wand in hand and his black Gryffindor robe trailing behind, blissfully unaware this would be our last family vacation together. We'd all had a fun time, actually, drinking large mugs of Butterbeer at the Leaky Cauldron and eating chocolate frogs in Hogsmeade Village, but as the weekend ended, I vowed to myself that next year, on my fiftieth, I'd do something for *me.*

I'd purchased tickets to Hawaii well before the Covid travel ban, and since I'd had to cancel them, I hadn't made an alternate plan. If I was to take my dead mother's advice and step out from behind the ghost and write my own story, I had to start living one, and turning fifty quietly indoors didn't qualify; even I knew that. What to do? Flying wasn't an option. Traveling to a destination that attracted more than a small crowd was also strongly unadvised. And there were the Northern California fires to contend with, specifically the Kincade that was currently burning hot down the north end of our county and blanketing the region in thick smoke. There seemed to be only one safe directive: head west, toward the river and the beach. After a quick search online, I located a forest retreat in Guerneville, home to Armstrong Redwoods and the meandering Russian River, and where I rented a cabin for Derby and me on the outskirts of town. We'd be insulated and protected from rampant disease and spreading wildfires, and still be out in the world, on a vacation, albeit far from Maui.

Ferngrove Inn was more stunning in real time than online, which is typically not the case, and I was happily surprised. The main house, resembling a Swiss chalet, sat at the base of an ancient redwood grove surrounded by an equally established fern-and-flower garden packed and still blooming with towering sunflowers, dahlias, blue and pink hydrangea, climbing yellow roses, and a mass of morning-glory vines.

"Wow," I said, wide-eyed as we pulled in.

Derby rolled down the window and leaned out. "Which one is ours?"

Alongside the main house sat a series of tiny yellow cabins with slanted, shingled roofs, each with its own tiny chimney and front porch. "Oh, who cares?" I said. "They're all so cute." I pulled into a parking spot as Derby instructed, "Get the cutest one, Mom. I'm gonna scoot."

I made my way toward the office door nearly engulfed in wisteria, while Derby pulled his Razor scooter and helmet out of the trunk and made his way to a high spot toward the back of the paved parking lot. He was wearing his favorite Hawaiian shirt, the one he reserved for all vacations, no matter the location, and I could easily spot him from a distance. I rang the bell and greeted the woman at the front desk, and before she could get her words out—"Welcome. Checking in?"—a blur of hibiscus print flashed past the office window. No more than five minutes later, I had room keys and a map of the enchanted grounds in hand, when Derby zoomed by the window again.

For the remainder of the afternoon, until the fog moved in and eclipsed the sun, Derby continued to delight in this simple outdoor activity, scooting down the forest hill at breakneck speed, waving wildly every time, happy to show off for me as I sat on our little porch, sipping chilled wine.

That night, we squeezed into an old double bed that creaked every time one of us moved. It was bothersome and also funny, and we made a game of it—lying as still as possible until, inevitably, one of us moved an elbow or an ankle and the bed gave us away.

"Whoever makes it creak next owes the other person five dollars," Derby challenged.

"No way I'm playing that game."

"C'mon, Mom, it'll be fun." He turned to face me in the darkening room. "Are you holding your breath?"

"Yep."

"You look constipated." He burst with laughter, more at his use of the word than at my expression, and the bed *creeeaaaaaaked*.

I smiled triumphantly. "You owe me five bucks."

"Noooo," he protested. "We didn't officially start the game yet. We have to do it again!"

The next day, we swam in the outdoor heated pool, sharing the rectangular space with an older couple and a family of four who kept to the shallow end. Due to Covid, the inn was operating at half capacity, which meant a maximum of eight guests and only three to four cabins in use at a time. It wasn't quite like sitting poolside in Maui, but it was a step up from the Slip 'N Slide in our side yard.

"What game do you want to play today?" I asked as we plunged into the deep end with the pink-and-white striped inner tubes I'd picked up at the local hardware store.

"Wet cat."

"What's that?"

Derby explained he was a cat that had fallen into a pool, and I was to rescue him and swim him over to the ladder before he drowned. I'd never heard of this game but I indulged him anyway. "Okay, how does it start?" He slipped out of his inner tube and began flailing around breathlessly treading water "Now, swim me over to the edge," he instructed. I secured him under the armpits and began kicking us to safety.

"Why are you making that face?" I asked when he glared at me with mad eyebrows. "Am I hurting you?"

"No, Mom." He rolled his eyes. "Wet cats are grumpy."

Later that afternoon, Gretta and Derby's cousins joined us for a surprise swim and birthday dinner. Gretta picked up pizza and a chocolate cake with candles, sodas for the kids, and a bottle of wine for us. As the sun began to fade, the kids played hide-and-seek, slinking behind redwoods and crouching behind sunflower stalks, while Gretta and I sat in the grape arbor under curling fall leaves and twinkle lights.

"How are you doing?" she asked.

"I'm really glad you're here," I said, and admitted, "It's kind of a sad birthday."

She topped off my wine. "I know, and I'm sorry. She should be here."

"Jenni called early his morning with my first birthday greeting of the day, and to rub it in that I was turning fifty. Usually, it was Mom who called first, all cheerful and bright, and when I realized she wouldn't be calling this year or next year, I thought, I no longer have a mother to watch me grow up."

Gretta looked at me with a shared understanding.

I took a sip of wine and watched the kids run past. "I wish it were different; I wish she were here, but the truth is that Derby is the kid. And I am the parent who gets to watch him grow up."

"That's sweet," Gretta said. "Even though what I think you're really saying is that it's time for us to start acting like adults."

"Hey, you can do whatever you want," I laughed. "I'm simply considering that maybe it's time for *me* to stop identifying so closely with the bereaved daughter bit and step into a more mature role. I am fifty, as Jenni pointed out."

Gretta held up her wine glass. "Cheers. To grown-ass women."

On the morning of our third day away, we packed up and left the forest for the coast, stopping several miles down the road in Monte Rio, where we found an unmarked path down to a hidden beach along the river, and where we ate turkey sandwiches and dipped our toes in the cool current. From there, we drove the narrow, shaded roads through Occidental and Freestone, passing through Valley Ford and then further west, toward Dillon Beach. I'd splurged on a coastal cabin with a view of the bay, and on this beach, unlike Bodega Head, Derby could run free like an unleashed golden retriever, splashing safely in the surf and diving into the thicket of tall dunes, and where when we wanted a break from the sun and the sand, we could wander into the bougie market up the road and order soft-serve salted-caramel ice cream cones and espresso drinks all afternoon.

That night, as he and I lay awake in the loft bedroom with a horizontal view of the water, I said, "Hey, buddy, did you have a good birthday?"

"It was okay."

"Next year, let's have a big party with lots of people."

He rolled over and faced me. "Did you have a good birthday?"

My heart tightened. "I did."

"You seem kind of sad."

I looked at him in the moonlight and decided not to lie. "I am sad. Not as sad as I was, and not sad all the time or the sick kind of sad, but the kind of sad when you miss someone. I missed having Mutti here on our birthdays, but"—I reached out and tousled his hair—"you know what I did love about my birthday?"

"What?"

"Being with you."

"Ugh, you say that every year."

"It's true, plus this year we got to swim in a warm pool in October and play 'squeak the bed' for five bucks. What more could I ask for?"

He rolled back toward the water with sleepiness in his voice. "Mom, you're so weird."

"Thanks, buddy."

"It wasn't a compliment."

I closed my eyes and smiled. My fiftieth was layered, kind of like a lemon cake, both sour and sweet. It was still worth eating, although chocolate was better.

* * *

"So how was it?" B asked the following week.

"I loved being with Derby, out in the world again without masks, breathing fresh ocean air, and at the same time, it was my first birthday without her, and a big one. I'm not sure if it was harder than the first Mother's Day or her August birthday. They all seem to be running together."

"The first year after losing someone you love is the hardest because you're experiencing so many things without them for the first time. The second year will be easier."

"If you say so, although it wasn't only that. Something weird happened. We were driving out toward the coast, and I went a different way than I usually go. The backroads of the West County all weave together and at one point, I thought I'd gotten us lost and the GPS wasn't working because of spotty service in the redwoods, and I kind of panicked."

"That you were lost?"

"Yes, but it was a bigger sense of lost. It was like lost-in-the-world lost, like I'm all alone and in charge here. I'm the adult. There's no higher-ranking adult above me to call. And what if we get in an accident, or I have a stroke while I'm driving? Who's gonna find us? I mean, who's coming for us? I started feeling skittish and fearful, and I didn't want Derby to catch on, I didn't want to freak *him* out, so I kept driving, praying I wouldn't black out and collapse on the steering wheel."

"I know what this is," B said. "The existential midlife moment."

"Is it the moment that directly precedes a stroke?"

"It's more apt to trigger an anxiety attack."

"Better, still not great."

"Listen, this is normal midlife stuff we didn't have to confront when our parents and our grandparents were still alive, when there were generations above us residing at the top. When we realize *we* are the top, and there is no longer a buffer, that we are as high as it goes on the family tree, and we're alone in the world in a way we never were before, it can create the kind of existential angst you're talking about. Most of us convinced ourselves that our parents would live forever, that they'd always be around, and until we experience the death of Mom and Dad, we're all still kids."

"Gretta and I were just talking about this! That maybe it's time to grow up."

"I hate to break it to you, but you are grown up. I think the difference this year is that you're being called to trust yourself, to trust you will not die without your mother. You can stand in this world on your own two feet, and you can mother yourself."

"Become my own matriarch?"

"Yes, why not, and who better? What do you need from her now that you cannot give yourself? Your mother is gone, but you have *you*. And you already know how to be a mother because you're one to Derby. There's no reason why you can't extend your own mothering to yourself."

"I'd always thought mothering was a top-down relationship, not a mothering-myself kind of deal."

"It's a new dynamic, but think about it," B said, his excitement mounting. "This is the moment when Sam the fifty-year-old walks eight-year-old Sammy back from the edge. This is the moment when Sam the adult gets into the driver's seat and takes the wheel, puts the pedal to the metal and drives little Sammy out of the Jack in the Box . . ."

"It always comes back to the cheeseburger."

"Hey, whenever I can work it in, but seriously, turning fifty represents an unraveling from old habits, old roles, and old stories. It's the midlife point for all of us, and it's a big opportunity for growth, not only for growing up, but for growing in all directions. Fifty is *big*. Welcome to adulthood."

To Clench or to Hold

"Welcome to adulthood," I recited in the mirror the next morning. As I took stock of my midlife face, I thought about what B had said, that fifty represents an unraveling from old habits and old stories, from who we were in our twenties, thirties, and forties. I resonated with this concept, yet one question loomed: Once I unravel, who will I be left with? I knew that my contemporaries, Jennifer Aniston, Tina Fey, and Lauren Graham had each crossed over this milestone a few years before me, so perhaps I would unravel into one of them, and that wouldn't be so bad. In the meantime, until my red-carpet metamorphosis, I supposed I could go ahead and make a few age-appropriate shifts to commemorate the new decade.

Shop for new bras. True confession: I still had a few holdovers from a decade ago.

Get a new haircut, one that didn't reflect a pandemic.

Invest in expensive skin serums, or something on sale from Sephora.

After completing my list, I recognized all items as vanity pursuits, but in my defense, hadn't I done enough inner work over the past eight months? Wasn't it time and didn't I deserve to obsess about my outsides? Wasn't that *big* enough? As I began rationalizing an afternoon spent shopping online and purging my closet, Jenni called with an announcement—the housing market was heating up, especially in Sonoma County where a large population of young professionals were migrating north from San Francisco and Silicon Valley, and where they could ride out the pandemic working from home with more square footage and fresh country air.

"Maybe it's time," Jenni said.

To sell our parents' house? This registered as an adult move, a significant and legitimately *big* event. I put overpriced serums on hold and agreed to meet my sisters in Sebastopol the following afternoon to discuss.

Since Mother's Day, we'd resumed our meetings on the side deck of our parents' house, getting together throughout the summer months to discuss the continuous Business of Dying, and to catch each other up on our separate lives. Today's agenda item was singular and pressing, so after taking our seats at the patio table with the red umbrella, I said what we were all thinking: "I will miss meeting here."

Jenni offered, "So, let's meet here as much as we can, while we still can."

"And how long do you think that will be?"

"The real-estate agent came by earlier this week to look at the yard," Gretta said. "She'll want to do some touch-up landscaping, but she thinks it's in pretty good shape.

The real-estate agent, a mutual friend we'd all known since junior high school and who'd always been a big fan of Mom and Klose, had become a successful Realtor in the area, and she'd generously offered to help us sell the house.

I looked beyond our table at a few late-blooming roses and a cluster of pink hydrangea. In early October, the leaves on the

Meyer lemon tree were bright green, as was the wisteria vine that wound its way up the porch railing. The only sign of fall color were the fanned leaves of the ginkgo tree—not quite there but hinting towards brilliant yellow. I felt similarly to how I did when Jenni first introduced the idea of selling the house in February. I was saddened by the idea of losing accessibility, not only because it was our family retreat, but also because it was all we had left of them, on a physical level, anyway. Even though I knew better, even though I knew they were no longer residing in the shadows of the house any more than Mom was haunting the cliffs of Bodega Head, I could still feel them both here. Sitting out on their deck, pouring wine in their kitchen, or thumbing through old issues of *The Atlantic* allowed me a little more time with them.

I well understood this trick I played on myself—the purple toes, the forwarded mail, the untouched house—all physical representations that helped fill a void. The house created a false sense of their presence, yet I knew their absence was real. Klose was not positioned in his favorite chair, watching the news, and Mom wasn't sing-songing in the side yard. For seven months, the house had been standing vacant, and the real-estate agent felt strongly that if we acted now, we'd sell quickly and make a generous profit.

"What landscaping does she want to do?" I asked. "I hope she won't want to get rid of Mom's geraniums." I motioned to a cluster of oversized pots filled with the Patriot red varietal. "Although, if she does, I'm happy to take them off her hands."

Gretta perked up and pointed toward the window. "In that case, I've got dibs on Daddy's bird feeders."

And that was how it began. The dismantling of a home.

* * *

We agreed a systematic approach was the only way to tackle two stories full of belongings; everything either had to go to someone or somewhere. We wiped clean the whiteboard and started mapping the materials in question. Items marked with blue tape were for things we wanted. Donation boxes for books, CDs, clothes, tools, towels, and linens were marked separately for Goodwill, hospice, and the local homeless and women's shelters. Smaller piles were created for items that friends and family had specifically requested—the *Je suis Charlie* artwork for a friend in Denver, the painting of the Dordogne for a neighbor, Klose's corduroy and motorcycle jackets for his brother. Larger furniture pieces, like the antique banquet, the marble side table, and the art deco glass lamp were tagged by the real-estate agent to remain in place for staging the house. We would have less than a month to box up and remove everything we wanted before the professional home organizer would arrive with her cleanup crew to pack up and haul out whatever remained. We understood that the Organizer could save us a lot of work by doing the preliminary sorting and labeling for us. "For an additional fee, I can take care of it all and you won't have to trouble with any of it," she explained. We appreciated the offer, but we'd declined.

"It should be us who initially decides where their things go, don't you agree?" I asked my sisters at our next Sunday-afternoon meeting.

"Absolutely." Jenni said. "To anyone else, it's just stuff. We know the story behind everything in the house, and we know what was most important to them."

"And I want to spend the extra time going through it." Gretta pulled a Graham Greene book from the shelf. "It's important to me."

Where the Organizer would have happily saved us the work of combing through the bathroom and the basement, the hall closets and the silverware drawers, we mutually agreed that packing up the more neutral rooms first would help to ease us into the entirety of the job.

"Not as emotional," is what I'd said.

Jenni and I started in the bathroom, and within a few minutes, we were laughing over our discoveries. "Five unopened tubes of hydrocortisone cream in one drawer," Jenni mused. "Is there something else they weren't telling us?"

"Oh, Jesus." I rolled my eyes. "Please, no more secrets."

Jenni worked her way to the back of the drawer. "Oh, and looky here, someone was stockpiling TUMS."

I'd been in this bathroom more times than I could count, but I'd never looked so closely at its contents, and here we were, combing through it inch by inch and drawing conclusions about our parents' personal habits and hygiene. I was wrong to think that emptying their bathroom would be impersonal. A bathroom reveals the private details of a person's life, it identifies a daily routine unique to the user, and I could easily see Mom reflected in the bathroom mirror, fussing with her hair and leaning forward to apply her favorite L'Oréal lipstick. I was wrong to think that packing it up would be unemotional, and as I left Jenni at the sink and climbed into their tub, I regretted throwing away their last sliver of soap, still stuck to the bottom of its dedicated dish. I hesitated with the half-empty bottles of shampoo and conditioner and the towels hanging from hooks on the wall. It somehow felt wrong to deconstruct their well-worn lives.

They'd custom-designed and paid handsomely for their recessed tub with the lapis-colored tiles, and it was "well worth it," confirmed my mother, who loved to indulge in a midday soak. The long, rectangular design was equally appealing to Derby and his cousins, who fought to squeeze in together and sink to its deep bottom. Frequently, after family dinners, Klose would turn the faucets on high and declare: "Bath time!" and the kids would strip naked and begin a chase around the house. "Wrong way!" Klose would redirect as they rushed past him into the back bedroom, shrieking. "This way," he'd point as they ran in the opposite direction. It was a popular bit, one that lasted for several minutes, until the kids tired out and filed dutifully into the bathroom, jumping into the tub and laughing hysterically as water splashed over the sides. I smiled at the memory, then felt hollowed by it. This process introduced a new layer of finality, of days gone by, impossible to retrieve or recreate.

"I think I need to move into another room," I said to Jenni. "This one's getting to me."

Jenni nodded. "I'm almost done. Only one more drawer of Band-Aids and mystery multivitamins to go."

I joined Gretta in the kitchen as she was stacking dishes on the counter. I moved to the cabinets above the stove and started in on the spice shelves, pulling out a clear jelly jar filled with red pepper flakes. I stopped. How many times had I watched Mom pinch a generous helping onto the pasta dish she was making? Beyond garlic and basil, this was her go-to spice. "Can I please have this?" I turned to Gretta, holding up the jar.

"If I can I have this." She held up a coffee mug that said World's Greatest Dad. "I gave it to him."

Jenni appeared in the doorway, interrupting our exchange. We froze with items in hand. "I'm taking the red chili flakes," I confessed.

"And I have Daddy's mug."

"You little thieves."

"What do you want?" Gretta grabbed a stack of mismatched dish towels off the counter. "We have plenty of these."

"Nice try, but I don't want their old rags. I would, however, like to take that." She pointed to the square wooden island on wheels that Klose made when we all moved in together in 1978.

"Hmm." I looked over at Gretta with a conspiring grin. "Only if you also take all the knives in the top drawer."

"That's right," Gretta said. "The dull knife collection goes with you."

"How about I take one dull knife, the dullest, and the cleanup crew can have the rest?"

"Deal."

After our first full day of sorting and packing, the three of us collapsed on the couch.

"It feels weird," I said. "Packing up their lives."

"We grew up with so much of this," Jenni said. "I mean, really, how long have they had that bookshelf?"

"That bookshelf predates IKEA. That's how long." My eyes landed on the spine of *African Queen,* the 1951 Hollywood classic with Katharine Hepburn and Humphrey Bogart that we watched as a family every year.

"We're not only packing up *their* lives," Jenni said quietly. "We're packing up our childhood."

That was the reason why we had to do it. To leave this job for someone else would have felt negligent, as if we were allowing strangers to burglarize our house and steal our past.

"At some point, before we pack up too much," Gretta said, "I think we should invite the kids to come pick something for themselves. They haven't been to the house since . . ." She sighed. "Well, since Susan died, and we're packing up a big piece of their childhoods too. They'll want to see these things again before they're gone."

On the drive home that evening, I wondered if we were doing the right thing by selling. Was it too late to change course and keep the house in the family? We'd entertained the idea early on, and Gretta concluded it wasn't big enough for her family of four and Jenni already had a house one town over that she didn't want to leave.

"You and Derby could live here. It's the perfect size for two people," they'd both suggested.

I'd considered it. They were right that it was a good fit for Derby and me, and while I loved the house, I worried that living in it would prove difficult, that I would long for Mom even more if I inhabited her vacant space, especially during the days and nights when Derby was with his dad and I was alone. What would it be like, I wondered, to move throughout these rooms? I imagined a cinematic scene where I dressed myself in Mom's full-length mink coat, wandered from room to room in red lipstick, becoming like the reclusive, tragic daughter, Edith Beale, from the documentary *Grey Gardens*. Mom would laugh at this mock image of me, although she'd be quick to point out that Little Edie and Big Edie lived together as a mother-and-daughter pair, refusing to leave the estate and each other, even after it fell into horrid disrepair. It was only when her mother died that Little Edie sold the house and left. I wasn't sure of her reasons why, but I imagined they mirrored my own: I couldn't live in my mother's house if she was no longer there.

⋆ ⋆ ⋆

"Well, it's finally happening," I said to B on Wednesday. "We're selling the house. And let me tell you, what an undertaking. We spent an entire day boxing up the bathroom and only one portion of the kitchen."

"That's some heavy lifting," B empathized.

"I'll admit that part of me wants to keep the house and everything in it as it is, just as they left it, like a shrine or a museum I could visit forever. And if the mortgage was paid off, we'd probably keep it."

"You could charge an admission fee to friends and extended family to offset the monthly payments."

I laughed. "Not a bad idea, but I know selling is the right thing to do. It's a sad thing, though."

"It's another ending. And closure is important, not only

for you and your sisters, but also for your mom and stepdad. Physical material holds energy, and that extends to their personal belongings. Their stuff grounds them in this world, so you help to release them by tying up their loose ends, by giving their things away, by moving them out of the house. It's an act of generosity to bring closure to their lives. Think of it as, *you're welcome*, not *I'm sorry I'm giving away your outdated CD collection*."

"For sure the CDs will go, but we're not giving everything away."

"Of course, you'll want to keep some things."

"So far it's only red chili flakes."

"A curious choice, and I'm sure you have your reasons. Moving forward, notice what you pick up. It will be tempting to pocket things, many things, and I would caution you to be mindful of what you take. If you don't set boundaries, you'll transfer their energy into your own home."

* * *

The following Saturday, as my sisters and I continued the work of going through every cabinet, shelf, box, and drawer, reconciling every napkin, greeting card, bottle of ibuprofen, packet of TUMS, pot holder, and thumbtack on the wall, I noticed how easy it was to cling to and wrap around certain things, for instance: a wooden figurine of the "Man at the Wheel," a gift from New England Nancy, who loved to send knickknacks from the North Shore. The six-inch figure that was likely bought in the famous seafaring town of Gloucester looked like a first cousin of the bearded man in the yellow rain slicker from the Gorton's fish-stick commercials. I picked it up because it reminded me of all my trips back East with Mom, and because she loved it even though it was tacky, and because it had sat on her kitchen windowsill for as long as I could remember. I stashed the fisherman in my bag and continued the slow process of sifting, organizing, labeling, and discarding.

Later that evening, after I returned home and positioned "Gorty" at the helm of my own kitchen sink, I immediately questioned my decision. He didn't fit on the windowsill, nor on my mantel, or on my office bookshelf, or anywhere. Gorty was out of place in my own home because, *dummy*, I would have never bought this figurine for myself! And why, I asked myself now, was I adding someone else's knickknacks to my own mantel? At some point, and hopefully much later than sooner, Derby would have to do the same for me. He'd be the adult child confronted with a houseful of his late mother's stuff, and did I really want to anchor him to a wooden fisherman in a yellow coat?

"Sorry, Gorty," I said to the figurine, "but you don't belong here." I stuffed him back in my bag with the intention of returning it, which I did the next visit, except I swapped it out for something else I didn't need: a Venetian carnival mask in the shape of a cat face with wire whiskers. I brought the mask home, only to declare, again, this is not me. I returned it in exchange for a Pennsylvania-Dutch hand-painted dish of a man on a green tractor that, once unpacked, I flatly rejected. I did this again and again. I brought home their faded yellow-and-white striped duvet cover and returned it. I brought home their red coffee thermos and returned it. And finally, I brought home Mom's flannel pajamas with the periwinkle print and knew as soon as I slid them into my own dresser drawer: I will never be able to wear these. They belong to her.

* * *

"I don't know how to do this," I said to B, explaining my back-and-forth dilemma.

"If you don't discern what you take and what you leave behind, your mother will continue to be everywhere, overshadowing your life, so I commend you for taking all those things back. Also, keep in mind that if everything is special, then nothing is special. So, as you go through the house, notice what is most meaningful and special to you, and leave the rest."

"That's the problem. It all seems special until I get it home."

"Okay, then try this: When you pick something up, notice if you clench it or if you're able to simply hold it."

"As Derby would say, 'what's the diff'?"

"When we hold something tightly, it communicates a resistance to let go, but when we can hold something loosely, in the open palm of our hand, there is more freedom, more release. The next time you pick something up that you think you want to keep, notice how you hold it in your hand, and ask yourself: Why am I holding onto this? Is it to hold *onto her*? Am I clenching it tightly because I'm afraid to let her go, because I want to freeze her in time, or am I taking this because it holds a happy memory, and having it brings me joy?"

I recalled taking Mom's Cabochard perfume several months ago. That was definitely a white-knuckle moment, and I was entitled to at least one of those, right? Because that perfume was *mine*, and I had no intention of bringing it back.

"I'll try it," I promised B, and the next trip to the house, I considered the subtle distinction—to clutch or to hold?—as I confronted Mom's office.

Before Mom and Klose moved into the house, they'd paid for the construction of a small studio in the backyard that served as his-and-her writing offices. Mom's was on the north side and Klose's was on the south, and you could pass between the two through an antique swinging saloon door. I'd left her office untouched until now because it was so distinctly her space, and also because it was an overwhelming task. It was filled with hundreds of books by mostly female and feminist-leaning authors, along with stacks of her own. There were magazines, newspaper clippings, framed photographs crammed on every shelf, and quotes and arty postcards tacked to the walls. A calendar of Paris bookshops hung frozen on the month of February and an NPR tote bag full of empty notebooks and Sharpie pens had been tossed, as if only yesterday, into a chair. Two metal filing cabinets and half a dozen full file boxes sat along the back wall, and on her desk that looked out onto the back garden, she'd left an empty coffee cup, along with a stack of hand-edited pages, Post-its with computer passwords were scattered here and there, and a list of phone calls to return.

Mom had written countless columns, at least two books, and a stage play in this space, and I considered it sacred. It was the one room I had not entered since That Day, and I stood in the middle of it now, engulfed in the past, unsure what to keep and what to let go. I felt burdened by the weight of boxing it all up and lugging it home. My own office was cramped already, but if I didn't take it, then what would become of it? I struggled with its likely resting place: her lifetime of work tossed into the recycling bin. I slunk down on the floor and attempted a calming breath. *Notice when you are clenching, holding tightly, wanting to freeze her in time.*

Three hours later, after sifting through dozens of folders and picking things up and putting them back down, I landed on a minimalist approach. I took a quote by Virginia Wolf and another by Joan Didion that she'd written on index cards and tacked to the wall; her copy of Anne Lamott's *Bird by Bird* and Natalie Goldberg's *Writing Down the Bones;* and because I couldn't reasonably lug them all home, I randomly selected one full file box of her old columns, printed out and marked up by her own pen. In her bedroom, I chose the antique rhinestone pin that was Grandma Helen's and that Mom wore every Christmas Eve, and from the kitchen I took her bright yellow teakettle and a selection of her favorite teas. There were other things, too—an iconic sidewalk café scene painted by San Francisco artist Maurie Lapp; a bright blue bowl that I'd given her one birthday and had always coveted for myself; a leopard-print Le Bag that was back, or surely soon to be back, in style; and finally, I took her white binder full of *Fantastic (mostly) Recipes*. After I brought it all home, I was pleased to discover everything fit well in my space without becoming a copycat of her space. It blended in and felt true to me, while also reminding me of Mom, of our life together and of happier times.

⋆ ⋆ ⋆

The following weekend, I brought Derby along with me, gently warning him on the drive over, "The house is going to look a lot different from the last time you were in it. Mutti and Grandaddy are gone, you know that, and we've also started packing up their things. It might look empty, and if you don't like it, we can leave, okay?"

"Okay." He nodded solemnly. "Will the cousins be there?"

"Not today. It's just you and me. I plan to spend a couple of hours packing, and you can help me or you can look around and take a few things if you'd like, things that mean something to you."

"The TV?" His interest piqued.

"I was thinking something smaller, something that reminds you of them."

"Grandaddy loved watching the news."

This was an indisputable fact, and still, "Something smaller," I repeated. "Something you don't find in every home."

Derby entered the house similarly to how I had many months ago. Quietly, carefully, with trepidation. His eyes wandered around the lifeless living room that was filled with boxes and packing tape, and at the now-bare walls that were once crowded with photography and artwork.

He looked up at me. "This is kind of sad."

I ran my hand over his head. "I know, buddy, it is."

I expected he might ask to leave, but he surprised me by bravely walking forward into the house and declaring over his shoulder, "I'm going to start in the guest room, and then go down to the basement."

"Okay," I encouraged. "Let me know what you find."

Derby found two crystal goblets and a sterling silver Queen Anne decorative serving tray that I'd not seen in my lifetime. Mom was informal; she served tea on whatever napkin was lying around and drained her tea bag directly into her cup.

"Where'd you find those?" I asked when he proudly presented them.

"In the basement. Can I have them?"

"Where are you going to put all of that?"

"On my bookshelf," he said as if it were obvious. "With my other antiques."

After an hour in the basement, he seemed to have forgotten all about the TV, and I wasn't about to remind him. "Okay, if that's what you want, they're yours."

"And also, this." He pulled on the strap of a leather messenger bag slung low across his chest.

"Hey, that's what Grandaddy took to the newsroom every day." I unzipped the weathered front pocket and peered inside. "Look, one of his old reporter's notebooks. And his pens." I pulled one out, rolled it between my fingers. "Insisted on a felt tip, nothing else would do."

"So . . ." He nudged me toward an answer. "Can I have it?" The heavy bag tugged on his small frame and the strap was too long. Where most kids would prefer a designer backpack, Derby wanted this.

"Sure." I smiled. "He would love for you to have it."

After another thirty minutes of boxing up old pots and pans and silverware that didn't match, I called from the kitchen: "Okay, I think that does it for today. Wherever you are, let's get ready to go."

Derby slowly emerged from the bedroom, cupping something in the palm of his hand.

"Mommy," he asked faintly. "Can I also have this?"

"What is it?"

He opened his fingers to reveal a tiny ceramic bird, a little house finch with a red breast.

"That's cute. Where'd you find that?"

"On Mutti's dresser. It was in a basket of jewelry. Its wing is broken."

"Oh," I said, leaning in to look. "It is broken, isn't it?"

"I'll fix it," he insisted. "Can I have it?"

I looked into his tender, earnest face and thought, *Baby, what's broken here is not yours to fix,* but since he wasn't clenching the tiny bird, he was holding it in his open palm, I acquiesced. "Yes, you can have it."

That night, Derby stuffed his pajamas, a pair of clean underwear, and a copy of *Diary of a Wimpy Kid* into Klose's leather newsroom bag and said, "I'll use this for sleepovers." He then retreated to his desk with a tube of super glue to mend Mom's bird wing. As he waited for it to set and dry, I boiled water in the yellow kettle and set out two cups. I'd taken the kettle because it matched my own kitchen, and because Mom and I liked to drink tea together. In fact, I only ever drank tea at her house, most often during an evening visit where we snuggled together on the couch and watched *Call the Midwife* or some other PBS series. Since she'd died, I'd stuck strictly to my morning coffee, but tonight I bravely pulled two bags of Sleepytime out of the nearly empty box I'd taken from her kitchen cabinet and called to Derby, "I'm making tea!" He soon joined me at the kitchen island and stirred in two drippy spoonsful of honey.

"Are you drinking tea or drinking honey?" I teased.

"Mom!" he said with sudden excitement. "You know what would go perfect with this?" He dropped his spoon before I could answer and ran back to his bedroom and returned with the platter.

As we sat on the couch, watching an episode of *Modern Family* and sipping from tea cups that we carried in on Derby's treasured find, already shined with a thick slather of Goddard's silver polish that he'd unearthed from the back of the linen closet, I missed Mom in the room with us, and when Derby laughed and spilled a mouthful of honey down the front of his T-shirt, I understood we were carrying a tradition forward. We were ritualizing loss by giving it new life.

⋆ ⋆ ⋆

It had been a full four weeks since we'd started, and true to form, my sisters and I had *gotten it done*. Except for the pieces that the real-estate agent wanted for staging, the house was empty as we gathered one last time on the side deck.

"I brought this," Gretta announced to our family of five adults, three kids, and two dogs. "It's one of their old coffee cans that I filled with photos of them, an old baseball they used to throw to Olivia, a couple of Daddy's pens, his favorite yo-yo, and a rock from Susan's collection. I thought we could dig a hole and bury it as a tribute to their life here."

"It's like a time capsule," one of the kids said. "We did this at school."

"Where should we bury it?"

"I was thinking in the front garden," Gretta said and I suggested, "Under the persimmon tree."

Gretta's husband was elected "digger," and after he broke through three feet of solid ground, we stood in a loose circle and dropped in the can. After it was buried, Gretta kissed her hand and touched it to the loose ground. Jenni and I followed her lead, then one of the kids broke the silence. "Is it time for pizza yet?"

We ate off paper plates and drank wine from glasses we brought from our own homes. It would have been an unremarkable meal, except it was our last one together in this spot, the one where we'd shared countless meals. I quickly did the math. We'd gathered here as a family for nearly thirty years, and while I knew I'd see the house again since Miriam lived over the fence, I would likely not enter it. After it sold, it would no longer be theirs. It would no longer be ours. That door would close.

I broke from the group as the sun began its descent behind the redwood tree to take pictures of the red umbrella, the planter boxes filled with purple petunias, and the blue gate at the front. I gazed upward at the redwood tree, searching for the owl box that Klose made from plywood and straight nails. He'd climbed an extension ladder to perch it between two high branches, and I prayed the new owners wouldn't tear the whole thing down. I looked around at what Mom and Klose had built, not only owl boxes and sitting benches and a garden of flowers and herbs, but a life that had meant something to a large community of people. I wondered if they were here with us now, visiting from another time zone, dropping in to thank us for releasing them from their outdated collection of Frommer's travel guides and foreign-language pocket dictionaries. I was enjoying my mystical moment of closure when Jenni pulled me and Gretta aside with worry. "I'm already kicking myself for all the stuff the cleanup crew hauled away. They probably donated most of it to the local Goodwill. Maybe we should go find it and buy it all back."

* * *

"It's done. Three offers, and the house sold in a week."

B whistled. "California real estate."

"We went through everything—files, drawers, cabinets. We literally touched every piece of clothing, every plate, every book, every bottle in the medicine cabinet, and now it's all gone."

"How do you feel?"

"There's some relief," I admitted. "And also, I feel worn out."

"Unwinding someone's life is energetically heavy, and you did it for *two* people. I bet you do feel worn out. Your body will need some time to process the work you've just done, which is what I want to talk to you about." He paused.

"Yes?"

"You know that my wife, Ariela, works with grief too?"

"Vaguely."

"I take a cognitive approach to creating pathways for healing, and Ariela is a sematic intuitive healer. She works with moving the energy of grief through the body. This is an important next piece for you because ultimately, you want to feel better, not think better. You'd really benefit from a session with her."

"Wait a minute." I stopped him. "Are you breaking up with my grief? Are *you* ghosting me too?"

The Darkest Night of the Year

Ariela HaLevi answered on the first ring. "Baruch said you might call. I'm so glad you did." Her voice had grounded resonance like B's, although it was less direct, softer.

"I'm not sure how much you know about my story," I began. "Or how much B has told you."

"I only know you've been working together. I don't know details. We share a marriage." She laughed lightly. "But it doesn't extend to client confidentiality."

I gave Ariela an abridged version of the past ten months, highlighting the main events: suicide, stark solitude, my seeking resolve and a new sense of self. "I think that's about it."

"Well, that's enough," she said with palpable warmth. "I lost my mom too. Three years ago. I've been where you are, and the wound from losing our mothers runs deep. On top of that, your mother's act of suicide created an additional trauma in your body, a huge hit on your nervous system."

I remembered back to the initial shock. It had felt like I'd been hit by a truck.

"Our bodies often hold onto grief and trauma. It can physically get stuck and stagnate in our bodies, and so what I help people to do is move it through the body, out of the cells, so you can heal."

Trauma stagnating in my cells? That didn't sound good. "On a scale of one to five, how worried should I be?"

"You're going to be okay," she reassured. "No need to panic. It's a process, and today I want to start with a simple body-scan exercise to identify where you're holding heavy emotion in your body. A lot of the time, we don't actually know how our bodies are feeling because we're so stuck in our heads."

I couldn't disagree that a disproportionate amount of my attention was focused above my neck.

"Close your eyes," Ariela said, as if she were tucking me into bed, "and feel into your body. Is there an area that feels tight or heavy, constricted or in pain?"

I took a deep breath and thought about it.

"Try not to think about it," she interrupted, as if reading my thoughts. "*Feel* into your body."

I took another deep breath. "My chest," I said. "It feels heavy."

"Good. Anywhere else?"

"My jaw," I said, once I realized I was clenching it. "And my neck, it's always tight, like I'm being strangled."

"Good," she said. "Anywhere else?"

I took another deep breath and stretched out my fingers. "My hands. I tend to clench them. B's been working with me on that."

"This is great awareness," she congratulated me. "Okay, now I'd like to walk you through a visualization exercise you can do any time on your own to help you unlock the grief and trauma being held in those parts of your body."

I eased back against the couch cushions.

"Close your eyes again and take a few deep breaths. Feel into your heart, the fourth chakra, the seat of love. It makes sense that you feel a heaviness here, a protectiveness after losing your mom. Your heart is vulnerable and scared. You're learning how to parent and protect yourself in the aftermath of her leaving, and . . ."—she paused to underscore—"it's also a scary time in the world. So many of us have turned inward to keep ourselves safe from sickness and fear, and if we aren't careful, we can close in on ourselves to the point of shutting down. I want you to imagine a flower blooming in your heart center. Can you pick a flower?"

"Uh," I stumbled. "A rose?"

"Perfect. Imagine a rose blooming in your heart, and as you breathe in its wonderful scent, imagine it spreading love and kindness throughout your entire body, and as you breathe it out, you extend love and kindness to others."

I really wanted to open my eyes and take notes, but I had the Spidey sense that Ariela would catch me in the act. I opened one eye and quickly shut it.

"Next, let's move up to your throat. I can feel the tightness too. Wow, it's like your vocal cords are about to explode. This is the fifth chakra, the center of communication, and when it's blocked, we cannot find our voice, speak our truth. Imagine another flower blooming here, releasing its grip on your neck."

"California poppy," I said without hesitating this time. It was an obvious choice; their bright orange blooms are loud and impossible to ignore.

"Perfect, and now let's move outward to your hands. Open your palms and imagine rich soil growing there, the symbol of new life." She paused, grew quiet. I held my hands open and waited. "Okay, now you can open your eyes. How was that?"

"Good. Different. It took me a minute to get out of my head."

"It's a different practice from what you do with Baruch," she acknowledged, "and it's a good time to introduce it. As we head toward the darkest time of the year, the winter solstice, your body is calling you to move through your pain and grow something different. In the days and weeks ahead, make a practice of growing your garden. When you notice your hands are clenched, when you're holding tight to control, open your palms and imagine heaping handfuls of rich soil. Imagine being vulnerable to new life. When your throat tightens, when you find yourself pushing up against other people's voices and start to lose your own, loosen the vines around your neck and invite your poppies to grow wild. When your heart constricts or grows heavy, imagine that blooming rose in the center of your chest. As we close out this year, there is still a lot of uncertainty and fear out there, but shutting off and shutting in is not healthy for any of us. What if opening the windows and doors to your heart was the key to feeling safe, less isolated and alone?"

What if? I had no answer.

She continued, "Embrace the stillness of winter and this dark time of reflection. Invite yourself to listen to your body, to the whispers inside and underneath. Listen for a new voice. Not your clients' or your mom's, but yours. What does she say? Listen to the whispers of your soul. They're at the root of your healing."

As it was after my first session with B, Ariela's soothing words left me feeling better than before our call, although her suggestion was provoking. Could I really grow a garden within the confines of my middle-aged body? Could my soul act as a soil booster that inspired wild growth? I thought back to the raised bed in the corner of my yard that was crumbly old dirt until I scattered a packet of seeds and raked them in.

That night, as I lay awake in the dark, I imagined the outline of my body as the edges of a planter box that held me safely within. At first try, my unruly mind drew the perimeter of an old wooden casket sitting heavy in the hard dirt until I intentionally reconfigured the shape. I extended the edges in all directions and turned the soil over until it was rich and dark, ideal for planting. I took several deep breaths, as instructed, and willed my spirit to untangle itself and grow. As sleep encroached, I remembered the last thing Ariela had said before we'd ended the call: When you take sanctuary within yourself, the world can be falling apart around you and you will be okay.

A Holiday to Remember

The following morning, it was there. A tall and slender green stalk with a delicate white flower blooming at its tippy-top. The single stem was reaching upward out of the window box that, along with the potted geraniums, I'd taken from Mom and Klose's yard.

"Look at that!"

I'd stashed the weathered box in a corner of my patio, certain the soil was dormant, and now a narcissus had arrived, signaling, not only the early days of December, but also apparently my internal growth. *Dang, visualization was fast-acting.* I smiled at the surprise arrival before I understood its alternative symbolism—if the Naked Lady was Mom's birthday flower, the narcissus was her favorite holiday varietal, which meant another first was right around the corner: Christmas minus Mom.

"I love the holidays," I said to B on Wednesday. "But I almost don't want to deal with them this year."

"Then don't," he said, if it were that easy.

"I have Derby to think about."

"True, and you're not the only parent who would rather not

deal with the holidays. Why do you think we eat and drink, overspend, and busy ourselves so much around this time of year? It's called avoidance. Avoiding people who are no longer here. Avoiding people who are still here. Avoiding ourselves. For a lot of people, it's a deeply painful time, and I say this to validate how you're feeling, and also to challenge you. Rather than avoid it, what if you went into it? Allowed yourself to feel what's painful?"

"Your wife is encouraging me to release the pain."

He laughed. "Using our modalities against each other. Maybe I shouldn't have introduced you, after all. Well, I'm certain she'd agree you can't release it until you feel it, and that won't happen by binge-watching holiday movies and eating plates of fudge. If you want to come out of this holiday feeling better than going into it, and not repeat the grief next year and the year after, then you have to sink into it."

"Sounds festive."

"It doesn't have to be dark. Give Derby the lights, the sweets, and the magic, and while you're creating that for him, can you also give yourself what you need?"

"I'm not sure what I need. I only know I can't pretend it's Christmas as usual."

"Then what if you engaged in the aspects of the holiday that felt right this year, and disengaged from the things that don't? That's not avoidance. That's called intentionality, when your choices are a true reflection of what you need. Being clear-eyed about skipping something because you're not ready for it is different than unconsciously avoiding it. Make sense?"

After we hung up, I made a list of holiday traditions that felt good, or good-*ish*, to engage in this year:

- Get a tree and decorate it.
- Play Christmas music (with the exception of all versions of "Joy to the World" and "Silent Night").

- Host Christmas Eve dinner.
- Bake cookies (probably, maybe).

Next, I made a list of long-standing holiday traditions I did not want to engage in because I didn't feel either willing or ready:

- Overly accommodate others (unwilling).
- Wear a smile when I don't feel merry (unwilling).
- Watch *The Snowman*, Mom's favorite winter movie (not ready).
- Attend any production of *The Nutcracker* (over it).

Finally, I made a short list of what I needed this year:

- Permission to cry into a fruitcake or a peppermint mocha.
- Permission to lie on my couch in between Christmas morning and Christmas dinner.

This last one felt important to me. I frequently spent the entirety of Christmas Day driving from one house to the next to see every family member who lived locally, followed by lengthy phone calls to family out of state. This tradition dated back decades, to the first Christmas after my parents divorced, and while I'd developed a muscle for visiting Mom's house, Dad's house, grandparents, and aunts and uncles in between, I found it exhausting and performative. What if I gave myself permission to stay put this year? To give myself a few hours in the middle of the day to reclaim this time for me?

As the days drew closer to the twenty-fifth, I felt good about my plan. Excited, even. I'd cleared it with Derby's dad and the rest of the family, and to my surprise, they'd easily granted my request. I was grateful, suspecting I wouldn't be able to play the "dead mom" card next year without some amount of push-back, so I held firm to my blackout hours: No visits or visitors between noon and four on Christmas Day.

On Christmas Eve, however, my door would swing wide open. Since our Sonoma County pod had elected to receive the first Covid vaccine, it now seemed safe to resume the tradition of gathering under one roof. In past years, Derby's dad and I had hosted the holiday dinner, serving a hearty soup or a stew, loaves of fresh bread, and countless bottles of wine. The party started early, usually around five o'clock, when Klose, who was punctual on a regular day, arrived first. He'd show up with his twelve-foot-long collapsible table that we needed to elongate ours, and after hauling it up the flight of stairs to the main room, he'd inevitably look around and say, "Where is everyone? Let's get this show on the road." Once the rest of the party arrived, we'd sit together as a family, eating and drinking for hours, and after the table was cleared, Derby and his cousins would slip into holiday-themed jammies and pile in front of the TV, eating handfuls of See's Candies straight from the box.

Last year, Klose was markedly absent, but Mom was still here, and she arrived early wearing Helen's antique pin and her beautiful smile, and we opened a bottle of wine and stood together in the kitchen stirring soup. "To my man," she said. "And to us," I toasted back.

* * *

For as long as we'd hosted the event, Derby had declared Christmas Eve his "favorite day of the year."

"Why do you love it so much?" I asked him on the eve of the upcoming eve.

"Because everyone will be together in our house." He looked at me and corrected quietly, "most everyone."

"Well, your dad will be here, and Miriam and her family, and your aunties and their families, and their dogs will be here too. It'll still be a party. And I thought we could do something to honor those who aren't here."

"Like what?"

"Well, you know how Granddaddy was kind of 'whatever' about Christmas, and Mutti was *really* into it?"

"Oh, yeah, what was that thing he always said once all the presents were opened?"

"He'd stand and announce: 'Well, that's another Christmas under our belts. Let's clean up!' Then he'd pull out a garbage bag and start collecting all the wrapping paper off the floor—most of it recycled newspaper—and the room would be picked up in less than five minutes, I think because he was quietly cleaning up the whole time we opened gifts. And then Mutti would sing, 'Oh, Klose, don't be such a Grinch,' and she'd skip into the kitchen for more coffee and brandy."

"And what's your idea for this year?" Not unlike his grandfather, Derby was eager to get to the point.

"I want us to make memory ornaments to give everyone tomorrow night."

"No, not a craft project," he groaned.

"Oh, come on. You used to like doing stuff like this. Go get your colored pens and the glitter."

He reluctantly pushed up from his chair and headed off to his room, and when he returned to the table, I was waiting with paper, scissors, and string.

"We'll cut out little snowflakes and decorate them. Then we'll write a memory on each one, things Mutti loved about Christmas."

"What about Granddaddy?"

"We'll stash a garbage bag near the tree."

"Okay, fine." He sighed and plopped down in his chair.

Despite his initial resistance, he soon rallied and cut out twelve snowflakes that he sprinkled with blue glitter. I wrote *Remember* at the top of each one and he filled in the memories:

Remember,
Winter walks in the fog
The dance of the Snow Queen
Boeuf Bourguignon
The smell of narcissus
Hot brandy and a book
Ribbon candy
Remember,
To host your friends and neighbors
To give to those in need
To make snow angels
To sing out loud in church
To light a candle for someone you love
Remember,
It's a wonderful life.

On Christmas Eve, after a hearty helping of Brazilian beef stew and several bottles of red zinfandel and mixed chocolates and new jammies for the kids, Derby and I passed out the paper ornaments for everyone to hang on the tree, and after the crowd departed at ten, I crawled into bed, drowsy and contented. Derby woke me up an hour later. "Mom." He tapped me on the shoulder and whispered, "I can't sleep." He crawled in next to me and put his head on my pillow. I kept my eyes closed, pretending to be asleep, and he tapped me again. "Mom, wake up. I can't sleep."

I wrapped my arms around him and mumbled, "Close your eyes and sleep here with me, then."

He cuddled close and settled in, and five minutes later, "I still can't sleep."

"Honey," I pleaded. "You must try. Santa can't come until you're asleep."

Like many kids, Derby's sleep pattern was disrupted on

Christmas Eve by eager anticipation and, in his case, half a pound of See's Candies. I had learned from previous years that it took him significantly longer to fall asleep on the twenty-fourth than on a typical night, and I had to wait him out before stashing gifts from Santa under the tree. In fact, through years of trial and error, I'd learned the safest bet was to go to bed at the same time as him, and set my alarm for *much later*, when I could slip out of bed and quietly position unwrapped gifts without him waking and me getting caught. Midnight was too early—I'd heard him stumbling out of bed for "a drink of water" around that time—and five in the morning was too late since he'd likely be bright-eyed by then. After several close calls over the years, I'd discovered that three a.m. was the optimal time to drop Santa's gifts, and I was committed to this holiday schedule, despite the stress and fatigue it created for me.

But what now? This creature lying next to me would very likely stir when my phone alarm signaled me to drag gifts out from underneath the bed. I could turn it off, but then I ran the risk of sleeping soundly through the night and ruining Christmas. I lay next to Derby, listening to his breathing. If I waited for him to fall into a deep sleep, I could probably slither out of bed undetected, slip the gifts under the tree, and be back underneath the covers in under five minutes. And then, if he woke up any time between now and sunrise, I could physically restrain him if he tried escaping for an early peek. This, I determined, was my best and only plan.

One detail I had working in my favor was the gift itself. This year, Derby had asked Santa for a Nintendo Switch, a handheld gaming system that came packaged in a relatively small and slender box. The year before, he'd asked for a light saber, a much larger item and harder to hide and disguise, and the year before that he'd asked for a mechanical walking T-Rex that made sporadic roaring sounds without warning. When the plastic carnivore turned on from underneath the tree with bright flashing lights and hunger groans before daybreak, I'd frantically jumped out of bed and yanked the batteries from its chest cavity before it woke my sleeping child.

This year, Derby's father and I had every intention to secure the popular Switch, the gift that—in 2020—every kid in America was asking for. He'd put it at the top of his Christmas list before Thanksgiving, and by Black Friday they were already sold out. According to Amazon, the Switch was on back order with a shipment schedule delayed into January.

I tried to sound reasonable when I called Derby's father and said, "I don't care if we have to hijack a container ship, we need that Switch." After calling every big-box store in the North and South Bay, he located one that had just been returned to a Best Buy. He called me with the news. "The guy on the phone said he'd hold it for one hour before he adds it back into inventory."

"Can you go get it?" I'd framed it as a question but meant it as a directive.

"It's over sixty miles away." He said it as a statement but delivered it in protest.

"Our kid needs a win this year." And in case that wasn't clear, I leveled, "Seriously, Santa needs to show the fuck up."

Derby was nine, not an unreasonable age to stop believing in Santa, and I'd become aware that the seed of suspicion and doubt had already settled into fertile ground. Of course, as parents, we don't know exactly when this story begins to be challenged, but I was fairly certain it could be traced back to St. Patrick's Day. The Irish holiday, which I'd stopped observing in my late twenties after beer-guzzling benders and green cropped tops lost their appeal, was still wildly celebrated in elementary schools. Not the black-out partying, but the folkloric aspect. I knew this from Gretta, who talked without enthusiasm about all the overtime hours she spent setting leprechaun traps in her classroom. The basic concept, as I understood it, was to create a rainbow trail to trap this mystical creature with bait, using things like gold coins, four-leaf clovers, and sweet treats. "Leprechauns are very tricky," she explained to me, "so they rarely get caught." To prove to her young students that a leprechaun had visited their classroom before smartly escaping, Gretta would leave green sponge-paint footprints on the desks, the chalkboard, the windows. "Leprechauns are also naughty, so I throw a bunch of rainbow confetti and green glitter on the floor and toss around the papers on my desk and turn over the trash can. It's a shit show, but the kids love it."

Since Derby had started kindergarten, he'd also been introduced to this spring tradition and agreed it was a lot of fun—until earlier this year, when things changed. Had it been a normal year, St. Patrick's Day would have been celebrated on or around March seventeenth, but this year, it landed at the onset of the state's mandated shelter-in-place order, which meant the school celebration was put on hold because, well, the whole world was on pause. When the kids returned to Zoom school in April, the celebration was rescheduled to boost morale amidst global uncertainty. Unfortunately, not everyone got the memo.

"The leprechaun came today." Derby dropped his head and began to cry. "But not to Dad's house."

"What happened?" I asked, trying to quickly catch up. I'd picked him up from his father's for the next few nights with me and on our drive across town, he explained that when he'd turned on his iPad and shown up to Zoom class that morning—surprise!—it was St. Patty's Day in April and all the other kids, in their separate square boxes, were showing off their leprechaun traps and all the goodies that had been left behind for them overnight. Things like candy and stickers and green footprints all over the walls.

"And he didn't come to your room?" I pictured the regretful scene, twenty-six kids crowded onto a computer screen, all of them gobbling chocolate coins, and Derby sitting alone with nothing to show. My heart broke, and I wanted to kill his father. Although, to be fair, I didn't know this belated holiday was happening either, and if Derby had woken up at my house, I would have failed the assignment too.

"I'm so sorry, honey." I put the car into *Park* and faced him. "I'm not sure what happened."

"He probably just missed it," he whispered, referring to the leprechaun. "Maybe he doesn't know I live there, too, and . . ." His voice broke. "He probably can't get to all the houses."

Derby was trying to explain this oversight as he wiped away tears. He was trying to justify being left out and forgotten. "Probably because I didn't set a trap," he said with defeat. "It's okay, Mom."

"No," I returned, my voice rising more than I'd intended. "It's not okay."

I hadn't planned to pull the curtain back, to expose this Irish masquerade, but I wasn't going to sit still and allow my child to feel like he wasn't deserving of a leprechaun visit, because this was about more than being dismissed by a green fairy with an orange beard. Derby felt inadequate, unworthy. And worse, I sensed his acceptance of it. He was trying to talk himself into expecting less, into being the kid who's skipped over, who's not deserving as all the rest.

"Honey, I have to tell you something." I paused. "There is no leprechaun."

His brows cinched together. "What do you mean?"

"I mean, there is no leprechaun. The parents do it."

His eyes widened, betrayed for the second time today.

"And Daddy must have forgotten, and I'm so sorry. I'm sure he didn't mean to forget. Parents make mistakes. We mess up sometimes."

"I can't believe this." His voice ticked up a notch.

"Well, it's true, and you need to know so you don't think there's something wrong with *you*, that this is your fault and that's why the leprechaun didn't come." I met his eye. "You weren't skipped on purpose. We just forgot. You deserve a pot of gold just like everyone else."

Derby sat quietly, digesting this new information, and I watched as his expression shifted, moving the puzzle pieces to form a new picture. "What about Santa?" He turned to me with alarm. "Is that made up too?"

"No," I answered as fast as I could. "Santa is *definitely* real."

As far as I was concerned, leprechauns were fringe fairies. Santa was the embodiment of magic, of possibility and hope. He sat at the top of the mythical creatures' glass pyramid, and I wasn't ready to have that shattered. Not this year. Not when Derby had recently lost one grandfather to cancer and his Mutti to suicide. He needed to believe in something magical because in the real world, he'd been forced into a separate box. Death was a part of his young life. At nine, Derby knew shock and loss and the unpredictability of relationships. He understood the people you love will leave some day, and that without warning or intending to, the people you believe in the most may disappoint and hurt you, so if I could preserve his winter wonderland and save Santa for one more year, I damn well would.

⋆ ⋆ ⋆

I lay next to Derby and listened to his breathing grow deeper with each breath. When I felt certain he was asleep, I slowly slid out from under the blankets and pulled the Nintendo Switch from under the bed. I tiptoed into the living room where I placed it under the tree before returning to bed as quickly and as quietly as I could. It was only after my head hit the pillow that I realized I'd been holding my breath. I lay still until my heartbeat slowed, then I closed my eyes and hoped to sleep.

Somewhere between five and six o'clock, I was awoken by a gentle tap on my shoulder. I opened one eye. Derby was standing next to the bed.

"You're up."

"Santa came." He smiled in the early light. "Come see."

I followed him out to the living room where he proudly pointed to the floor. "Look, I got the Switch."

"Oh, look at that. You did."

"Can I open up the rest?"

"Hold on." I laughed. "We have to wait for Daddy to come over. And I need to make coffee, a lot of coffee."

As I padded into the kitchen, I glanced back at Derby sitting under the tree in his new jammies, wearing an expression of delight. At least, that was what I hoped it was. I desperately wanted for him to still believe that sometimes you get what you ask for, that the thing you want most doesn't pass you over. It magically shows up at your door.

* * *

At noon, I nudged Derby and his dad out of the house and wished them luck on their afternoon endeavor: putting together a 7,541-piece Lego of the Millennium Falcon, the storied starship that Hans Solo flew in Star Wars. While I would have liked to watch Derby tackle this auspicious project, the noise level associated with seven thousand Lego pieces divided into countless plastic bags would hinder my nap. I stretched out on the couch and gazed up at the tree. Mom's memory ornaments hung throughout the pine boughs, and as I read them, I allowed myself to miss her. I invited the sadness of her absence to fill my heart and sit heavy inside me. I held it there until the discomfort began to settle and then, as Ariela had coached me, I visualized a bright, white rose bloom in the center of my chest.

Breathe in, breathe out.

I appreciated the poetic imagery of the exercise, although I wasn't too sure it was working, until an interesting thing happened. For a moment, my grief lifted and something else slid into its place: an understanding that wrapped around me like beautiful twinkle lights. While I missed Mom here with me, she'd left her favorite things behind, and these memories and traditions were now mine, and fast becoming Derby's, and nothing, not even suicide, could take them over the cliff. While our snow globe had been shaken and the scene hadn't quite cleared, that didn't mean we had to give it all up. Our family had changed, yes, but we were still here and we didn't have to live on the outside, feeling separate and alone. We could still believe in a magical world. That was our choice to make, and after the storm of this first year settled, I intended to make snow angels. I pulled a blanket over me and because I was tired from playing Santa, I drifted off easily and didn't wake up until four.

By Now

Less than a week later, we celebrated the new year with thick steaks, chocolate cake, and a Mandalorian marathon. After dinner, Jenni stopped by for a few rounds of laser tag with Derby, and at midnight we all three skipped out onto the porch to beat pots and pans with wooden spoons and holler into the dark and empty streets: "Happy New Year!" Then, after Derby returned to school the following week, and without a holiday to distract me, I slipped back into my office chair and wrote the last two chapters of the manuscript I'd been working on since early spring. The day I hit *Send* to my editor, releasing me from what my literary agent playfully refers to as "book jail" and which feels uncomfortably close to the truth, it was well into February.

⋆ ⋆ ⋆

It was a wet and foggy Sunday when I met Jenni and Gretta at the Laguna Trail in Sebastopol.

"I'm taking next week off," I said as we weaved our way through the mist.

"What's the occasion?" Jenni asked.

"Well, you know, Mom's year anniversary."

Jenni stopped in the middle of the path and turned to me. "I knew it was coming, but wait—are you taking the whole week off?" She turned to Gretta. "Do we get to do that? Are you taking it off too?"

"I'm not taking the full week off, but Friday I've called in for a sub. Maybe I'll ask for one on Thursday too."

"I hadn't even thought to do that. I didn't think I could."

"Aren't you the boss of your organization?" Gretta pointed out.

"Yes, but still, I feel like people think that 'by now'"—she emphasized with air quotes—"after a full year has passed, I should be 'past it' and moving on, not taking more time off."

"I get that," Gretta said. "No one says it, but it's implied."

"Or," I added, "it's encouraged with comments like, 'It's *so* good to see you smiling again' or 'We've really missed you' when what they're really saying is: 'We're over it, and we've gotten kind of tired of you talking endlessly about your grief.'"

"Right?" Jenni laughed. "Like there's an expiration date and after a year, the expectation is that you ought to be healed and 'over it,'" she said again with emphasis.

"Do you?" I asked. "Feel healed . . . and over it?"

"No." Jenni stopped abruptly again. "Not at all. I still have days when I'm in fresh shock, like it just happened. Honestly, I'm still in disbelief that it did." She stared out across the Laguna, and muttered to herself, "Seriously, who jumps off a cliff?"

Where a year can seem like a long time since reactivating your gym membership or going out to the movies, there was, as Jenni said, an extra unbelievable-ness to this year marker. *Had a year passed already? Wasn't it just yesterday that she was still here?* And as much as I, too, wished to be over it and moving on, in a lot of ways, I felt like I was finally getting the hang of it, learning to live with loss like one might adjust to arthritis—because you know it's not going away, you buy yourself some nice hand cream and make lifestyle adjustments.

"There's a name for it," I said. "It's called the 'deathiversary'."

Gretta turned up her nose. "I don't like it."

"Never heard of it," added Jenni.

Attention Target: one more underrepresented sentiment to slap on card stock and monetize.

"So, what are we supposed to do?" Jenni asked. "Throw a deathiversary party? I can tell you how many people will want to come to that: none."

"I was thinking of hosting our family at the end of the week for something less morbid, more celebratory. I plan on making Mom's famous Senegalese soup, the spicy peanut one."

"Mmm," Gretta's mouth turned up in delight. "I love that one."

"Well, okay, that's it." Jenni struck a defiant pose. "I'm taking a couple of days off too. Fuck it." I nodded my approval.

"No one else is going to give you the time or suggest or even anticipate that you need it. You have to take it."

⋆ ⋆ ⋆

My primary intention for taking a full week off was to give the year anniversary my focused attention, similarly to how I responded on That Day. The moment deserved my presence and my respect, so if I could adjust my schedule and throw some extra time at it, I would. Yes, I was aware I'd already devoted many hours to grieving over the past year—sitting alone and staring into the void on countless nights, pacing the floors in detective mode throughout the days—and that, perhaps, a full week was excessive and maybe I just needed time off from deadlines and work demands, and a deathiversary was a convenient excuse. Either way, I'd made my decision: The week was mine, and what was the harm? I wasn't asking anyone else to join me.

I appreciated that the rest of the world had other things to do, and that was fine by me because for the activities I'd planned, I didn't require their company.

On Wednesday, I said to B, "I'm taking the week off to mark the one-year anniversary."

"Good for you."

"You don't think it's indulgent?"

"The one-year anniversary is the most significant, and in the Jewish tradition we have a name for it, *yahrzeit*, and it both commemorates and concludes one full cycle of grief."

"Well, okay," I cheered. "That means I'm right on schedule, and I can buy myself an anniversary pair of shiva sweatpants."

"Now, hold on." He laughed. "Shiva is over. That lasts only the first seven days after someone has died, and it's meant to provide the living with a pure and dedicated stretch of time to focus solely on bereavement. Most people don't do this; they hurry back to life. *Yahrzeit* honors the natural rhythms of loss that ebb and flow throughout the first year."

"I'm into that, and then what? After the year marker, please don't tell me we're supposed to be 'over it' and moving on?"

"Anyone who says that has never lost someone significant, and if they have, they may have moved on, but they haven't moved forward. There's a difference. Moving on is incomplete. It's what we do when we try to outrun or hide from grief. It's what people do when they don't have time, when they skip over, avoid, or numb their pain. Moving forward is what we do after we've spent the time sinking into the loss, looking at it, not past it. Carl Jung referred to this as 'making the darkness conscious,' and I'd add that it's only after we've become conscious that our grieving feels complete."

"Will there be a completion certificate after all of this? I've always prided myself for being a good student, so at this point, I'm not going to ditch class. But can we speed things up?"

"You'll get there, and the time you've spent already is not for nothing. It's a tribute to your relationship, to your connection to your mom. Really," B lightened, "I hope my own kids are as messed up over my death as you've been over your mother's. I should be so lucky that they mourn me for a year."

* * *

In the spirit of Jung, I decided to tackle the darkest activity first: Empty the drawer. For the past year, I'd shoved the most painful evidence of Mom's death to the back of my dresser drawer. I felt safe knowing it was all in one place, and at the same time, it unnerved me, and I avoided it like a child might fearfully refuse to look underneath the bed or in the back of the closet. In fact, I'd been that kid. At my dad's house growing up, the entrance to the attic was in my closet and after *Poltergeist* hit the big screen in 1982 and I watched in horror as little blond-and-blue-eyed Carol Anne was sucked into an evil vortex in the back of hers, I never opened my closet door again; or, at least, not in that house. Now, I was an adult with a spacious walk-in and nearly four decades of avoidant behavior behind me, and still, I recognized my slight regression, the temptation to slip back into the old shadows of fear.

I opened the drawer and steadied. C'mon, Sam, you can do this. There's nothing to fear here. No surprises. Nothing hiding in the dark. Only the note, the obit, her journal, some photos and jewelry, and—*oh,* I had forgotten about this—my hand pulled out something shoved to the back: a plastic Ziploc bag. Her effects. I held it up and examined its contents, my mind traveling backward in slow motion, working to fit this detail into the timeline. When had I received this? Was it the day after? Or the day after that? It was the sheriff, the one who'd been at the scene, who'd called me and said he'd wanted to drop it by. He'd seemed insistent on driving over to the house to give it to me. Was this protocol or his own personal contract? I'd agreed, still in shock and not understanding how these things worked. Klose died in a hospital. There was nothing to take except for his wedding band, which Mom put on her hand before she left his bedside. Mom's death was different. There had been a 911 call, a boat rescue and a helicopter, and her Toyota to tow down the hillside. The sheriff had her purse, he'd said on the call, along with her cell phone, and some other things he wanted to hand deliver. I'd met him in front of the house, in the middle of the walkway. I think I shook his hand. I don't remember what he looked like, only that he was kind. He handed me Mom's purse and the plastic bag. "What's this?" I'd asked.

"Her effects," he said with an awkward mix of authority and apology.

I remember staring at the bag and thinking this moment made no sense. How had I landed in a crime series? These were the wrong lines, the wrong characters. I took the bag and said, "Thank you," unable to say more. Looking back, I wish I'd asked him questions. He'd been at the bluff, he'd seen her body, he'd talked to the women who'd seen her jump. Maybe he could have helped me understand some things, but I hadn't thought to ask him because, in that moment, I hadn't accepted that she'd died. I took the bag from the sheriff, dropped it into my purse and carted it home.

Later that evening, it fell out when I went fishing for my phone. I stared at the plastic bag with the case number written in blank ink: # *200000196*. I ran my finger under the plastic seal until it opened and out slid her gold wedding band. It fell into my hand, wet, and I'd gasped. I sat silent and unmoving, reeling from her proximity. The ring was still wet from when they'd pulled her from the water; that was how recently it had been on her hand. I thought, *she is so close to still here.* I held it in my own hand, disbelieving, feeling the wetness on my own skin. *She is so close*, my soul howled, *and I am too late.* I slipped the band onto my own finger in a desperate effort to connect to her, to symbolically hold her hand as she floated in the waves of the Pacific. I pulled out her watch next, the band also soaked. It had stopped at 2:10 p.m., two hours after she'd been pronounced dead. I'd hurriedly returned the watch to the bag and zipped it shut, foolishly believing that if I could keep it from drying, I could somehow preserve her or keep time from ticking another minute forward and advancing away from my mother.

I recalled this scene now, a year later, as I held the bag up to the light. Why am I doing this? What is the point? The memory was uncomfortable and my instinct was to shove it back in the shadows. That *is* the point, I answered my own question. To look at it. To face the monster. And then, to put it in its rightful place: the past. I opened the bag and slid out her watch. It had grown mold; of course it had. I'd returned it to the bag when it was still wet, holding the saturation of the sea, and it had had a year to ferment. The time was still stopped at 2:10, although the face had become clouded and hard to read, and the band nearly black. It was a grotesque artifact, deserving of a burial. I held it lightly in the palm of my hand and spoke directly to it. "I see you. I feel you. And now I am putting you down." I slid it back into the bag and set it aside. I'd decide what to do with it later, but it wasn't going back in the drawer.

* * *

The following morning, I congratulated myself for tackling the most challenging item on the "anniversary" menu, determined to spend the remainder of the week on lighter fare. On Tuesday, I revisited Mom's favorite indie bookstore in Sebastopol and bought myself a stack of new novels. On Wednesday, I visited her neighborhood bakery and bought fresh bread and scones. On Thursday, Derby and I drove out to Doran Beach and searched for sand dollars and kicked our feet in the surf. On Friday, I hosted Miriam and a few more of Mom's friends for wine in my sunny side yard. And on Saturday, I invited the family over for Senegalese soup and a candle ceremony.

The ceremony was—no surprise—inspired by B, who explained we each suffer two deaths: the first, when our bodies physically die, and the second, when people forget our name.

"When we are no longer remembered," he said, "when our name is no longer spoken, we have truly died."

"Jesus," I said. "That's dramatic."

"Jesus doesn't have that problem."

"What do you suggest for the rest of us?"

"Say their name, speak it out loud, tell their stories. Vow to remember. This is how we keep our loved ones alive. Also, as you close the circle on this first year, consider how you might carry Susan's flame forward. This goes beyond the material. I'm talking about her fire, her essence. Your mom was big and bright, she was your sun—and how she died was destructive. In addition to remembering our loved ones in their full light, it's equally important that we let the hurtful pieces burn out. Think about what aspects of her life you want to carry forward and pass on to Derby, and which ones you'd like to actively extinguish."

On Saturday evening, I passed a ceremonial white candle to everyone in the family, and as we lit our individual flames and spoke their names out loud—Klose, Granddaddy, Daddy, Bob, Susan, Mutti, and Mom—the light grew and we formed a circle. As I looked into the faces of my family, I understood that collectively, we were the guardians of their legacy, and the fire we each chose to carry and bury would impact the generations ahead of us. I focused on the flame of my own candle and made a mental list. Bury: secrets, shame, silence, stigmas and that moldy watch. Carry: empathy, fairness, generosity (Klose scored especially high in these categories), and for Mom, I vowed to carry forward her active curiosity, engagement, great humor and love of life.

My anniversary week was dripping with symbolism and I didn't care who might roll their eyes because on Sunday morning, I woke up revived and spent a solid hour seriously considering that I abandon my ghostwriting career and manage grief tours. Perhaps I could partner with a few of those Sonoma and Napa Valley wine expeditions? The marketing copy wrote itself: *Make a memorable anniversary trip with our Luxury Van that can accommodate twelve grieving family members. In between tastings and discounted bottles of wine, we'll visit some of your loved ones' favorite destinations, from bookstores to beaches! Wherever you are on your grief journey, we'll pair you with the best experience.*

To close out my week, rather than flesh out a full marketing plan for Grief and Grenache, I landed on my final symbolic gesture: the garden. It had been nearly a year since I'd planted Mom's wildflower seeds, and it had yielded a rainbow of color. I expected some of the heartier perennials to return, and I'd bought a packet of hummingbird attractors to fill in the empty spaces. As I worked my hands into the soil that was no longer crumbly and dry, but soft and lightly soaked, I smiled at the memory of myself in the early weeks after I'd raked in those first seeds. They'd responded quickly, peeking their little green heads up for air, and at first, I'd taken offense. How can you thrive, I accused, when she is gone? You're just showing off! Throughout the spring and well into the late summer, I'd wrested with two contrasting realities: unapologetic beauty alongside the finality of her life. Despite my internal struggle, the garden continued to grow. I mean, really, it just wouldn't let up, and when one day a particularly delicate primrose caught me in an unguarded moment, I was struck with the supremely obvious: the garden was simply a reflection of the beauty of our relationship, cultivated over a lifetime, and as long as I continued to tend it, our garden would thrive. It had taken me three seasons to appreciate this, and now, as we were on the cusp of spring, I further understood that if I unclenched my hands and allowed myself to feel the sunlight, perhaps I could pop my head above the surface and breathe again.

Big Small Moments

"What now? I've made one full loop around the sun. Deathiversary complete. What's next?"

"Are you back for another assignment?" B chirped, like he were offering me a second scoop of ice cream.

"Depends on what it is."

"You honor those you've lost by grieving them, and then you honor them by living."

"Hmm, I'm not sure what living looks like on the other side of all that's happened in the past year."

"What if moving forward into the unknown was your next 'big' event?"

"It doesn't have the drama of a phoenix rising from the ashes, but . . ."

B interrupted. "Can I point out the obvious here?"

"Yes, please."

"The big event was your mother jumping off a cliff. That's *BIG*."

"Oh, come on," I protested. "Why does this story always have to come back to her? Are you saying Mom stole my big event?"

"No," B steadied. "That was her big event. What if your big

event is to *not* jump? What if your big event is to make a different choice than your mother made? What if your big event is to say yes to life? What if your big event is to simply say yes to you?"

I sat quietly on the other end of the line. I had experienced suffering that brought me to my knees, where my only hope was to somehow get back up and eventually, *please, God,* survive. I'd plodded through the days and now, a year later, I was no longer doubled over; I was standing. I had a bit of a survivor's limp, but I was deliberately facing forward. "I've made it this far," I said. "What if my next move was a small step? What if I start by reopening the door? Is that enough?"

"Yes. Open it wide and see what comes through."

In the days that followed, many things came through my open door. Another "please renew" subscription from *Yankee* magazine, three Amazon boxes, a lizard missing its tail chased by a predatory cat—and then, on Friday, Derby brought home a new friend from school.

His name: Phoenix.

I'm a dedicated learner. That doesn't make me quick. I was only beginning to understand that redemption stories don't always unfold the way you expect they will.

⋆ ⋆ ⋆

It was officially spring again, which allowed me to leave the door open without generating a regrettable heating bill, and I was thankful for the fresh air that had a rejuvenating effect. I was breathing deeper, with more ease, and the tightness in my throat had loosened up. I opened the windows in my office to release the winter's stale air and to encourage the outside elements to filter in. I detected a physical lift, I really did, a rising of my spirit, yet I was hesitant to trust it. Was it real? How long would it last? If I depended on it, would it flee? As my reliable self-doubt conjured up a storm cloud, another horrible moment to disrupt my life before my next pedicure, a bright blue jay landed on the crooked arm of the budding peach tree outside my window. It gave me a long side-eye before ascending to a higher branch on the sunnier side of the street. My interpretation: Hey, knucklehead, you've come through a dark time, and if you haven't noticed, the sky has cleared. Get outside and feel the light on your face.

⋆ ⋆ ⋆

That evening, I shed my isolation sweatpants and zipped into slim-fitting denim to meet a girlfriend for dinner.

"I haven't seen you in nearly a year!" LeLe squealed as soon as we locked eyes. "I already ordered us wine. Sit down!"

I slid in next to my friend at an outdoor bistro table decorated with twinkle lights. I'd known LeLe since the seventh grade, and while our lives had taken us in many different directions over the decades, it only took one glass of wine before we exemplified the popular adage about old friends—"It's like no time has passed"—and we were giggling and making a scene.

"Let's get right to it. Can we address the elephant in the room?" She took a hearty slug of wine.

"Oh, shit," I braced, "don't tell me you voted for Trump?"

"No!" She nearly choked. "Can you imagine my family of radical dissenters marching around in MAGA hats?"

To her point, the last time I'd seen LeLe was at a local production her brother was directing, a satire about totalitarian rule in the Emerald City.

"What elephant, then?"

Lele dropped her gaze. "Your mom. I'm so sorry, Sam. And I'm sorry I haven't seen you sooner."

I took her hand. "Thank you, and I understand. It's been a crazy year for all of us."

"So, how are you? I mean, really, has it been hell?" I appreciated that she wasn't asking me if I was *better now* or crossing her fingers under the table and hoping I was *okay.*

"Well, since you've asked, I'm working on a new lifestyle brand called SOS, Inc.—Sisters of Suicide. Catchy, right?

"Oh, you're bad." She laughed loudly. "But you've earned it."

"My grief counselor isn't entirely on board. He's encouraging me to retire my orphan identity, although I feel like I've finally got it down."

Her eyes flashed a knowing sadness. Under different circumstances and several years prior to Mom's death, she'd also lost a parent unexpectedly. "You know I get it."

"I do."

LeLe invited me to share all the gritty details of the past year, and I provided some until I suggested we change subjects. "Our dead parents shouldn't monopolize our entire conversation," I said, and she finished, "Not unless they're going to show up and pay the bill."

For the next two hours, we talked about parenting, politics, pets, and Pilates until I felt satiated, and not only from the shared plates; our conversation had filled me from the inside out. When we got up to leave, LeLe gave me a tight squeeze.

"It really is like no time has passed," she said, "and every time I'm with you, I'm reminded why I was so smitten with you in seventh grade and bored with everyone else. You're still *you.*" She kissed my cheek. "And your skin looks amazing, and I kind of hate you for that." As she walked away, she called back over her shoulder, "Call me soon."

On the drive home, I reflected on what LeLe said, *I'm still me.* I felt heartened, and relieved, too, that my longtime friend could still see the parts of me she'd always loved, although the truth was: I was only parts of me. There was no returning to the me before That Day, and since the candle ceremony, I was more mindful of the parts I didn't want to put back in, destructive traits I shared with Mom—hiding, half-truths, false happiness. I'd started to regard my personal rebuild like any good home restoration. You wouldn't ask your contractor to tear out the old kitchen counter tiles, only to put them back. Cracked, gray tiles belong in the dumpster, along with outdated habits and old stories. I was resigned that any attempt to rewind myself to a previous life was futile, and I surprised myself when I realized I didn't want to.

★ ★ ★

Several of my girlfriends argued that my home restoration wouldn't be complete without a new love interest to brighten my doorstep. Even I had to admit that as naturally skilled as I was at introverting, I'd finally had enough alone time. It hit me on no particular afternoon—I was lonely. I traveled from room to room like I'd done for months, and while my home was busy with bright colors and fashionably mismatched patterns, it was suddenly still. And even with the excess of throw pillows I'd ordered on the regular from Wayfair, it emanated an emptiness. Like waking up from a hazy head cold, I refocused and saw my isolation in a new light. "Damn," I remarked out loud, "I've been hiding away in here for too long." *Maybe I should invite someone in?*

When I conceded this to B, he did a verbal double-take. "What? This is news. Now, this is *big*."

"Calm down. No one's getting married. I'm just saying that I'm 'open' to the idea of meeting someone. I haven't done anything about it."

"It's still big," he insisted. "I'll remind you that for the past year, you've been emphatic that you weren't interested in a romantic relationship, and I've understood your hesitance given all that you've lost, and your opposition has been clearly noted. For you, opening up is a big step."

"It's a soft open," I clarified. "Not a door-thrown-wide situation."

"One lock at a time."

B likening my heart to a big-city apartment door with a series of locks, including a dead bolt and a chain, wasn't an exaggeration. Since Mom's suicide and my divorce, I'd been resolutely disinterested in dating. Opposed, even. I told myself and anyone who asked, "Are you dating yet?" that I didn't have space for anything more. I'd spent the last year learning how to live with my loss, how to carefully hold, carry, and tend to it. I'd made a lot of room for its unrelenting presence, and I told myself I didn't have room to allow anything else in. Moreover, I didn't believe I could afford to let any of me *out*. It was too risky. My wounded heart rested on flimsy pick-up sticks and any clumsy move, on my or anyone else's part, could inflict further cuts and bruises, and I wouldn't endure any more pain.

I'd tried out my anti-dating argument with LeLe when we'd been out to dinner. "And really," I'd said, "who wants to get involved with a divorced, likely menopausal, daughter of suicide—"

"Sister," she corrected. "Sisters of suicide, if you want to stay on brand."

"Sister, daughter, whatever. I'm a handful right now. I'm not light dining. Truly, I can't promise I won't start crying or yelling after two glasses of wine."

"Oh, I like a mess," Lele leaned in with delight. "I'd totally date you. You sound fun."

"The night is still young," I promised. "But, really, please stop me after two glasses."

I'd been holding firm that I wasn't ready. I wasn't interested, available, or emotionally able to let someone new into my life, but what if that were no longer true? If I removed the first lock on the door with a heartfelt intention to open up, would the

Universe do the rest? Would it bring me a partner for simply being brave?

My friend Karen laughed out loud when I suggested this. "Woman, you need to get online."

"I was afraid you'd say that."

I hadn't dated since 2005, and the landscape had changed dramatically since then. Gone were the days when you met another human at, say, the taco truck next door to your office or at the finish line of a 10k when you're handed a Dixie cup of electrolyte water by a nice man with whom you start up a breathless conversation. Sure, these types of introductions still happened, but they were now considered antiquated and increasingly far-fetched. I understood that one increased their chances of meeting someone—and, better yet, of meeting someone with similar interests, aligned politics, and even a shared regional accent—when they curated this person online. But I'd been offline for over a year. I'd retreated from social media after That Day and I'd stayed away, and at some point, it felt too overwhelming to jump back in. I struggled with The Post that warranted my return. Beyond an arty pic of my morning avocado toast, I'd come up with nothing. Perhaps dating apps would finally draw me out of obscurity? I was hesitant. From what I'd been told, this process required a cheeky profile and catchy copy that, if you asked me, seemed like one more tedious writing assignment.

"Is the old-school form of dating really dead?" I asked Karen. "Where you put on your best lipstick and make eyes across the hotel bar?"

"Trust me, this is better," she said. "And you don't really want to troll for guys in hotel lobby bars, do you? Online dating is way more efficient. And dignified."

Is it?

Although I trusted Karen because, as far as I could tell, she'd cracked the code. Utilizing her professional expertise in art direction and online marketing, she knew how to write engaging copy and choose the best profile pics to make the best match.

"It's all about natural lighting and not trying too hard," she said.

It could have been the image of her laughing joyfully with her eyes closed, or the story of her driving from California to Utah to buy underwear—whatever it was, the man she'd been dating for over three years now, and with whom she'd just bought a house that combined their four kids, she'd met online. I was willing to take her advice.

"Tell me what you're looking for," she said as we strolled through our adjoining neighborhoods.

"I know what I'm *not* looking for," I said, flipping her question. "It's good to set boundaries from the start, don't you agree?"

"Boundaries are good. Go on."

"Okay—no addictions, no angry temper, and no mystery amount of debt."

"That's fair."

"Also, no snoring."

"Good luck with that. Most every man over the age of forty snores. Do you want to date someone still in college?"

"Oh, God, no. That presents different problems."

"So, maybe reconsider snoring?"

"Fine, with limited overnights."

She smiled. "Is that it?"

"One more—no Beach Boys."

"Oh, come on." She stopped. "You're drawing a line at The Beach Boys?"

"Karen, more people ought to draw that line."

She steered us across the street. "Why don't we focus on what you *do* want?"

"Hmm." I softened. "Kindness. And competence but not overconfidence."

"Make it a positive," she redirected.

"Funny. Observant. Engaging. Has his own interests."

"All good."

"And he loves his mother." As I said it, my voice cracked. For anyone lucky enough to still have one, they ought to love her madly.

"Of course, and you probably want someone who isn't a stranger to grief too, someone who understands loss because they've been there, which"—she raised a finger to emphasize her next point—"is most divorced men over forty. That might make up for the snoring."

"Heavy breather, heavy griever," I said and we both laughed as we turned another corner, returning to my house.

"I think it's a great list, Sam. Call me next week and I'll help you create a profile, and then"—she gently elbowed me—"you can start making dinner dates on Open Table."

Her optimism was encouraging, but as soon as I returned inside to my empty isolation chamber, I froze. We'd neglected to explore the second half of the dating equation—what was *I* bringing to the table? Besides declaring myself available, which was a notable commitment to those who knew me, what did I have to offer? Tips and tricks on how to fast-track a death certificate? The name of a good divorce lawyer? An increasingly erratic nine-year-old? There ought to be more on the menu. I kicked myself for being the only woman I knew who hadn't yet enrolled in a frequent-flier program. At least then, I could offer up a free companion pass to Hawaii.

⋆ ⋆ ⋆

I lay in bed that night, turning it over. What do I have to offer? I fretted like a school girl who's forgotten her homework, her jacket, and her lunch—I have nothing!—until a wiser voice reframed the question. I was beginning to recognize this voice. It was the one that had taken a back seat at the Jack in the Box and gone quiet, the same one that had struggled for many years to speak up and be heard. The one that had become the voice for other people, the ghost who articulated other people's truths but who suppressed her own. It was my voice, my inner voice, my true voice that was becoming far less afraid, much more vocal. And tonight, it said, would you stop making this about *you*, and ask a better question: What does love have to offer?

What Does Love Offer?

My favorite photograph of Mom and Klose was taken in Germany. I'd snapped it the summer after they'd moved to Darmstadt where Klose had taken a staff reporter position for *Stars and Stripes*, the American military newspaper, and where Mom continued to write a weekly column for the paper back home. At Mom's invitation, Gretta and I had flown over to "traipse around Europe and use our guest room as home base." We were barely twenty when we moved into their little flat with our stuffed suitcases and American hair dryers, and with only a few years of college French and Spanish between us, we'd braved the overnight trains to Amsterdam, Paris, Interlaken, Lake Como, and Rome, always returning with travel stories to share. Mom and Klose listened attentively as we recounted the highlights: washing our dirty feet in a classy Parisian bidet, eating gelato as our main meal in Italy, and bunking in youth hostels up and down the rail line. We'd had our adventures, yet my favorite part of the summer wasn't our freedom away from them but squishing into their little rental car and traveling to nearby villages together, where the four of us would wander the old streets, searching for the best café and sitting uninterrupted for hours, observing local customs and eating foreign foods we grossly mispronounced. On one such weekend getaway, we'd discovered a walking path along an unhurried green river, and I'd snapped a picture of Mom and Klose reclining on a bench along its bank. In it, Mom is flashing her signature smile as Klose lies across the full length of the bench with his head resting in her lap. Above them, the delicate branches of a willow tree swirl in the breeze as Mom runs her hand through his chestnut hair. It is a moment that perfectly captures their ease and effortlessness together, their mutual adoration of one another. Wherever they were, Mom and Klose created a palpable energy between them, unseen but felt, and if that's what love has to offer, I want what they had.

"I loved coming to your house as a kid," Lele recalled. "I can picture it still—your mom and Klose sitting in the living room, each with a glass of wine, usually reading the newspaper and talking about current events. They had this really cool thing between them, and also they welcomed everyone who came through the front door. I always secretly hoped they'd ask me to move in." In the newsroom, Bob and Susan had the same affect. "I spent a lot of time with them over the years, as friends and colleagues," Miriam said, "and I think their partnership was most evident in their writing. They were such different types of writers—Bob was an investigative reporter and your mom was an outspoken columnist—but there was never any doubt how much they respected each other's work. They weren't exactly Joan Didion and John Gregory Dunne, but kind of. Susan asked Bob to edit everything she wrote, and if he suggested she cut something or change it, she did it without question. She trusted him absolutely. Not every couple has that level of confidence in each other, and I always found it remarkable."

Long after they'd retired from newspapers and Klose had gotten sick and he was in and out of hospital rooms and everyone's nerves were frayed, they remained a united front. Mom was with him always, taking copious notes as the rotation of doctors offered their ever-evolving prognosis, frequently stopping them mid-sentence. "Can you please repeat that so I can write it down?" with Klose jumping in right behind her with, "You can't get anything past her, doc. She's a stickler for the facts." Most mornings, Mom was there, delivering hot coffee to his bedside and pulling *The New York Times* out of her canvas tote bag, along with fresh socks and his toothbrush if he were staying another night. The day after he had neck surgery to cut the cancer out of his spinal cord, I found them in his room, watching CNN. The Notre Dame Cathedral in Paris was burning, and they sat together on his bed, rapt as the flames erupted. "What a shame that something so beautiful can be destroyed," Klose said as Mom rubbed his arm. "It'll be okay, babe. Maybe all is not lost." On a different day, I discovered them laughing behind the privacy curtain as they fumbled with his oxygen tank. "It's not a rocket ship." Klose chuckled as Mom turned every knob with exaggerated confusion. "Oh, yeah? You try making sense of this." She tossed the manual in his direction and like a true baseball fan, he caught it. "Hey slugger, you oughta stop throwing things or they'll throw us out of here." I remember I'd smiled at their banter, at their ability to make this scene—one that was undeniably critical—a funny moment. I left the hospital that day, reluctant to drive home. I sat in the parking lot with a pit in my stomach: my marriage would never make it that far. My husband and I couldn't laugh in the face of something as dire as lung cancer. We weren't laughing on good days. A week later, we agreed to separate. I'd finally accepted that my marriage was over, and I admired that Mom and Klose always found their way back.

On the day before he died, Klose looked up at Mom from his hospital bed. "Hey, you know what day it is, don't you?"

"Our thirty-eighth-year wedding anniversary." She smiled down at him and smoothed his hair.

"We've had fun, haven't we?" His eyelids were heavy and he reached for her hand. "Yeah, babe." She placed her hand over his. "We sure have."

For their anniversary, Mom had made reservations for a celebratory weekend in Gualala on the coast and she'd hesitated to cancel. He'd been moved to the ICU the day before and we were all in and out of his room like an army of attendants, attempting to keep up his morale as the projections became more and more grim. Out in the hallway, Mom pulled me aside and whispered, "I really hoped we could get away." His kidneys were failing and they'd called in a palliative care team, and she said this as if it were still a possibility that he'd get out of bed and they'd make it up the coast in time for the sunset.

Watching Mom lose Klose on top of losing my own marriage had created some, let's say, new relationship misgivings. And the more I thought about it, I wondered if it wasn't that I didn't have anything to bring to the table, but it was that I brought too much to ask some unsuspecting new man to hold.

"Divorce. Cancer. Suicide. Perimenopausal rage. They're all on the menu. What do I lead with?" I asked B.

"Good question. Is there drinking involved?"

"Definitely."

"Try warming him up with politics, then take his temperature."

I laughed, because can you imagine? I wouldn't dare introduce any hot topics, not on a first date, anyway. I didn't want to come off as a heavy burden, and I also didn't want to be disappointed if "unsuspecting new man" fell short. I was warming to the idea of someone who could hold my pain, although not in the way that they'd try to fix me or make me feel better, but to be someone with whom I naturally felt better. This required opening up and trusting, and I was shaky on both points. Outside my small pod of friends and family and grief counselors with solid credentials, I hadn't opened up to trusting anyone in years.

"Then why do it?" B challenged.

It would be easy to continue to isolate, working from home as a full-time ghostwriter who needs little to no interaction with other people to create and complete work. It would be easy, except it was no longer enough.

"I'm afraid to remove all the locks, but I'm more afraid of what will happen if I don't."

"One lock at a time," B repeated. "And I think you might be surprised at what your heart is capable of holding. One of my mentors, Rabbi Menachem Mendel, said, 'There's nothing more whole than a broken heart.' What if you have more to both give and receive because of what you've lost, and not the other way around?"

"I guess we'll find out."

One positive about online dating was that it functioned as an efficient vetting process. Once I created my cheeky profile and uploaded some photos, I sat back and let the matchmaking algorithm do its thing. While most people primarily filter for age (no more than ten years older or younger), location (no more than a full tank of gas away), and scan for obvious red flags like overuse of controlled substances and excessive wear of cycling shorts, I was hyper focused on character. Do his eyes convey kindness? Is his smile trustworthy? Does his posture communicate dependability and an overall fortitude and stamina for the uncertainties of life? A tall order, maybe, and hard to discern from a series of selfies, but I was a novice, and I figured you have to start somewhere.

Round One:

There was the man who talked nonstop about his ex-wife.

The man who couldn't find a wine he liked from a menu of one hundred.

The man who wouldn't laugh.

The man who was recently widowed.
The man who lived too far away.

No one's perfect, especially me, so I was willing to give these guys some slack, but as I said, I was new to this game and not yet able to discern when, and on what points, I ought to tighten up. I enlisted my friend Dan, who I'd known since high school and who had become a successful talent scout for comedians. We'd split from our spouses around the same time and I knew he was also dating again. I called him one night, after returning home from dinner.

"What if he doesn't make me laugh?" I asked Dan.

"Lose his number."

I knew this would be Dan's answer, which was why I called him. I wanted him to validate my own conclusion.

I added, "My date also confessed he's an open-mouthed sleeper. To be fair, I'm pretty sure I drool, but I don't lead with that."

"Well, as someone who cuts a few logs, I'd like a pass on that one. But the first—not funny—unforgiveable."

Round two:
There was the man who wanted an open relationship.
The man who didn't want kids, his own or mine.
The man who checked his phone.
The man who never called back.
The man looking for a one-way mirror.

Of all my suitors, this last one was the most interesting to me. We discovered a lot of shared interests, and every time we landed on a commonality, whether that was spicy guacamole, crowded city bookstores, or estate sales, he became visibly delighted, but by the end of our evening together, I had the uneasy sense he was looking for someone to reflect his interests back to him, rather than become interested in *me.*

"Sounds like one of your clients," said B. "He's looking to you to be his mirror."

"Except he's not a client. We were on a date."

* * *

Several years ago, I was riding in the car with a client who suddenly turned to me with apology. "Geez, I've been talking all about myself for hours, and I realize I don't know much about you."

Her comment caught me off guard, and I froze. *Was this a trap? What did she want to know?* After all, I was accustomed to our exchange—I asked all the questions, and she did all the talking, and in this particular case, she'd generously flown me in from out of state to stay at her house for a full week to shadow her at her place of work. We had been together, nearly unseparated, for five days. We'd shared all of our meals together. I'd met many of her family members, and even her housekeeper. I'd slept on her beautiful sheets and used her scented soap. I'd roamed the hallways of her three-story home and helped myself to countless Keurig coffees in her sunny kitchen. She was absolutely right that I had remained relatively silent about my own life as I learned all about hers, and she was not the exception to this rule. Since becoming a ghostwriter, I'd cultivated a similar relationship with dozens of clients who told me their stories and rarely asked about mine. This one-sided conversation is what enabled me to write in first person, as them, and I hadn't met another ghostwriter who described a different dynamic. "While you're working together, it can feel like there's something real there, something reciprocal," one of my ghost-friends said. "But as soon as the manuscript is done, that connection is almost always dropped. It's like, *thanks for listening, bye.*" She was right that the relationship between client and ghost was intimate, and that level of closeness could last up to a couple of years if you were with the person from the book-proposal phase through publication and publicity, which I often was. For this extended period, the client received the majority of my focused time and energy, too often bumping friends and family members out of line, and that was because writing their stories extended beyond full-time hours. To best channel their voices, my habit was to also think about my clients morning, noon, and night, to hear their words as my own and anticipate where their story might take me next. This was how it worked. The role of the ghostwriter is to mirror the client, to reflect the person across the table, while remaining unseen and unheard on the other side, and I'd rarely questioned this relationship. In the context of my most recent date, however, I wondered if I'd unconsciously accepted that this was how *all* relationships worked. Over the years, my job had served to reinforce my childhood belief that my greatest value was my invisibility, and if I wasn't careful, I risked repeating it in the dating world. I'd attract men who wanted a ghost.

⋆ ⋆ ⋆

"I have no more time for this," I announced to B. "The next guy who talks my ear off for two hours and then leans back and takes a sip of his small batch whiskey, and says, 'You're really sweet for listening'—that's a direct quote, by the way—I'm turning over the table like a New Jersey housewife and walking out of the restaurant."

"I'd like to see that." B laughed. "And I like this new track. This is what can make dating in midlife so rewarding. At this age, you're no longer looking for the big wedding, or someone to have babies or to even share a mortgage with. You're looking for a partner in the pure sense, an equal who sees you for who you truly are. The catch, however, is that if you want to be seen, it starts with seeing *yourself*. Are you ready to do that?"

Mirror Return

Since buying that first antique mirror with the piecrust beveled edges, I'd kept at it, and still new to the world of collecting, I didn't yet know the rule about when to stop. In other words, how many mirrors are too many? They were now hanging in every room of my house, including hallways, above the kitchen stove, and behind bathroom doors, and given its cozy footprint—950 square feet—I was, quite actually, living in a House of Mirrors. It's true that mirrors create the illusion of a larger space and they're experts at bouncing light and brightening a room, and this was my argument for collecting so many. Did my surplus of reflective surfaces allow me more opportunity to look at myself? Sure, although I understood that B's challenge had little to do with checking my hair as I passed from room to room. He was encouraging me to look *into myself.*

Nevertheless, since I had so many visual aids, I figured, why not utilize them? I positioned myself in front of the mirror with the best natural light for looking into my own eyes, and was immediately distracted by my chin, a mound of formless flesh that had begun its inevitable descent during lockdown. I'd conveniently hid it under a mask for months, tucking it into a synthetic hammock, but now that the world had "opened up," I couldn't hide the slide. I did that thing where you smooth the skin back, hoping it'll lock in place and stay that way, and redirected my attention to my countenance, as a whole. I saw myself and I saw Mom shining through. There was no denying the resemblance. Even Jenni had remarked on it recently when I'd met her for coffee in dark glasses and a sun hat, calling the look-alike "startling" and I wasn't sure how to respond, settling on: Thank you and I'm sorry.

As I looked at myself now, I thought about how Mom had started avoiding mirrors toward the end, gagging at her reflection whenever she was caught by one. "I used to love my looks," she admitted sorrowfully one afternoon as we combed the racks at a consignment shop. "And now"—she held up a red knit top and scowled in the mirror—"I've lost them." I'd interpreted her comment as vanity talking. She was getting older, she'd grown thinner and her hair was, as always, giving her fits. It was more than that, though; she was finding it harder to hide from herself, and she didn't like me looking too closely either. On that final Friday, the one when I last saw her, she stopped mid-sentence: "Is something wrong?" She'd caught me silently watching her, holding up a mirror with cracks in it, and the unspoken directive was to put it away.

My mother had worn a mask, presenting herself as the Susan she thought the world wanted to see and hiding the parts of her she believed they would reject. She'd done such a masterful job of exhibiting airtight confidence and capability throughout my entire life that when an alternate version appeared, I rejected it, moved it out of the frame, and waited for the Susan we all recognized to return. She sensed this, I think, that many of us were holding our breath, riding out her bad patch along with her until she got better. And when she didn't rebound and only became fearful she was getting worse, she still tried to maintain a brightness that people expected from her, myself included, and I regretted this now. This had been an unfair expectation, although a predictable one. I'd been raised under the canopy of her sunlight, and when she faded, the little girl in me felt left alone in the dark, on the edge of a cliff calling out to the setting sun, *Come back! I'm lost without you!*

B asked me in one of our first calls: Had I unconsciously dimmed myself for Mom? I learned early on that playing small was a safe bet, that fading into the background so the grown-ups could talk was a solid survival skill, a means to win favor in the room. I'm not sure when this dynamic took shape or how and by whom it was imposed, but as far back as I can remember, I was cast as the supporting actress who doesn't hog the stage, who allows the spotlight to land on someone else. That became my role, and I allowed it. Retreating into the shadows was easy for me because Mom was blazing bright for the both of us. Her natural ability to radiate allowed me to sit back and bask in her light, rather than to rely on my own. I can recall countless memories of me as a kid, relaxing into her on a couch or sitting in the chair right next to her, reluctant and shy, as she spoke in her infectious and animated way to whomever was in the room. In this repeated scene, my participation wasn't noteworthy, but I always had the best seat in the house. As her daughter, I enjoyed preferential treatment, a lifetime invitation to soak up her shine. So, in answer to B's question, I hadn't dimmed myself for *her,* so much as I dimmed myself because being close to her felt special.

My mother modeled vibrant positivity and her sunny outlook created a beautiful world for me, and as one of her most adoring fans, I tried to please her the best way I knew how, not only by sitting stage-right, but also by turning my negativity down. Over the course of her successful career, Mom interviewed and wrote about a diversity of people who'd suffered or were struggling in one way or another. She was an expert at drawing out a hard story, listening with compassion, leaning in and asking to learn more—except she didn't welcome it from her young daughter. "Don't be so sensitive," I remember her saying. *Be more like me.* I'd wanted to be more like her and I was ashamed that I couldn't as naturally reach her high notes, and certainly not sustain them. Anger, disappointment, sadness, frustration, fear, insecurity, and failure are big feelings for a kid to suppress, so I learned to dim in other ways—by numbing with alcohol by the age of fourteen, by dissociating from my body with unprotected sex at fifteen, by practicing indifference to others and actively denying my own needs, by hiding my true self away in oversized clothes and under heavy makeup. Self-forgetting and denial were my best defenses throughout my teenage years. It was how I handled setbacks and confusing social circles throughout my twenties, and by the time I hit my thirties, I'd swallowed my feelings and buried my hurt for so long that I'd lost sight of the girl who had once attempted to interrupt and speak her mind. *Who was she? Had she ever existed?* By then, I was wearing my mother's mask of clear confidence and strength, the woman who doesn't ask for much, who takes care of herself and contorts herself to fit in with the crowd with an almost mechanical persistence.

It wasn't until I had my own child that cracks in my own façade began to appear. By his pure energetic presence in the world, Derby's arrival released raw emotions within me that I didn't want to suppress: joy, wonder, awe, love and passion, and also a fierce and protective rage, a new and uncensored boldness. Derby birthed a tempest of emotion within me that refused to be stifled or easily contained, and once the chaos of new motherhood settled, I was forced to acknowledge where I'd been holding myself back, masquerading as someone different from me. At that point in my life, my marriage was my most shameful falsehood, and facing this truth was terrifying because once the mask reveals itself, you have an important choice to make. Leave it on or rip it off.

I'd left it on. And while I'd since worked through the reasons why I remained for as long as I did, I wished I would have had the courage to speak up before that fateful viewing of *Trolls*. But we cannot rewind. We all operate on our own timeline, and since my divorce, I'd afforded myself some grace for finding my way back to the mirror eventually, where I could face myself without skulking in shame, and since Mom died, I'd made a hobby of amassing reflective glass, an unconscious effort, I supposed, to become more comfortable with visibility. And still, I intuited that there was something more for me to *see*.

Oh, mirror, mirror on the wall, who am I without the mask?

In Matt Haig's *The Comfort Book*, he writes that the cure for loneliness is understanding *who we are*. When I first read this, I underlined the quote and dog-eared the page, certain it was the riddle that opened the secret chamber. I'd always equated loneliness with a longing for the company of others, and I'd gone on a recent string of first dates with the hope of meeting someone who might offset my solitude. I was still optimistic that dating was a worthwhile endeavor, although meeting *him* wouldn't be the cure for my loneliness because—cue the chamber door—what I was lonely for *was me*.

Mom had wanted to hold on to "the old me, the one everyone loved, the one I loved." In her suicide note, she'd referred to the version of herself that she could no longer find, that was "already dead." She was searching for the *before* Susan who hadn't become sick. She was longing for the woman who was able to effortlessly glide through the world, sunny and bright. In one of her last journal entries, she'd written, "I can't keep pretending." My mother was desperately looking underneath the bed and in the back of the dresser drawer for her mask and she couldn't find it. I believe her feverish search led her to the edge that day, while I sought an alternate path.

I was suddenly clear on this! I didn't want to refasten my mask because what had been an effective survival skill for much of my life—numbing my vulnerability and silencing my voice—had ultimately worked against me. What had once felt safe had become detrimental to my happiness. It kept people at a distance, prevented true intimacy, and it disconnected me from myself. Furthermore, hiding in the shadows to avoid conflict with others had created heavy conflict within me. It kept me in a perpetual state of self-doubt, questioning my feelings or deeming them wrong, and suppressing my intuition or acting counter to it. I no longer wanted to present a fictitious me. I wanted to recover the original.

I'd confused myself for so long, thinking it was all or nothing, high shine or muted tones, and I was mistaken. We are all light and shadows and shades in between, and I needed to release both my mother and me from our false mirrors. Mom was brilliant, a kaleidoscope of light, and also, darkness was a part of her. It could have been there all the time, lying dormant until it eventually stirred or perhaps it crept in one day unannounced. I remember her saying to me, years ago before Klose got sick, "I'm afraid that if I go in too deep, I won't be able to get back out." I'd thought it was a curious insight, and not fitting of her, the always upbeat. It was in response to a conversation we were having about cognitive behavioral therapy, and I was promoting its positive outcomes. She didn't elaborate on her comment and so we moved on, yet she'd revealed something there, a glimpse underneath the mask.

I leaned forward into the mirror and said, Mom, I see you, and I see me, and we're okay. The stories we tell about ourselves can change. We get to be both, light and dark. It's not either / or.

Turned up bright or turned down low. We are whole. Our struggles don't make us weak, unworthy, or defective. Daring to be real is what makes us exceptional.

★ ★ ★ ★

"I did your mirror assignment," I reported back to B on Wednesday.

"Oh, yeah? And what did it reveal?"

"My big event."

"Please don't say plastic surgery."

"My chin is a clear candidate, but no. My big event is to tell the truth even when it's terrifying, to scream out loud when life pushes me to the edge. My big event is to stop the cycle of presenting falsely, of hiding in plain sight."

"Your mother's death has provided you with an opportunity to do what she couldn't, and you do this, not in spite of her suicide, but because of it. Nice work. So, what's your next move?"

"I haven't gotten beyond tossing out my stockpile of N-95 masks."

At Last, a Memorial

After mom died, I thought I'd feel abandoned and alone forever. What mother leaves her child? I feared a deep loneliness would live within me, in my blood and bones, for the rest of my life. But if loneliness is a result of self-abandonment, self-betrayal, and self-forgetting, then it's within my power to be the cure. If I have me, I'm not alone. If I speak for myself, I'm not unheard, and if I step forward and let myself be seen, I'm not a ghost. My mother didn't abandon me; she abandoned herself. I'm still here. I am my own light source. I am a sun and a moon. I am light and dark and shades in between. Mommy, you are gone, and I miss you. This is how it will always be. I will miss you forever. But I am here, and I've missed me more.

These were the thoughts I woke up to the next morning, and as I sat up in bed, my next move was clear. It was time for the memorial. It was time to honor the full life, the unfiltered and beautiful complexity of my mother, and to give her community the opportunity, finally, to gather together and collectively say goodbye. I sent Gretta and Jenni a text: *I'd like to start planning the memorial. The weather is nice, most people are vaccinated. What do you think about an early-summer event, somewhere outside? I feel ready, do you?*

We met a few days later in my side yard under a new red umbrella, a tradition I'd determined to carry forward. "I'm thinking something casual. Wine in the park. Good food. And we could time it to her birthday and call it a party. What do you think?"

"A celebration of her life." Gretta smiled. "I like it."

"And how about this? We release balloons at the end and sing happy birthday."

My sisters exchanged a look.

"What?"

Jenni shook her head. "Balloons are cancelled."

"Really? Who are we offending with balloons?"

Gretta pointed upward. "The environment."

"And very likely every left-leaning, planet-loving, climate-conscientious person living in the West County, which is pretty much everybody," Jenni clarified.

"Okay, so . . . confetti poppers?"

"Not unless they're biodegradable."

I rolled my eyes.

"How about bubbles?" Gretta offered. "Bubbles are the new balloons."

Jenni nodded. "Good call. We also need to think about individual dishes, nothing shareable because, you know, the new variant. People are worried about their food touching other people's food. Maybe we should scrap food altogether?"

"So, no birthday cake either?" I was quickly deflating.

"Cupcakes!" Gretta squeezed my arm. "We can safely do cupcakes."

* * *

"That's your plan?" B said on Wednesday with undisguised mockery. "Cupcakes in Covid-safe liners, a couple of glasses of wine and, what did you call it? Some light reminiscing?"

"What's wrong with that?"

"Look, I've presided over hundreds of funerals and memorials and trust me, free flow is not your friend at this type of event."

"But we don't want to do some formal, stuffy thing. It's been over a year and we just want to create a space to finally come together."

"Understood, but still, people need structure at a memorial. Whether it's a small group or a big crowd, there will be a lot of emotional energy that comes through the door, and that energy needs a container or it can quickly become unhinged. Now, this doesn't mean you have to create an elaborate or highly formal thing, but it's best to give people something to *do*, something for people to focus their energy on. That's why services work. There's a program, music, and candles, and a focal point like a casket or an urn. Where are your mom's ashes, by the way?"

"In the back of my closet."

"We'll table that for later. What's your plan for speeches? Who's addressing the crowd?"

"Umm, we talked about inviting people to bring something of hers to read. A column or a quote or a passage from one of her books."

"That's a great idea but give them a maximum word count and a time limit or you'll have someone who goes on for forty-five minutes and who will, very likely, veer off script and break down in tears."

"Oh, shit, really?"

"I've seen people fall apart at the podium more times than I can count. And also, you need a mic. Nothing worse than people mumbling inaudibly. And you need chairs for older people."

"Chairs? It's going to be outside in a park, and all her friends are older people."

"Then pray for shade."

"I'm glad you're telling me this, but it's kind of freaking me out."

"You'll be fine. You really can't fuck it up because unlike a wedding, a memorial is already a fucked-up event. Although," he tacked on, "you ought to think about a water station and positioning yourself near a bathroom."

After I hung up with B, I immediately called the park to inquire about the site we'd reserved: yes to running water, yes to nearby bathrooms, yes to picnic tables, and yes to shade. No to microphones, speakers, or any type of "sound amplifier." That left my sisters and I to do the bulk of the projecting and invite our guests to do something else.

At our next planning meeting, I suggested, "Since we have a gazebo on site, what if we built a Dia de los Muertos-inspired altar and invited people to leave a personal memento, meaningful object, or a photograph of times they spent with Mom? This will give them something to do, to contribute."

"Love that." I wasn't surprised by Gretta's reaction. She honored the tradition in both her own home and in her second-grade classroom every year. "There should be lots of flowers," she said, "and I'm happy to make the arrangements. Marigolds are customary, but since it's her birthday, what if we featured naked ladies?"

"Now, that's a party." Jenni winked.

"Problem is that they can sometimes be hard to find at the flower market."

"No problem," I said. "They're blooming up and down the back roads to the coast."

"And I pass them every morning on my bike ride between Santa Rosa and Windsor," Jenni added.

"Okay, then," Gretta directed. "If I can't find any to buy, prepare to forage."

With our revised plan in place, I sent a Save the Date to Mom's nearest and dearest:

> *After a dark year for so many of us, and in celebration of what would have been her 78th birthday, we invite you to join us for a party in the park to celebrate the life of Susan F. Swartz. The Dia de los Muertos-inspired altar we aim to create as a community is to honor her memory, release her spirit, and bring peace and closure to the living.*

A few days later, I was back in my favorite antique shop when I discovered a vintage sign that read: *COMPLET.* I recognized it as French for 'complete' and was struck with the idea of placing it on Mom's altar. I hesitated only because I wouldn't want people to interpret it as insensitive or flip, but I finally bought it because it spoke to me. Later, I looked up the translation: *Complet*, as in a '*Hotel complet*' (with no rooms available); *les oeuvres completes*, as in the complete works of M.F.K Fisher; and *une liste complete.* This fit Mom perfectly, enthusiastic list-maker and avid fan of cozy hotels, eating well, and all things French. Further down the page, *complet* was more broadly translated as: Full, Whole, Missing and Wanting for Nothing. The definition didn't describe how Mom left the world, but it did describe how she lived on her best days, of which there had been many, and I hoped her community could finally release her from her worst moment and remember her full life. "After all, people are not a la carte," B said. "We are whole beings, so we ought to love the whole, not only the parts."

⋆ ⋆ ⋆

Two days before the big event, and on Gretta's charge, we initiated Operation Belladonna. After toast and coffee, Derby and I set out in earnest with an empty hatchback and a pair of gardening shears. I took the two-lane road out of town that quickly turned toward open fields, dairy farms, and a scattering of homes set back behind oak and eucalyptus trees. We hadn't driven for more than a few miles before Derby pointed. "Over there!" I slowed down at a clustering of naked ladies on the edge of the road, blowing bubble gum and flirting with the golden grass dancing on either side of her.

Hello, girls.

I put the car in park and reasoned this wasn't private land. We could probably cut a few. I prompted Derby, "Go!" and he was out of the car in a flash, crouching at the base of the tall cropping with his clippers, and seconds later, he opened the hatch with a victorious smile and a fistful of flowers. "Got 'em!" We repeated this stunt more than a dozen times, careful to avoid residential property, to cut sparingly, and to not deplete the late-summer harvest for other travelers on their drive out to the beach. By noon, the trunk was piled high, the rearview mirror reflecting a cascade of pink, and I drove straight to Gretta's to offload our bounty. Derby and I threw open the front door with our arms overflowing—"Look at what we got!"—quick to discover we hadn't been the only foragers at work. Gretta's dining room table was covered and she'd run out of vases to keep the flowers from wilting. She instructed us toward the kitchen. "You can put yours in the lobster pot on the stove until I can figure out a plan."

The house was humming with a mild current of chaos. Every available surface was crowded with naked ladies toppling over each other, while Whitney Houston—*I'm every woman!*—blasted overhead. The cluttered kitchen smelled of butter and sugar, and Derby's cousins sat perched on stools, smearing a variety of frostings on cupcakes at the direction of Auntie Jenni wearing a trucker hat and oven mitts.

"Come help us!" his cousins called to Derby.

As he ran into the kitchen, Jenni backed into Gretta, flipping a platter of finished cupcakes off the edge of the counter, including one that landed in the open dishwasher. "Oh, shit!" she hollered, a household profanity that immediately signaled,—food on the floor!—and Lulu the labrador bounded into the kitchen. As she chewed cake out of the silverware holder and licked frosting off of the floor, Jenni turned to her niece and nephews for a teaching moment. "This is the beauty of having a dog. They're happy to clean up your mistakes. But as you can see, we're gonna need another batch of lemon, on the double."

* * *

Early the next morning, Derby and I met Gretta and the kids to begin dressing the space. The park was dewy and dark as we got to work laying out bright tablecloths, hanging birthday banners and crepe streamers, and assembling over twelve dozen cupcakes—dark chocolate, vanilla custard, lemon curd, strawberry, carrot, and red velvet with sprinkles—on a variety of cake stands and antique platters under the shade trees. As Gretta added a few finishing touches to her flower arrangements, tucking in Queen Anne's lace, amaranth, and bunny tail grass to accentuate the pink, long-legged star at the centerpiece of every vase, I built the altar in the gazebo. Loosely following the customary design, I created a wide base covered in white lace that I adorned with photographs, votive candles, clusters of tomatoes and fresh fruit, stones, crystals and sand dollars. I added stacks of Mom's books and bracelets, along with a package of clam broth that I positioned next to a photo of her and Nancy wearing sun hats. I stacked a smaller pedestal atop the base that featured the largest bouquet of them all, a golden urn packed with roses, hydrangea, sunflower, grape vines, pomegranates, white daisy, and more naked ladies. As the morning fog began to lift and the sun stretched its light throughout the park, people began to appear at the periphery of our space, out for their weekend morning walk with a friend or a dog or a young one asleep in a stroller, and many of whom stopped to look at our creation and inquire about the occasion—Is it a wedding? A bridal shower? A birthday party?

"A celebration of life," we answered back.

"Beautiful," one woman said, smiling up at the altar before moving on.

By ten o'clock, Jenni arrived with the bubble machines, along with a couple of Klose's old newspaper buddies who got to work setting up the bar. They uncorked Sancerre and red zinfandel as Gretta scattered the custom coasters she'd designed. To Life, they said in a variety of languages. *Salud. Prost. Cin-cin. Santé. Gan bei.*

"Okay," I turned to Derby—"it's time to change into our party clothes."

"Finally."

Derby had been waiting all morning to slip into his new black blazer and red tie. We'd gone shopping earlier in the week and he was clear. "I want to dress up for Mutti." I wanted to dress up too, but struggled to land on the appropriate mood: casual dressy? Dressed-down formal? Traditional all black or its converse, all white? I pulled a shirt from the rack, a white blouse with embroidery around the scooped neckline and frayed edging along the bottom hem. "What do you think of this?"

Derby made a face.

"You don't like it? Doesn't it look like something Mutti would wear?"

"Mom," he groaned, "wear something *you* would wear."

"Okay, wise guy." But he was right to call out my automatic habit of mirroring her, rather than presenting as myself. I returned it to the rack and selected something I would wear: a fitted white linen tee that I could dress up with jewelry. Casual dressy, it was decided.

We walked back to the site in fresh clothes and to greet my friend, Alec, who'd offered to play an acoustic set of Beatles songs, and that was when I noticed the first of the guests arriving. They drifted forward through the trees, some faces tentative, others eager, still others stricken, solemn, and slow. After a year of isolation, I was suddenly surrounded on all sides by people who loved Mom, many who'd known me since I was a child younger than Derby and whom I hadn't seen since Klose's memorial, if not further back. Their faces pressed in on mine, and as their tears welled and their hands gripped me, they spoke. *I still don't believe it; I cry for her every day; I wish I would have known she needed help.*

B had warned me to be careful. "You are simply holding space for them. It is not yours to do others' grief work. Just be with them." I understood the importance of setting this boundary, but when a woman I recognized from the *Press Democrat* leaned toward me and put her hand to her heart and choked, I couldn't help but hold her grief as my own, understanding finally how a single suicide impacts a large community. Over one hundred people filtered in through the trees and over the lawn, dragging their heavy hearts, their shock, and their unresolved questions still begging for answers. It was not my solitary loss, I'd known this, but because the pandemic had prevented us from gathering until now, I'd mostly grieved alone. Today, we were finally together and I felt an unexpected relief from their company. One by one, I was greeted by faces familiar who held out their offerings: small bundles of lavender, wildflower seeds, bottles of wine, love letters, and poems. This is why people gather when we lose one of our own, I thought. It's not to create ritual for ritual's sake. We do it because our grief needs a witness. We do it to remind each other and our children that we aren't alone, that our pain is shared, and while the act of gathering doesn't release the ache, it validates it, gives it a home with other people who feel messed up too. I hadn't wanted a memorial, not at first. I'd been so bitter and mad, stubborn in my stand that she didn't deserve it. *Too bad for you*, I'd sputtered at the time. *We just had one for Klose and you weren't supposed to die, so you'll just have to wait.* And then the pandemic made the decision for us and I shoved her memorial to the back of my dresser drawer, along with the other sad things. It had been postponed for longer than I'd expected, and in that time, my rage had simmered, and I was grateful it had because as the park swelled with people, I understood the importance of this day. Of course, Mom deserved a memorial. We all did. Surviving suicide is too hard a journey to navigate alone. We had, because we had to, and now our lonely grief was being made visible and whole.

After allowing for the inevitable last-minute arrivals, my sisters and I ascended the gazebo steps to begin the service. Alec strummed the final note of "Let It Be". We cued a family friend to signal silence with a swift tap to her Tibetan singing bowl and I began. "Thank you all for coming. It's wonderful to see so many of you again after such a long time, and it's a testament to Mom that you are all here, especially those who have traveled far." I looked out over a canopy of straw hats and spotted a couple from Kansas, her college roommate from Denver, and a girlfriend who had driven up the coast from Mexico. "Mom wouldn't want to miss a party with all her favorite people, and yet it is what she wanted. When she and Klose originally put their trust and estate papers in order, she sent this casual note to my sisters and I: 'Dearest family and friends, in the event of my demise, a party or memorial would be nice, with seasonal flowers, food and wine—preferably a tasty but reasonably priced California Sauv Blanc or French Sancerre that I loved except for the predictable migraines. Also, music, maybe dancing and something spiritual, something hopeful to be read.'"

I stepped aside and Gretta stepped forward and read Mary Oliver's *Instructions for Living a Life*. By the time she finished, the crowd had grown still, and in that silent moment, a walnut broke free from a tall branch above and fell onto the head of a friend sitting at one of the front tables. It made an audible crack, and she exclaimed, *Oh!* and then she laughed. "It's Susan!" And with that, the somber moment shifted and Jenni said, "Susan leaves a rich legacy of the written word. We're grateful to access her that way whenever we want. Of course, we all miss talking to her. Luckily, some of her Susan-isms are deeply embedded in our memories and family culture, and we thought we'd share some with you now."

Gretta and I squeezed in to Jenni's left and right, linking arms and holding each other up as we'd been doing since the third grade, and together we recited some of Mom's favorite phrases from memory.

You're only as old as your spine.
Smiling is the best facelift.
Walk tall.
Make a friend wherever you go.
Drink your water.
Look at the sunrise.
Look at the sunset.
Oh, the snow!

Oh, the moon!
Smell the air.
Ask questions.
Make a list.
Write it down.
Who's making the coffee?

Laughter rippled through the crowd, and Jenni continued, "Our parents talked and dreamed periodically of moving to Lawrence, Kansas, or further east to Massachusetts. Not because they didn't like it in Sonoma County, but because they so valued their community here, and especially Susan, who thrived in community with all of you. She loved her groups: the writing group, book group, transitions group, her walking group, improv group, stepmothers group, her biking, water aerobics and yoga buddies, her Spirit Rock friends, her neighbors and newspaper friends, her supper club, her sister district activist friends, the Village network and the Margaristas, who planned book events while sipping tequila and lime. We're happy you're all here today representing her extensive community, and we invite you to stick around and share stories, eat a cupcake, and have a glass of wine."

I raised my own. "Let's please toast to the juiciness, to the richness and fullness of Mom's life," and as glasses were raised, Jenni whistled. "Hit it, kids!" And Derby and his closest cousin jumped to attention to perform their critical task. They flipped the ON switch to the three bubble machines stationed at the base of gazebo, and within seconds, a rush of bubbles filled the space and spilled out over the crowd, eliciting a collective "Ahhhh!" and causing a few dogs to jump for them midair. "Group hug," Jenni opened her arms and pulled me and Gretta in tight. "We did it." We'd turned a tragedy into something joyful. And with the big talks and toasts out of the way, the mood relaxed. Sancerre was poured. Laughter swelled as stories were shared, and the kids climbed trees and guzzled soda from tall branches. It was just the kind of party Mom loved, and I imagined she was with us, her spirited energy bouncing from tree to tree and group to group, kissing everyone on the cheek before they finished their last sip of wine. *Happy birthday,* I whispered. *Complet,* she whispered back.

★ ★ ★

Later that night, I went to bed with a sense of completion myself. I felt resolved; peaceful, even. Until midnight, when I woke up feeling very sick. I leapt out of bed and ran to the bathroom, and without going into graphic detail, what happened over the next few hours might best be described as a purging. A colonic. An exorcism. Where one could point to the excess of wine and chocolate frosting as the offending combination, I believe I was struck by something deeper. It was as if everything I'd been holding for over a year—the anger, guilt, confusion and heartbreak—was released. By morning, I was depleted and physically wrung out, and also I felt lighter—obviously, from an absence of fluids—but that wasn't only it. After dropping Derby at his dad's house, I took my routine walk around the neighborhood and realized what it was: I didn't feel Mom's presence on me in the way I had before. I stopped in the middle of the sidewalk and took stock of this new sensation—autonomy, alone-ness. It was the reverse feeling of being followed; you know, when your body absorbs the energetic weight of someone who is close by, a block behind you or walking next to you in the shadows. You can sense them even if you can't see them, and then you turn a corner and unlock your front door and suddenly, you don't feel them anymore. It was like that. Except I hadn't been aware of Mom's trailing presence until it was gone. Part of me felt liberated I finally had my body back! While another part of me wanted to hold on: *Don't go, please don't go! I don't want to feel lighter.* I stood frozen in place, unsure of what to do next. I forced myself forward and by the time I reached the end of the block, I relented. *Okay, yes, fine, go on. It's time for both of us to walk on separate sides of the street.*

⋆ ⋆ ⋆

No longer weighed down by my mom's spirit stalker, I returned to the house inspired to release another energetic layer. Her ashes. They were stored in the same box that Joe at Pleasant Hills Crematorium had delivered to us before lockdown, over a year ago. Gretta and I had arrived together to pick them up, and as we sat in his somber parlor of an office signing release papers, we'd had to stifle our laughter every time he referred to the ashes as "cremains."

"Isn't that a dried fruit snack?" I whispered to Gretta.

"No, that's Craisins," she whispered back and started to giggle.

"Oh, right, dried cranberries, not to be confused with the currant or the crouton."

"Stop," Gretta warned.

I elbowed her. "Think we should tell Joe it's confusing? What happened to good old ashes?"

"I'm not telling him anything." She elbowed me back.

"Ladies," he interrupted. "Just one more signature, please."

We scribbled our names at the bottom of the page and he showed us to the door.

I'd assumed responsibility for Mom's "cremains" and because they were in a box too big to shove to the back of my dresser drawer, I'd found a spot for them underneath my winter coats, where the top of the box had been collecting dust and cat hair for over a year. I slunk down to the floor and pulled it forward.

"Yuck," I said in reference to the surface muck, and also to the contents inside. I could think of other projects I'd rather start on a Sunday, although in the spirit of release, this was the obvious choice. I carried the box into the kitchen and plopped it down with a thud. It was sealed shut with fancy tape that I slid through with a kitchen knife. Once the edges were loose, I slowly opened the lid, not sure what to expect, but surprised to find a plastic bag, also sealed shut, like chicken breast cooked sous vide. *Hmm*, I pondered, and fumbled around in a drawer, looking for scissors. I cut across the seam until it popped open and then I peered inside. There were her cremains, although I preferred to call them ashes, and they were gray and sand-like, as you might expect. There were also a lot of them, and I reeled at my understanding of why this was. I was staring at the condensed sum total of my mother's body.

"This is bullshit," I said out loud.

I stared at them some more, not sure what to do next. What was my plan? I'd only thought this project through as far as opening the box. Now what? My sisters would kill me if I took the whole box and drove it out to the coast, dumped it on the beach, and let the tide take it away. They, I knew, wanted to be part of the ceremonial release party although we'd never talked about what type of party that would be, or when we'd throw it, and here I was now with the box open on my kitchen counter. What if I just took some of its contents for me, and left the rest for a bigger moment shared between the three of us? Yes, that was what I'd do. I would remove a handful now to plant in my garden and save the rest for later. The question was: How do you parse out someone's ashes? Put a portion into a smaller bag? Does this disrespect the integrity of the whole body? Would it split my mother's spirit in half, and cast her into disembodied limbo for eternity? Nobody teaches you these things. I rummaged around in another drawer until I found a box of plastic snack bags. Ziploc came out with this cute version of their ever-popular sandwich bag when Derby was a year or so old, and I liked them for stashing things like baby carrots and cashews for him on the go. My mother abhorred them, called them "ridiculous" and insisted "no one can fit *anything* in these ridiculous bags." How fitting, I smiled now, that I would put a pinch of her ashes in a snack bag, although this decision created a more pressing follow-up question: How does one transfer ashes from one bag to another? Again, I threw open a drawer and looked around. A ladle would be too big, a serving spoon too shallow and a soup spoon too small. My eyes wandered around the kitchen, landing on the plastic scoop I filled with fresh ground coffee every morning. Again, fitting. Mom was a coffee addict, so why shouldn't I scoop her alongside my Peet's Major Dickason's Blend?

"Here goes," I said, and dug into her ashes, only to discover that once penetrated and turned over, they emitted a miniature dust cloud, and when I attempted to dump the scoop into the mini snack bag, the sandy substance spilled over the edges and scattered onto the floor. "Fucking hell!" I screamed. "These bags *are* ridiculous!" After I tried again and created a further mess, I dissolved into tears. "Shit, I'm sorry, Mom." Her ashes were on the counter and swirling into dust cyclones on the floor. My snack bag contained the equivalent of less than one cup of weak coffee, and I felt like a failure. I could never get a job at a crematorium, if I even wanted one. Joe would never give me the important task of vacuum-sealing the bags; I'd only spill ashes all over his grief-stricken clientele. I sank into myself, a widening well of self-pity, until suddenly, I started to laugh. Because it was funny. And if she were here, Mom would throw her head back and howl. She would think it was the most hysterical and ridiculous scene, and it would go into the library of memorable moments that we shared and mutually agreed were top-notch comedy, even if no one else thought so. "You should be *here*." I laughed through tears. "You, of all people, would appreciate this." I held up the snack bag and cry-laughed again. "I mean, just look at you. You're a bag of bones."

* * *

"Don't take it the wrong way," I said to B on Wednesday, "but you're a solid consolation audience. I figured you would get the joke."

"I'll have to get myself a box of snack bags and start handing them out at funerals."

"Oh, maybe we can rebrand them, like they did with 'cremains'."

"Something between a baggie and an urn. Burgie, Uggie?"

"So, you don't think I'm making light of it?"

"I do think you're making light of it, and what's wrong with that? I counsel a lot of people who feel guilty about this, who won't let themselves go there. I once presided over a funeral where there were strict instructions to everyone in attendance that they *not* laugh, under any circumstances, which only tempted me to tell jokes."

"Did you?"

"No, but I do often tell the story of my hero, Viktor Frankl, who endured endless horrors in the Nazi death camps, and who said humor is the weapon of the soul. It's an act of defiance to laugh. It's a way to take back your power when confronted with darkness, with the grimmest of the grim. And that's what you're doing. You're laughing in the face of it."

"At this stage, it's what's working."

"You've learned by now that grief isn't linear, nor is there one way to go through it. I can't remember who said it—there's no right or wrong way, there's your way."

"Frank Sinatra."

"That's *My Way*. The quote I'm thinking of was Nietzsche, I believe, the philosopher, not the performer."

"Same diff."

New Loss, New Grief

I was having a pretty good time laughing in the face of death when Derby delivered a straight line. We'd pulled away from the school parking lot when he announced from the back seat, "Mom, I've been thinking about something."

"Thinking about what, buddy?"

"That maybe I don't want to tell you everything anymore."

I gripped the steering wheel and jerked up to the four-way stop. I glanced back at him in the rearview mirror. "Okay." I tried to sound cool.

"Are you upset?"

"No," I lied.

"I'm just thinking I want to keep some stuff to myself from now on. Not talk to you as much."

"Totally." I smiled and drove the rest of the way home rattled on the inside and trying not to show it. Once we walked into the foyer, I forced more coolness as I darted toward the bathroom, singing out over my shoulder, "Be right out."

I closed the door and burst into tears. *I don't want to tell you everything anymore.* His words pierced me. *I want to keep things to myself.* Sure, okay, but why? We're the mother and son who talk, who make up silly cat songs and hold hands. What happened? What's *happening*? It felt like a breakup.

My kid was nine and developmentally, it made sense that our open-ended conversations would change and that the stretch of our invisible string would be further tested by the impending double-digit years, and while I knew our bond was strong, his willingness to release our string, if only a little, hurt. I understood there were important brain functions at work in his rapidly elongating body, creating a natural separation that I ought not to take personally. I knew his emotional maturity wasn't about my shortcomings and still, give me a minute to catch my breath. After nine years, I'd learned there is no warning when our kids suddenly change a habit. Breastfeeding had been like this. He'd been latching on without complaint when one day, he was done. He turned his face away from me with distaste, as if to say, I'm not feeling this anymore. Do you have any bagels instead? Sleeping in his crib had been another quick change the night he figured out how to throw his leg over the side of the top bar and thump to the floor. From that moment on, the crib was dead and he slept in a bed. Carrying him on my hip had also come to a fast halt on no particular morning when he was all of a sudden too heavy and too squirmy for either of us to continue our daily gymnastics. These exchanges that a mother grows accustomed to and tricks herself into believing will continue forever suddenly stop, and we're expected to modify our behavior just as quickly to foster our children's growth. When my friend Lindsay was encouraged by her daughter's pediatrician to try baby-led weaning, the practice of letting babies feed themselves, she expressed her concern to me. "I don't think Lila's ready, and I'm afraid she'll choke if I start letting her shove yogurt into her own mouth. Isn't it okay that I feed her myself? She's only six months old."

"You get to do what's right for you," I defended, "and trust me, when she's ready to feed herself, she'll rip that spoon out of your hand and there'll be no going back."

I took several deep breaths behind the bathroom door and wiped my splotchy face. I looked into the mirror and scolded myself: Stop making this about *you*, Sam. Stop making this about what you're losing. Derby is asserting his independence, and he ought to be congratulated for asking for what he needs. I opened the door and found him in the living room, stretched out on the couch. He sat up, scanned my face.

"Are you okay?"

"Yeah, I'm good." I sat down next to him, picked up a throw pillow, yanked at the tassels.

"No, you're not. God"—he huffed—"I knew I shouldn't have said anything."

I felt small and found out, but I willed my adult self forward. "Listen to me." I leaned in and met his eyes before he could look away. "You do not have to tell me everything. Of course, I love how we've always talked to each other about all kinds of things, and I hope we always will. But as you get older, there are going to be things you want to keep to yourself, and you get to do that. You get to have things you only share with your friends. I'm here either way, okay?" I poked him in the ribs and he tried not to laugh. "Jeez, Mom, okayyyy."

⋆ ⋆ ⋆

I'd been proud of my ability to recover and sound like a reasonable adult, but when B answered the phone, I regressed immediately. I recounted the car ride, the offending comment, my tearful retreat and our reconciliation on the living room couch. When I was finished, B said: "You have a preteen. You're lucky he talks to you at all."

"But we've always talked," I defended. "And now he's pulling away and . . . I can't lose anyone else."

"There it is," said B. "Think about what you just said. You're confusing his natural separation with the loss of your mother. Be careful of grouping them together because they're very different. What your son is doing is developmentally appropriate, not a betrayal or an abandonment of you. You're not losing him. He's just growing up."

* * *

This feeling, this moment, had happened before. It was two weeks after Mom took her life. I pulled up to the school at three o'clock and spotted a friend of Derby's playing in the adjacent park that bordered the blacktop. "Hey," I called. "Have you seen Derby?" He pointed to the play structure. I scanned for Derby's bouncy blond curls and blue backpack. I didn't spot him right away, and as his classmates filtered past me and dwindled in number, I became impatient, then anxious, when he didn't appear. I turned toward the open-air quad. Not there either. I peeked into his classroom. Not there. I walked back onto the blacktop. He wasn't anywhere in sight, and I started to become panicked and called his name, louder and louder as I walked in circles. When I returned to the front of the school, it was nearly empty, just a couple of girls playing in the park.

"Have you seen Derby?" They giggled and pointed to a cluster of trees in the corner. I marched through the grass and found him and his friend up in a tree, cracking jokes.

I commanded, "Derby, let's go!"

He registered alarm and climbed down quickly. We crossed the park in silence and once seat belts were on, I erupted. "You do not wander off. You do not disappear. I need to know where you are, always. And when I call your name, you come!"

"I'm sorry." He cowered in the back seat and his lower lip began to tremble. My reaction scared him, and I felt a rush of regret. He'd lost track of time. He was only having fun and I'd overreacted. I climbed over the front seat and squeezed in next to him. "I'm sorry, buddy. I shouldn't have yelled. I got scared. I thought I'd lost you, and I cannot lose anyone else."

I returned from the memory and said to B, "Derby and I have been through so much, and I've relied on him, rightly or wrongly, to ground me. He's been the consistent thread in a chaotic world and parenting him has given me something important to do, someone important to be. Showing up for him has kept me moving forward, and I guess what worries me is what happens next, now that our lives are becoming more stable and he no longer needs me as much as I need him."

"What happens next is the teenage years, and trust me, they aren't stable. There will be days when you *want* to lose him. I'm only half kidding. I've got four of my own and what I can tell you with certainty is that Derby still needs you, maybe now more than ever, and in the next couple of years, when his hormones take over, he'll push you away even harder. He'll act like he doesn't need you, doesn't like you, until he needs money, and my advice is to make him work for the money, and to let him know you're there for him always, and for free."

"A teenager with a perimenopausal mother. That's a lot of change."

"Change is good."

"Is it?" Maybe it was time to buy out of this popular self-improvement trope. It no longer held the promise it once did in earlier years, when one naively equates change with optimistic progress. After forty, the changes in my life had taken a sharp turn toward devastating and dire, and I wasn't looking for more change like that. I was done with positioning my phone on the edge of my nightstand with the ringer on, in case a sister were to call in the middle of the night—*Meet us at the hospital. Hurry!* I was done with waking up in the morning to instantly go into dreaded hyper alert. Is everything okay? Is everyone okay? Did anything happen overnight? I was done with my morbid thoughts, guesstimating the life span of everyone I loved and obsessing the most over my own and berating myself with questions like: Why did I wait until I was nearly forty to have a kid? What happens when I die? How old will Derby be? A young adult? A husband? A father? My worrying mind had had it. I said to B—

"I'm done with change."

"That's too bad. I'm afraid that change is out of your control."

Since turning fifty and selling the house, marking the year anniversary and hosting a memorial, I'd felt the good kind of change, a lightening of spirit, the return of hope and laughter. Positive change was stirring within and still, I was scared a lot of the time. I hated admitting this, even to myself. I was scared of life's implicit uncertainty. I was scared of what lurked behind the next corner. And I was scared to not be scared. I asked B, "Is it common for someone who's suffered a series of losses and grieved over a prolonged period of time to get stuck in a perpetual state of clenching? My fear is that if I release my grip, life will take something else from me. If I relax and stop worrying, something else bad will happen. I'll get breast cancer or Derby will be bullied at school or the cat will get run over by the recycling truck."

"In mental-health circles, you could be describing complex post-traumatic stress disorder, which is often identified by heightened anxiety, flashbacks, nightmares. And while you have suffered trauma, no question, I believe your suffering is tied more closely to your vise grip on what *was*, and not allowing what *is* and what can be."

"Profound." I took in his words. "Is there a fix? Shock therapy? Less gluten?"

"Accept that you cannot control outcomes or change people. You couldn't control your mother or change your ex-husband, and you cannot stop Derby from growing into a young man."

We cannot control what people will do. I knew this, but inconveniently forgot it every morning.

"You can, however, control your choices," said B.

"I want to feel safe in the world again, I do. I want to retire my worry and fear. I want to let go."

"Then you know what to do."

Sunday Funday

On Sunday, I pulled on the bright yellow T-shirt I'd overnighted from Amazon. In big block letters, it read: *Sunday Funday*. That's right, I was reclaiming Sundays. Because there wasn't a rule that they had to be shitty and reserved for the Business of Dying and isolated, indoor activities. Sundays were meant to be enjoyed outdoors and with others, which was why today, not only would I open the door, but also I planned to walk boldly through it.

I headed out into the bright blue day and toward town with my chin up, and when I passed the white steepled Unitarian church on the corner, the one that had piqued my interest for months with its bell tower that rang at noon and its newly restored stained-glass windows and a friendly welcome sign in the grass, I walked through its front doors. Out one door and through another. The service had already started so I slipped into a pew in the far back. The woman minister wore a purple tunic top and smiled warmly as she lit candles and chimed bells. I hadn't picked up a program, so I didn't know the context of her sermon, but it didn't matter; her words instantly resonated. "Remind yourself that you are not fear," she said. "Your essence is something more, your essence is safe, loved, and connected. Your essence is joyful, and our daily challenge is to remember this, especially in moments of difficulty. Rather than wait them out, or wait for them to go away, we must remember we are not what scares us, and to tap into our reserve within. You are safe. You are okay. Can you let yourself feel that?"

I inhaled deeply and did my best to unclench on the exhale, to let go of my tight grip on fear, on the unknown and unexpected, on the next bad surprise that might happen, or might not. I squinted up at the sunlight coming through a portal of emerald-green glass spreading sparkles on the floor. Could I allow myself to feel safe? Tucked into the creaky, soft pew in the back, I allowed myself some release. I allowed myself to trust that safety lived within the walls of the church sanctuary, and within myself. I wasn't sure how long I could sustain the feeling, probably another five minutes, or until the minister stopped talking, whichever came first, and then it was anyone's guess when the old tightening would return.

After the service was over and I said hello to a few familiar faces, threw back a splash of lemonade, and offered a promise to return, I skipped down the church steps and traveled further into town, toward another church, the one I frequented with regularity: the bookstore. Thirty minutes later, I emerged back onto the street with a stack of sale books when I caught myself thinking, hey, I'm still okay. And I caught myself remembering, this is my kind of day. In fact, it was my day, free of parenting and work deadlines, and why the hell shouldn't it be fun? I'd been holding myself back and holding myself in for so long, it had become my automatic habit to dread Sundays, and I'd forgotten that before Klose's cancer and Covid and my divorce and Mom's sad ending, I looked forward to Sundays. I called Miriam, "Can I come up?"

"Sure, do you have time? Don't you usually have a lot to do?"

"No. I actually don't have to do anything," I said, surprising myself. "I'm free."

When I arrived at her house, she had afternoon espresso and cookies waiting for me on her wraparound porch, and after we'd caught up on the Sunday *New York Times* book review and what we each planned to stream next on Hulu, I asked—

"After Nick moved out, when did you stop missing him?"

"What are you talking about?" She laughed at me. "I didn't stop. I still miss him, even though he's practically thirty and engaged."

"Derby's not even ten, but his shoe size has doubled in the past six months, and while I want to pull the string tight and keep him close, I know it's better to hold it loosely, right? How did you do it?"

"I got a dog." Miriam took a bite of shortbread. "It's not easy, Sam. You're entering a time of big push and pull. With Nick, I tried to give him space and also hold space for him whenever he needed me. And as he got older, his dad and I encouraged him to pursue the things that interested him, as long as he didn't leave the country without telling us or ever forget my birthday. What they don't always tell you about parenting is that, at a certain age, it's our job to back off and let them pull away. And this is important for a mother and son because if he doesn't pull away, you become one of those weird TV shows. And anyway, it's not all so bad. As Derby gets older, you can give your parenting energy to other things you haven't had the time for."

"If you're going to ask me to join your pickleball group, the answer is still no."

⋆ ⋆ ⋆

A few days later when I picked Derby up from school, I didn't immediately ask him a bunch of rapid-fire questions—how was school, what did you have for lunch, who'd you sit with, did anything interesting happen?—instead, I released the string, allowed for a little slack to form in the line, and let him come to me. Finally, after about five excruciatingly silent minutes, he chirped, "Dad taught me how to use his welder. We're making a sword."

"Oh, that's cool. I did some fun stuff too. I hung out with Miriam and I signed up for some fancy cooking classes, and I also called our music friend, Alec, and asked if he could teach me how to play the drums."

"Why do you want to do all that?"

"Well, because when you're with Daddy, I have time to do things just for me."

He was quiet again. I glanced back at him in the rearview mirror. We locked eyes and he scowled.

"What's wrong?" I kidded, "Come on, when you're at Dad's, do you think I just stay home, looking at pictures of you?"

"Kind of."

I'd loosened the string and he was pulling it back in.

"Don't worry, buddy, I'll always have time for you, and don't forget we'll be roommates when you go to college."

"What? No, we won't."

"Yes, remember, a few years ago, you invited me to live in your dorm. I wrote it down."

"Then I won't tell you where I'm going to college."

"Pretty sure I'll know since I'll be paying for it."

"Mom," he pleaded, "we cannot be college roommates."

"Okay, fine, but you have to at least go somewhere cool that I want to visit. Or where I can rent the apartment next door."

"Apartment, no. Visit, maybe."

★ ★ ★

That was Mom's line. She'd always said that if I moved away from her, to please choose "somewhere cool" that she'd want to visit. When I was accepted to a college in San Francisco, she voiced her approval. "Only an hour away and it'll give me an excuse to shop in the city." But when I got engaged and announced that my fiancé and I were moving to Austin, she clearly stated her disappointment. "Texas? I would have preferred Paris."

And now, she had moved somewhere far away that may or may not be classified as cool, and certainly wasn't easy to visit. As I rounded through the small town of Bodega, past the white steepled church on the hill and through a tunnel of eucalyptus trees, I slapped my own hand for what I was about to do.

Bodega Head was windy but bright, and as I hiked up the trail to the Fisherman's Memorial, I heard her almost instantly. "What are you doing back here?" She was standing in silhouette at the top of the cliffs, the sun enveloping her from behind, and when I reached her, I said, "I wanted to talk to you, and I thought this was the quickest shortcut." In the wake of Derby's request for distance and more autonomy, I was craving attachment.

"Sammy, I told you I don't live here. I only showed up because I felt your pull."

I smiled brightly. "Then, it worked."

Mom took a seat next to me on the ocean-facing bench, and instantly took my hand. "How are you, sweetie? Tell me everything."

"I'm doing okay." I pulled back, suddenly distracted by her clothes. "Hey, what are you wearing?" The white cotton sweater she'd worn in earlier visitations had gotten an upgrade. "Is that cashmere?"

"Nice, huh? It's Eileen Fisher."

"What happened to the other sweater?"

She leaned in. "I'll let you in on a little secret. When you're no longer in your body, you can dress yourself in whatever you want. I'm finally starting to get the hang of it."

I looked down at her pants. "You can choose from anything imaginable to wear and you still picked J.Jill jeans?"

"Some staples transcend."

"Debatable."

She laughed. "What brings us here today, besides your snobby fashion advice?"

"I haven't felt you in a while. Not since the memorial."

"I'm beginning my ascent." She tilted her head back and closed her eyes.

"What does that mean?"

"I'm getting stronger. I'm moving upward, further away from the density of your world and into another realm."

"Oh, it's *my* world now?"

"It is yours, for now." She looked at me directly. "So, be in it."

"I'm working on it," I sighed. "In starts and stops, open the door, close the door, push and pull, clench and release."

"I know life's not always easy, but the more you engage in it and leave the past behind, the easier it will be for us both to move forward."

"Move forward? Do you mean, away from each other?" I'd been okay with feeling her presence less, but my temptation was to hold onto some amount of grief as a way to keep her close. Not always there, but within reach. Because what was the alternative? Not feeling her at all?

"That's an illusion," she said as if reading my mind. "You will feel me more once you release what happened and allow what comes next." This sounded strikingly similar to B's pep talk. Were these two working together?

"And what comes next for you?"

"Free at last," she said with dramatic flair. "But not quite yet. We have a couple of things to still work through."

"Such as?"

"Forgiveness."

I turned to her, surprised. "I forgive you." Had I not voiced this aloud? It was months ago, after reading her journal, that I noticed an internal shift in my understanding of events and my response to them. My mother's sharp mind had become compromised, telling her lies, making her believe there was no other way to end her suffering. She was sick. There was nothing to forgive.

"What I meant was, do you forgive yourself?"

The question gave me pause. Did I forgive *me*? I wasn't sure. Had I known on that Friday that it was the last time I'd see her, I would have told her I loved her hair just the way it was and that she didn't need to cut it. I would have poured her one more glass of wine and asked her to stay longer. I would have hugged her tightly before she walked out the front door and told her I loved her without condition. "I made the mistake of thinking we had more time. That I could fix whatever needed fixing later. I regret that."

"Let it go." She touched her shoulder to mine. "And let me go."

I tightened, my body protecting itself from more abandonment, more loss. "But you're already gone. How much further is there?"

"I'm gone from my body, yes, but I'll stay tethered to this world until you tell me it's okay to lift off. You have to say the words."

I stalled. "And where will you go?"

"Higher, to meet the mother of all mothers, the big Mama of the stars. I've heard she's very chic, a cross between Mother Teresa and Meryl Streep."

"Holy shit!" I jumped up. "How did I miss it? It's Meryl Streep."

"No, sweetie," Mom laughed. "Meryl Streep is inarguably a divine actress, but she's not the Divine."

"She's your cell-phone password. Meryl Streep *is* your password, right?"

Mom squinted at me with confusion. "What does that have to do with anything?"

"Oh, trust me, it's relevant." I pulled out my own cell phone to leave myself a note: *Meryl Streep is favorite actress!* "I cannot wait to tell Gretta. You have no idea how long we've wanted to solve that mystery." I sat down again, feeling satisfied, and returned to Mom—"Okay, back to what you were saying. Once I give you the green light, you're free to join some kind of celestial social circle led by a Merylesque matriarch with great skin and hair, and I'm left here, motherless." I turned to her. "That doesn't seem fair."

"I'll still be accessible to you. I'll just be in another time zone, as you say. And a higher-class one than this interim place I've been inhabiting while I worked out some of my own stuff."

"Like forgiving yourself?" I turned the question back on her.

Mom nodded. "It's taken some time. And there's still more healing to do, for both of us, and we will continue to do that, side by side, in tandem, in different realms."

"What if I don't want to let you go? What if there are others who don't either?"

"We stay stuck in place."

"This is on me now?"

"Don't take it personally. Humans are stubborn. Hard to trust, hard to let go. And understand that we're not saying goodbye. I'll never be gone, gone. I'm in your bones, your blood, your cells, interwoven throughout your beating heart. I am connected to you always through our invisible string, through our love and through your memory."

I considered her words, what she was asking me to do. She sensed my hesitation and again, took my hand in hers. Her familiar speckled sunspots were beginning to form on my own.

"Sammy, I gave you all that I could, and I had my limitations, my imperfections, as you found out. I did my best, and now it's time for you to turn away from me and pull your energy back to *you*. Find comfort within yourself and trust you have everything you need to survive. More than survive, actually. Tell a story that goes beyond surviving, that is bigger and better than what we've left behind."

"I've been telling our story," I admitted.

"It's time to put it down. You've held this story close for a long time, a lifetime."

"Give up the ghost. That's what you're saying." I'd thought myself clever to turn this figurative phrase and apply it to my ghostwriting career and had only recently learned of its biblical roots: to die, to leave the body and release one's Spirit. I gazed out at the horizon and took a sharp breath of ocean air, and before I lost my nerve, I turned to Mom and said, "I am giving you my blessing to move on. Only, one thing."

"Anything."

"Don't be a stranger."

"Never." She leaned in and kissed my cheek. "I am always right here."

Epilogue: Hawaii

"What does 'virgin' mean?"

I'd ordered Derby a piña colada without the rum, and a mai tai for me with a dark rum floater.

"It's not important. Just drink it."

We'd arrived in Maui to celebrate our consecutive fall birthdays and upon landing, the weather deceived us. It felt like summer, and the open-air tiki bar we now found ourselves in was full of island guests in skimpy July attire, and as we sipped our fruity drinks, I ran through my list of must-do's: hike to a waterfall, drink fresh guava juice, swim with a turtle.

"Aren't we on vacation?" Derby eyed me while sucking down his drink.

"Yes, and?"

"Maybe lose the list?"

The studio apartment I'd rented was tucked into Napili Bay, a sleepy stretch of sand and surf north of Lahaina and Kaanapali, the largest tourist hub, and one I intended to avoid. Derby took charge of opening the door, his Hawaiian shirt already unbuttoned. "I'm jumping into the water as soon as I put on my swim shorts."

I stepped inside and took in the view from our oceanfront lanai. We weren't more than twenty feet from the water's edge, where a scattering of people floated in lazy water the color of turquoise brush strokes. This was a scene that didn't need filters or added saturation. It was already perfect.

"Wait for me!" I said and tore into my own luggage to find my suit.

We were giddy as we skipped onto the beach, tossing off our flip-flops and wading in without hesitation, and all the way up to our necks. It was still the Pacific, a body of water that hugged our home shores, but its' easy island warmth was foreign to me. In Northern California, you suit up with a hoodie and a scarf, and you keep your shoes on. You watch out for sneaker waves and barbeque far up the beach to avoid the biting wind. Not here. Napili Bay shimmered like jewels and encouraged us with its gentle rocking and sweet serenade to do as the locals and *hang up the hoodie and hang loose.*

And so, we did. We floated for hours, until our fingers and toes became waterlogged and froggy, and we retreated inside to our little oasis where we ate cheese and crackers for dinner and watched people wander up and down the beach until the stars came out.

That night, Derby fell asleep first and I lay atop the hibiscus-themed bedspread, listening to the waves outside. I'd opened the windows and pulled the blinds high to watch the night sky, and sometime after midnight, I was awoken by the surf crashing so loudly, I was sure it had breached the railing and was flooding into our apartment. I sat up, touched my feet to the floor. It was dry. I'd been so overconditioned by Derby's sound machine and sleeping apps that simulate waves that I no longer knew what the real thing sounded like. Assured we weren't floating away; I crawled under the cool sheets and fell back asleep.

The next morning, Derby tapped me awake. "Mommy, get

up. You have to see the sunrise." I perked up and padded out onto the lanai and was hit by the morning light, spreading upward and outward from the horizon like melting ice cream. "Wow! Who knew you could mix colors together like that? It's mind-blowing, and I haven't even had my coffee yet." As soon as I said it, I recognized the remark as such a Mom thing to say, and then laughed because she'd always pooh-poohed Hawaii. Said it was too hot, too touristy, too cliché, and "I don't do floral prints." For all her sunniness, she didn't like the tropics.

When I planned our vacation, I was conscious of creating new memories for me and Derby and building on our shared history where we were witness to each other's lives, the guardian of each other's stories, the setup for each other's jokes. On the morning of his birthday, we ate giant banana pancakes smothered with whipped cream, then found a stretch of beach where I could recline and read a novel while he played in the surf. I kept one eye on him and one eye on the page, and after he proved himself capable in the water, I relaxed into the sand with my hands held open. *Unclench. Release.* Hawaii, I concluded, was an effective tonic for practicing trust and a new level of optimism. After lunch, Derby said, "Let's go snorkeling." Our apartment came equipped with two full sets of gear, making my answer easy. "Let's go."

We pulled on the clumsy fins and waddled down to the shore. I showed Derby how to secure his mask and breathe through the tube. "Let's stick together and stay inside the bay. It's going to get deep, so wear your life vest." He gave me a thumbs up and we waded out until it was over our heads and we were breathing under water. The visibility wasn't great, but we could mostly see to the ocean floor and follow a school of iridescent fish weaving in and out of a coral reef. This was a new experience for Derby and he swam ahead of me, fearless and full of adventure until—he stopped. He popped his head out of the water and turned around to look for me. I swam over to him and pulled out my breathing tube. "What is it?"

His eyes were filled with fright. "Something swam under me."

"It was probably a school of fish." I sensed his alarm and hoped to quell it. There were a dozen snorkelers swimming in our general vicinity. The water was calm and I believed we were safe. "Should we keep going?"

He shook his head and held onto me. I submerged my face in the water, attempting to see what he might have seen. Was there something there? Or was he just scared? I lifted my head back out. "I don't see anything, babe. It all looks clear to me."

"*Please*, Mom, can we go? I don't want to be out here."

I understood well the fear of what we can't see, of what lurks underneath, of uncertainty, of what we cannot predict or control. I also shared his fear of sharks, and getting attacked by one was not a new story I wanted to tell. I imagined that our fellow snorkelers would wave it off. "There's nothing's down there, kid. Stop freaking out and keep swimming." I could similarly dismiss him, but I also knew from experience that when our fears take over and threaten to consume us, it doesn't matter if they're rational or real. When they're that big, they can become our reality.

"Okay, let's go." I took hold of his vest and swam us both to shore.

After we'd pulled ourselves out of the water and yanked off our rubber fins, we sat on a hill of warm sand and pulled our towels tightly around us.

"Sorry," Derby said shamefully. "I thought something was out there."

"It's okay." I took his hand and held it in my mine. "We can try it again tomorrow."

Trusting we were safe in the world was going to take more

time. That's not to say that we hadn't moved forward. Derby was a big-fourth grader, I was onto a new writing project, and we were in Hawaii. That wasn't nothing. And still, we had a ways to go.

"Mom!" Derby had wandered back down the beach. He was smiling and pointing toward the open water. "Look, it was a sea turtle. I'm getting back in."

"You want your flippers?"

"No, I don't need them."

He splashed into the surf and I watched him swim out to greet the turtle. "Hello, guy." I stood up and walked to the water's edge and dug my feet into the wet sand, letting the water wash over my ankles, and recede back.

While I could end this story by saying Hawaii ultimately healed us, that would be untrue. And too convenient. The truth is that we were taking our time, slowly wading in, stepping back, wading in again. Do you want to know the real story? The beating pulse of loss doesn't go away. It fades, goes quiet at times, but it doesn't stop. The missing of someone continues, and the missing is hard and long, a daily reminder that there are some sorrows we have to live with. The fear is not gone either. It's a regular visitor that tries to block the door, and you have to decide if you will move forward anyway. All these aches and pains are there, and that's all right with me because I don't want the scars to heal, not completely. They remind me that it all mattered, that the loss was significant because the relationship was true.

I looked out at the blazing sun with eyes wide open. I choose heartbreak. I choose unknowing. I choose aliveness. I choose life.

ABOUT THE AUTHOR

SAMANTHA ROSE is an Emmy award-winning television writer, author and a *New York Times, USA Today* and internationally bestselling ghostwriter who collaborates with celebrities, experts, entrepreneurs and industry leaders who represent a wide category of titles, including some that have been selected as Reese's Book Club and Target Bookmarked Picks. She is the principal of YellowSkyMedia, a boutique editorial agency in Petaluma, California, where she lives with her son.

Visit Samantha Rose Online

Yellowskymedia.com

IG samantharose_writer

Substack @bananarose

ACKNOWLEDGMENTS

It's been said that our personal challenges and our most staggering losses provide us with opportunities to grow, so in that respect I want to first acknowledge the sad event that propelled me forward to write this book: my mother's suicide. While this book is a personal account, my hope is that it can provide some relief and healing for anyone who has struggled or is struggling with their mental health. You are not alone and help is available. It is also for those who have survived unthinkable loss and feel isolated by grief. You are not alone, either. Open the door. Write it down. You may be surprised by who and what comes through.

Thank you, Rabbi B, for encouraging me in the earliest days to write about my loss, however difficult. My heart is full of gratitude for you—my guide, my friend, my hand in the dark. You were the right person at the right time and my life has been forever touched by you. Your words and the space you held for me every Wednesday were the greatest gift and this book is a tribute to you. That said, I wouldn't have made that first call to B if it hadn't been for Rebecca Rosen, who nudged me to do so and whose friendship and spiritual insight has changed the way I look at life and death and everything in between. We were brought together for a reason, a season and a lifetime, and I thank you for showing me a peek into another world and for instilling in me a new belief that our loved ones never die. And to Ariela, who brought together B's wisdom and Rebecca's insight to help me heal from the inside out. Thank you for showing me your open heart and for encouraging me to open mine.

To my surrogate mothers and newfound girlfriends—Miriam and Sara—I love you. You were there from the start and haven't left my side since and I feel so lucky to call you family.

An extended thank you to Barbara, Neva, Marylu and Helen, who also stepped forward to embrace me and who I consider to be some of the coolest women I know. Mom always picked the good ones! And to Karen and Sandie who knew Mom long before I even came along—you have both helped to fill her void and remember the best parts of her. You also tell the funniest stories and your humor brought lightness to a dark time.

Thank you to Chris Smith and the "Old Guard" at the Press Democrat who continue to respect and protect the legacies of both Mom and Klose. And to everyone in Sonoma County and beyond who attended their memorials—there are too many of you to count—but I can see your faces and know who you are and I am grateful for the support and love you have shown my family for years, decades, my entire lifetime.

And speaking of lifetimes, to my oldest friend Aza, who was the first to say what we were all thinking: this is SO FUCKED—thank you for breaking the silence. To my Austin besties—Leah, Sara and Trish—thank you for always making time for me, preferably at the onset of triple-digit Texas temps when we can share stories over margaritas.

Thank you to my trusted early readers: Lele, Lori, Amanda and Eve, for your wonderful feedback and encouragement forward. Gratitude also to my ghost friends who know well what it means to write in the shadows and meet a looming deadline. And to my Petaluma book group who cheered me on through the earliest drafts.

Thank you to literary agent Mark Tauber who believed in this book from the start and who championed my efforts to get it to a wide audience of readers, and to Sibylline Press who shared his enthusiasm for my ghost-grief journey and found a way to publish it nearly to the *day* of Mom's 5-year deathiversary date. A special call-out to Vicki DeArmon, Publisher and Production Manager extraordinaire for being all things at all times; Jen Safrey for your sensitivity to the subject and skillful editing; Anna Wilhelm and Hannah Rutkowski for your engaging book trailers and social media art; Alicia Feltman for the beautiful book cover; Sang Kim for keeping production moving forward; and Anna Termine for your efforts to find readers all over the globe.

A big thank you also goes to Jennifer Jensen at Co-Pilot publishing, Trish Collins at TLC Book Tours and to Courtney Cook, for joining in and lending your creative expertise to get this book into the hands of everyone who needed to read it.

To my Sonoma County family—Pops, my in-laws, my niece and nephew and specifically, my sisters Jenni and Gretta, who trusted me to share my experience of our family story and who helped me remember some of the more nuanced details of that first and most difficult year. The 3 Orphans After Party was formed by tragedy, but any party with the two of you is a welcome event. Thank you for standing by my side for 40+ years.

And to Mom, who was indeed my silent partner throughout the writing process. We are untouchable, always connected, and you will forever remain a central character in the story of my life. But, really, can you stop upstaging me?

Lastly, to Derby, who grounds me in this world and whose smile reminds me that there is only one choice: to live.

If you or someone you know is struggling with suicidal thoughts, confidential assistance is available through the Suicide & Crisis Lifeline by calling or texting 988.

BOOK GROUP QUESTIONS

1. Samantha Rose's mother's death came on the heels of the worldwide pandemic that forced the majority of the world to retreat and isolate indoors. Rose acknowledges that this surprise circumstance allowed her time and room to grieve that she wouldn't have been afforded in "normal" times. Why does there seem to be a cultural expectation to push through grief, noting for instance, relatively short bereavement policies in the workplace that typically afford employees only three to five days off, and often unpaid. How much time does grief need?

2. Like so many survivors of suicide, Rose struggled to make sense of the nonsensical, leaning into her training as a writer to help her to process her complicated feelings. If you have also wrestled with loss, what actions, habits or new routines helped you to process your grief? How have you witnessed others wrestle with loss? How does suicide make it a different kind of grief?

3. Rose is mindful of staying joyful around Derby, not laying her adult tragedies and challenges on someone so young. In an effort to protect and shield our children from hardship, do we unconsciously dismiss their experience? Is there an age or a stage in a child's life when they can hear the full story?

4. Rabbi B says that when we lose someone suddenly or unexpectedly, the first stage of grief is often consumed by the *how* of the death, and that it can take a long time to move through the "haunting of the how". If this resonates with you, discuss your own haunting of a loved one's death and if you have arrived on the other side of your initial shock,

outrage, confusion and hurt, what has filled the space? Compassion, empathy, forgiveness, simple distraction?

5. As Rose explores her mother's shame and secrecy around her deteriorating health and her perceived irrelevance in a world that still stigmatizes mental illness, Rose recognizes the similarities they share, specifically a resistance to asking for help. She wonders, "Maybe I wasn't above receiving help—I was afraid to ask for it, either because I didn't believe I'd receive it, or I'd be criticized, or worse, rejected for needing it." Discuss the stigma around asking for help, for women especially, and how we can push through our resistance, individually and collectively, to receive the care we need.

6. Rose explores the possibility of having a relationship with her mother after death. She writes:" I believe we each are permitted to have our own unique relationship with our dead loved ones, just as we did when they were alive, and the nature of that relationship is not for others to dictate or decide." If you have lost a loved one, in what ways have you continued the relationship? Discuss how this has helped or hindered your grieving process.

7. Rabbi B says that all of us have a fire inside and we keep our loved ones alive by carrying their fire. When you think about the legacy of a loved one you've lost, what aspects of their lives, the light and the dark, do you want to bury and which ones do you intend to carry forward?

8. After reading her mother's journal and returning to the site of her death, Rose suggests that her mother's suicide was an act of free will, that she was exercising her right to choose both how she lived and died. Rose acknowledges the controversial and sometimes polarizing viewpoints about the Right to Die

movement and that Rose's stance on her mother's suicide may be unpopular, and even contested, considering her mother's mental instability. Discuss: is it our birth right to assert personal freedom, no matter what the circumstances? What does it mean to live and die on your own terms and whether there are instances when you forfeit that right?

9. Rose writes that a primary reason for continuing the *conversation* with her mother had to do with remembering. "I hadn't anticipated what it would mean to lose the person who remembers with you because they share your history, they share your same stories. Mom and I had a lifetime of memories that belonged solely to us, and if I didn't continue to refresh those memories, I worried I'd lose them." Share with the group the name of an important person in your life who serves as your witness to your history. Is there a story, a scene or a memory that you'd like to pass on to others so that it's not forgotten whether that be through speaking it out loud or writing it down? Who, besides yourself, wants or needs that memory? If your loved one dies, are your memories like the trees in the forest—if it falls, does it really make a sound? Does anyone notice?

10. *Giving Up the Ghost* is about a ghostwriter who "ghosts" a ghost. Beyond that interplay, the narrative uncovers how Rose had retreated into the shadows of her own life and that ultimately, her mother's death was an invitation for Rose to reconcile with and heal her inner ghosts. Ask yourself: In what areas of my life am I living in the shadows? Silencing my voice? Burying my truth? And what will it take for me to give up the ghost? Can it be less extreme, less painful than what Rose had to go through with her mother's suicide?

Sibylline
DIGITAL FIRST

www.ingramcontent.com/pod-product-compliance
Lightning Source LLC
LaVergne TN
LVHW051108310125
802517LV00003B/3

* 9 7 8 1 9 6 0 5 7 3 6 8 1 *